Lifelines Through the Arctic

Lifelines Through the Arctic

By

WILLIAM S. CARLSON

DUELL, SLOAN AND PEARCE

New York

First edition

Affiliate of
MEREDITH PRESS
Des Moines & New York

Library of Congress Catalogue Card Number: 62-12167

MANUFACTURED IN THE UNITED STATES OF AMERICA FOR MEREDITH PRESS

VAN REES PRESS • NEW YORK

To MARYJANE and KRIS

Acknowledgments

A<small>T THE</small> invitation of Vilhjalmur Stefansson, the author and Major George Brodsky spent several months in Alaska and the Aleutians, during the latter part of World War II, gathering material for a human interest story of the Eleventh Air Force and the Alaskan Wing of the Air Transport Command. With the help of several officers attached to the Arctic, Desert, and Tropic Information Center, an Air Force organization I commanded at the time, the project was completed and a manuscript we called *No Mean Victory* was finished.

With the end of hostilities there was little interest in war narratives, and upon my separation from the Air Force and return to my post at the University of Minnesota, *No Mean Victory* was shelved as a classified document. Several years later the manuscript was declassified and made available to me for use in the preparation of this book with the understanding that it include material on the establishment of the northern route to Europe and postwar Air Force activities in the Arctic. Thus, only a small segment of Part II is drawn from *No Mean Victory*.

This book would not have been possible without the co-operation, patience, and gentle prodding of Major James Sunderman, Chief, USAF Book Program, Office of Information, Department of the Air Force, Washington, D.C. It was he who located the copy of *No Mean Victory* and was successful in arranging for its declassification after several others, including a three-star general, had failed in this attempt.

I am also indebted to other friends, too numerous to mention here, for encouragement, advice, and criticism during the life of the book in its manuscript form. The publishers made available to me the able editorial assistance of John Brick. To my secretaries, Ruth Niehaus and Margaret O'Connor in New York and Ada Skelding in Toledo, I am deeply grateful.

The chapter on Greenland was made possible by a grant arranged by John Gardner of Carnegie Corporation, and Greenland travel was facilitated by the assistance of Hans Christiansen of the Royal Greenland Trade Department and Per Norlin of Scandinavian Airlines System.

The bibliography gives an idea of my debt to those on whose published and unpublished work I have relied so much, and I note particularly my indebtedness to the anonymous historians of Air Force units whose typed manuscripts were made available to me.

WILLIAM S. CARLSON

Contents

Introduction   xiii

PART I.   LIFELINE TO THE UNITED KINGDOM

I	Pioneers of the Northern Airway	3
II	Hassell and Cramer	12
III	The Great Icecap	22
IV	The Search for Landing Sites	49
V	Building the Crystals	59
VI	"Bolero"	64
VII	Snow, Rain, Sleet, and Ice	69
VIII	The Weird Winter	74
IX	Beleaguered by the Icecap	82
X	The Suspenseful Rescue	90
XI	They Didn't Come Back	99
XII	Sweating It Out	103
XIII	Snow Man, Mint Julep, La Station Centrale, and Northice	109
XIV	Greenland Today	121

PART II. LIFELINE TO MOSCOW

XV   Northward to Nome   139

XVI   The Battle of Northwest Airlines   148

XVII Life in the Bush Country   160

XVIII Confusion Along the Alaskan Route   169

XIX   Alsib   178

PART III. LIFELINES ACROSS THE POLAR SEA

XX   The DEW Line, BMEWS, and Thule   191

XXI   To Keep Them Flying   203

XXII Ptarmigan   216

XXIII The Assault on the Arctic Ocean   225

XXIV Ice Islands and Ice Floes   239

XXV   Bravo   254

      Selected Bibliography   269

Illustrations

Following page 50

Greenlanders in Fragile Kayaks

Motorized Snow Sleds

Big Bombers Down on the Icecap

American and Soviet Fliers

A Shark-nosed Bomber

Vital Radar Watch

Along the DEW Line at Dawn

Massive Sky Scanners

Delta Daggers on Patrol

Radar Platform Aloft

Mileage Marker

Aircraft on a Pedestal

Snow Weasel and Helpers

Snow House on T-3

Men on Bravo

Introduction

THE BARREN and frigid wastelands of the Arctic and the vast ice-bound reaches of its polar sea have been a forbidding goal to intrepid explorers since the dawn of the great age of discovery when Norsemen, whose names are lost in antiquity, ventured with their slim and graceful craft into the treacherous northern waters. They were followed through the centuries by the great sailors of Western Europe, who probed the seas for the legendary Northwest Passage.

Wooden ships, no matter how iron-willed their masters, were always at the mercy of the cruel ice that could so easily smash them to splinters. It was only in the nineteenth century, with the development of steam propulsion and steel-hulled ships, that scientists began to journey deeply into the bleak frozen lands and to accumulate the geophysical data that enabled their successors to complete the conquest in the twentieth century.

However, it was not alone the scientist's quest for knowledge nor the lure of a vast unknown that opened wide the Arctic land and sea during the middle decades of this century. The exigencies of two of mankind's greatest conflicts have sharply focused the world's attention on the northland. During the turbulent years of World War II, the great powers expended vast resources in Arctic activities that were fundamental to the downfall of the Third Reich in Europe and Japanese imperialism in Asia. Now, two decades later, in the chill grip of the cold war the frigid Arctic has become the earth's most vitally strategic area.

The story of American military pioneering in north polar areas divides itself fittingly into three parts, for we have devised three lifelines through the North during these past twenty years. Two of them served us well during World War II; they were transport routes that helped immeasurably in throttling the Axis. The third lifeline waits. The earnest desire of its builders, and of the thousands of men who man it, is that it may never be called upon. If it is ever needed, however, the third lifeline is ready.

The first of the transport routes ferried thousands upon thousands of military aircraft across the North Atlantic to the United Kingdom; these were the planes that wrested supremacy in the air from Hitler's Luftwaffe and reduced his boasted fortress to rubble.

The second route was over the land of northwest Canada and Alaska. It carried American planes to Siberia and thence to Russia, where they helped to hammer Hitler's Wehrmacht into bitter retreat.

The third lifeline is designed to transport not planes but information. It is the gigantic radar network that stands sentinel across our northern approaches, ready to flash the warning that missiles and supersonic jets are hurtling toward us over the top of the world.

The men who built and serviced the remote stations of these lifelines—at the bleak edges of Greenland's icecap, in the rugged wilderness of the Yukon, on the drifting pack ice of the Arctic Ocean—endured bone-aching cold and maddening loneliness. They underwent dangers for which no previous experience or training had prepared them. They won few medals in comparison to the heroes of battlegrounds around the world, yet many of them died at their lonely posts or vanished forever over bleak lands or icy waves.

Their efforts have been eminently rewarding; they have helped insure our future security, and they have transformed a strange and forbidding land into a new frontier that men can traverse in relative safety, guided by science that they helped pioneer and protected by technology that they tested and perfected. This book is the story of those soldiers and airmen and of their achievements in opening the North.

PART I

Lifeline to the United Kingdom

CHAPTER I

Pioneers of the Northern Airway

IT WAS late afternoon of the twelfth of April, 1942. The instrument panel clock of a camouflaged B-24 Liberator showed 3:45 P.M.; the altimeter was fixed at 8,000 feet, and the air speed was steady at 250 miles per hour. The nose of the aircraft broke through low-hanging clouds. The huge four-motored plane, an early model of the bomber that was to perform so steadily in both European and Pacific theaters of war, hurtled over the choppy waters of Davis Strait, which separates continental North America from the vast frozen mass of Greenland.

As an observer aboard that aircraft, I stared forward through the pilot's windows for the first glimpse of the saw-toothed mountains of Greenland's western coast, beyond which lay the great flat dome of the Greenland Icecap, 700,000 square miles of eternal snow and ice, crevassed and ridged at its perimeters, and as much as two miles thick.

My anticipation was so keen as to be almost a physical sensation, for I had spent many months on that great northern island more than a decade before with geological expeditions from the

University of Michigan. I was longing to see it again, for it had always held grandeur and awesome beauty for my eyes, even though to most of its American visitors, before and since, it may have seemed a barren and lonesome land.

There was trepidation in my mind as well, because all of us aboard that great aircraft knew the vital importance of this single flight. We were pioneering the northern route to the United Kingdom; the Liberator that probed toward the ice-encrusted coast ahead was the first four-engined plane to essay so hazardous a mission. We knew something of the ferrying operation that was planned if we succeeded; it is unlikely, however, that any of us dreamed, during that first flight, of the thousands upon thousands of Fortresses, Liberators, Marauders, and Mitchells, which would roar through the Arctic air bound for Great Britain and the battle for the skies of Europe.

Anxiously, the aircraft's commander, Lieutenant Colonel Milton W. Arnold, peered ahead for landmarks that would lead him over the rugged coastal area to the one place within hundreds of miles where he could let the big plane down safely. He began his descent, then flattened out in a low-level approach to the crude new airfield at Narsarssuak, lying fifty miles up Tunugdliarfik Fjord in southwest Greenland.

The aircraft glided through a bewildering mass of mountains and fjords that lie to seaward of the Narsarssuak base, known as Bluie West One * in Army Air Force code.

The Liberator skimmed along the ice-covered fjord, flanked by towering snow-covered mountains. Its wheels touched the tilted, single runway, a newly constructed strip of steel matting. The plane rolled to a taxiing stop in the deepening gloom, and the first leg of the pioneer flight was completed.

That landing of a big bomber at Narsarssuak made no headlines in the nation's papers in April of 1942, for secrecy surrounded

* Geographical locations are used in this book. The AAF code name is not repeated after it is identified.

the Air Force ventures in the northland. It was nonetheless a triumph to men in Washington and London who received swift reports that it had been accomplished, and to officers, airmen, and ground crews in remote stations scattered from Presque Isle, Maine, across Newfoundland and Labrador, in Iceland, and at great air bases in the British Isles.

As we landed in the Liberator, the United States had been at war for four disastrous months. Pearl Harbor was slowly recovering from the crushing blow that had stricken it; the Philippines were conquered; the Japanese seemingly had the rest of Asia simply for the taking. In Europe, most of the continent was in Hitler's hands or in the ineffectual grip of his blustering ally, Mussolini. German divisions had raced deep into the Soviet Union with the same ease with which the panzers had swept through every defense that western Europe could muster. They had stalled through their first Russian winter, but now that spring had arrived, they were looking confidently toward the capture of Moscow and the subjugation of yet another nation. Disaster seemed to pile upon disaster for the Allies, and there were few signs that the great tide of Axis victory would ever turn.

There was no way for the troubled world to know it, but the landing of one B-24 in a white spray of gritty snow on the western coast of Greenland was one of those signs. The northern route was open. It could not, in honesty, yet be labeled an airway, but in another eighteen months it would be.

The flight to the United Kingdom by way of Labrador, Greenland, and Iceland never became a casual operation, but the Air Force worked near miracles in reducing its hazards and its difficulties. Later in the war, operations became scheduled and standardized.

Ferry crews were briefed in the comparatively mild atmosphere of Presque Isle in northern Maine. Briefing officers informed new crews and reminded the veterans that the scenery on the flight, if they saw any, would consist only of rock and snow and water and ice as the primeval wilderness flowed below their aircraft. They heard instructions which most of them already knew by heart; understandably, some of them dozed during the inevitable survival film: *Land and Live in the Arctic.*

The weather officer admonished them to ". . . watch for ice conditions . . . stay out of clouds and rain . . . check in at all range stations. . . ." But in the later years they seldom encountered trouble on the Greenland hop. In spite of weather second only to that of the Aleutians in its vile nature, and with terrain to match, the flights along the bulky and rawboned mountainous portion of Labrador, over the dreary tundra that stretched endlessly above the northern tree line, across the ice-patched waters of Davis Strait, and through the jagged cloud-bound coastal mountains of Greenland to the awesome icecap, all became not much more difficult than routine flights from New York to Chicago.

After the headaches and dangers of the early days following the flight of our pioneer Liberator, the northern route finally was tamed to the proportions of standard operation between great and modern airports, carved out of mountainsides and protected by the finest radio and communications devices. Pilots followed airway flight plans similar to those used by commercial airlines across the United States.

An airway, after all, is more than runways, taxiways, and parking stands; it is a complex combination of facilities and services, manned by experts who know how to co-ordinate them effectively. Its primary essentials are a series of adequate, strategically located landing surfaces that are superior in construction to the finest of automobile turnpikes, as well as buildings to house personnel and planes, fuel and storage facilities, spare parts, machinery, equipment, and services for personnel. Radio ranges, the electronic route markers of the upper air, must be installed and maintained, along with two-way radio equipment beween ground and planes.

Reliable communications are essential to an airway, as are meteorologists, who serve not only at the airports but at scores of remote places, some hundreds of miles from the air route. Additional communications must link these isolated weather observers to the airfields. Weather information is worthless unless it can be expertly interpreted by forecasters and, most important of all, relayed by radio operators to the pilots without delay. An airway has other highly trained specialists in various capacities who must be fed, lodged, clothed, and paid.

An airway prospect has never been more discouraging and logistically challenging at the outset than was the northern route to Europe with its crude and primitive landing strips in Greenland, first of all at Narsarssuak and Söndre Strömfjord on the West Coast, and later at Optimist on the East Coast. All were furnished with unlimited quantities of unpredictable and violent weather and rugged, desolate terrain. Although some of the handicaps were unknown, those of obdurate soil and climate already were part of the history of aerial exploration in the Arctic, a narrative that goes back to the nineteenth century.

In the early days, explorers had no thought of airways linking the world's big cities. There was only one goal for the air pioneers —the North Pole.

Salomon Andrée, a Swedish aeronaut and scientist, was the first to try to reach the Pole by air. He used a drift balloon, the *Eagle,* which was launched hopefully from Danes Island, Spitsbergen, a favorite starting base for polar attempts, on 11 July 1897. Andrée theorized that a favorable south wind would blow him over the Pole, across the Arctic basin, and on to Alaska or perhaps Siberia. The winds failed to blow, and Andrée and his two companions, after a 64-hour flight that carried them on a zigzag course of 500 miles, came down on the ice pack of the Arctic Ocean, 288 miles from their starting point. They made their way successfully to White Island where, apparently in good spirits and adequately supplied with food and clothing, they evidently died of carbon-monoxide poisoning in their tent. Their bodies were not discovered until August 1930.

Ten years after Andrée's unsuccessful attempt, an American newspaperman, Walter Wellman, built the *America,* a dirigible airship with three engines, for a voyage to the North Pole. He made two attempts, both from Spitsbergen. On the first, his craft was no sooner off the ground than it lost direction in a snowstorm. Two years later he failed again, but this time he did fly to a point on the pack ice sixty miles north of Spitsbergen, where the party was rescued by ship. Learning that Peary had reached the Pole by dog teams from Ellesmere Island on 6 April 1909, Wellman gave up any further attempts.

In 1910, on the recommendation of Ferdinand Graf von Zeppelin, pioneer of the rigid airship, a commission of German scientists was sent to Spitsbergen to study the possibility of establishing a base there for a Zeppelin airship. The commission reported favorably, but for a number of years nothing came of it.

Thereafter interest in lighter-than-air craft for polar exploration waned. The first heavier-than-air flying in the Arctic probably was done by a Russian, Lieutenant Nagurski, who made five flights in 1914 over the pack ice of Barents Sea. When the Norwegian discoverer of the South Pole, Roald Amundsen, returned from Antarctica in 1912 he began to lay plans for conquest of the North Pole by air. Forestalled by World War I, it was not until 1922 that he was able to purchase a suitable Junkers monoplane. He loaded it on his vessel, the *Maud,* for transport to Alaska. Amundsen's plan was to fly with his pilot, Lieutenant O. Omdal, from Alaska over the Pole to Spitsbergen, but the plane was damaged beyond repair on a trial flight. Also in 1923, a Dutch-American airman named Hammer made several flights over Spitsbergen in a seaplane.

In 1925 Amundsen teamed up with the wealthy American philanthropist interested in polar exploration, Lincoln Ellsworth, and four others, in an attempt to fly to the Pole from Spitsbergen. Two twin-engine Dornier-Wal flying boats were used. Within 136 nautical miles of the Pole engine trouble developed in one plane, forcing it to land in an open lead on the pack ice. The other aircraft made a precarious landing nearby. The engine of the disabled plane was beyond repair. After twenty-four days spent chopping a runway out of the rough sea ice with improvised tools, both crews got aboard the remaining plane and returned safely to Spitsbergen.

Then on 9 May 1926 Commander Richard E. Byrd, with Floyd Bennett as pilot, in a tri-motor Fokker, the *Josephine Ford,* made a 15½ hour flight of 1,330 nautical miles from Spitsbergen to the Pole and back. After this successful flight emphasis again returned, temporarily, to lighter-than-air craft.

As a result of his earlier flight, Amundsen concluded that an airship, with its ability to remain aloft for longer periods, was better adapted for polar travel than heavier-than-air planes. He was successful in raising funds for the purchase of an Italian semi-rigid dirigible, the N-1, which he renamed the *Norge*. Its designer and pilot was the Italian airship expert, Colonel Umberto Nobile. The *Norge,* with Colonel Nobile as pilot, Amundsen, Ellsworth, and a crew aboard, left Spitsbergen only two days after Byrd's polar flight. The expedition flew over the Pole and was brought down at Teller, Alaska, after a flight of 72 hours covering nearly 3,400 miles.

Only two years later Nobile became the center of controversy when the dirigible *Italia,* which he was commanding, became the first major casualty of polar flying. Amundsen and the crew of a French plane were lost in a rescue attempt, as were a Swedish scientist and six men in the dirigible's gondola, which broke loose from the airship and was never found.

G. H. Wilkins, Australian born veteran of the Arctic, and Carl Ben Eielson, former teacher and Alaska's most celebrated aviator, made a spectacular flight on 15 April 1928, in a Lockheed Vega monoplane from Point Barrow to Spitsbergen, a distance of 2,200 miles, in twenty-four hours. Wilkins was knighted by the British crown for his achievement in making the first flight across the Arctic Ocean from America to Europe.

The flights of Amundsen and Ellsworth by dirigible and Byrd, Wilkins, and Eielson by airplane were milestones not only in polar exploration but in aviation as well. These successful pioneers showed the way for those who followed. Since 1925 few expeditions have ventured into the polar regions without supporting aircraft. The early flights produced very little of scientific value although they did arouse public interest and enthusiasm for polar aerial travel.

In the meantime air routes were being developed. The large bodies of water, particularly the Atlantic and Pacific areas, were the principal obstacles. But even though they were hazardous, they were not considered insuperable problems. By 1924 many great trail-blazing flights included the spanning of the Atlantic in one jump. Nevertheless, aircraft lacked sufficient range to make flying the Atlantic the routine matter it is today. Attention turned to routes where over-water hops could be reduced to a minimum— along the Great Circle Route over the northern latitudes. The first aviators to circumnavigate the globe by air, the "Round-the-World Flyers" of the United States Army, in 1924 selected a route that began at Seattle, followed the west coast of Canada and Alaska, the Aleutian Islands, the peninsula of Kamchatka, and the Kuriles to Japan. Then the flight plan carried the planes to Shanghai, Burma, India, and to Europe and England. They also crossed the Atlantic via the northern route—from England to Iceland, then to Greenland and Labrador.

Three years now went by before Colonel Charles A. Lindbergh's historic flight across the Atlantic revived interest in a route that could be safe and commercially economical. While Lindbergh's flight and succeeding ones proved that the two continents could be linked by airplane, a direct hop of 4,000 miles without a stop was too long and hazardous to be commercially practical. It had to be broken into sections, with refueling stations along the route, since fuel and crew took all available space on the long hop. Attention turned again to the islands of the Atlantic. A great circle of the earth, from the Great Lakes region to Europe, swings far north of the regular steamship lines—far enough to take in Greenland. With the commercial plane then being flown—one requiring that no single link in the transportation system be more than 1,000 miles long—it was obvious that Greenland must be an important part in the solution of the problem.

The northern route of the 1920's, lacking suitable air fields, required an amphibian type of plane. The numerous lakes of Canada, Greenland, and northern Europe, as well as the wide sea reaches, would permit planned or forced landings along almost the entire route. From Detroit or Chicago, the first lap of the journey would carry the plane to the Hudson Bay post at Melville Lake on the western end of a long Labrador fjord, the present location of Goose Bay airport. With a high percentage of clear weather, this area was a good take-off point from America to Greenland. The hop then would be about 400 miles over Davis Strait to Greenland's west coast. From there the plane would climb over the steep coastal ranges and fly over the great, flat icecap. A forced landing undoubtedly would be possible on the hard surface. Angmagssalik, on the east coast, could serve as a refueling station on the planes' way to Iceland. From Reykjavik, already used as a seaplane base by the "Round-the-World Flyers," the route would be by way of the Faeroes to Edinburgh and London. Having selected this logical route, the proponents still had to convince the world of its practicability. Pioneer test flights by capable flyers were the obvious answer.

CHAPTER II

Hassell and Cramer

THE PIONEERS proved to be Bert Hassell and Parker (Shorty) Cramer and, after one abortive flight, Cramer and Oliver Pacquette. I was deeply involved in these two historic early attempts to reach Europe by way of Greenland in 1928 and 1931, while I was a member of the University of Michigan Greenland Expeditions under the leadership of the famous geologist, William H. Hobbs.

In the spring of 1928 Bert Hassell, an experienced aviator, had made plans to fly from his home in Rockford, Illinois, to Stockholm in a single hop of 4,200 miles. His proposal was considered so completely foolhardy that no one would back him financially. Finally, someone brought him some good advice instead of mere warnings: he was urged to break his flight into two parts with a refueling stop at Mount Evans, a scientific observatory that had been established by the University of Michigan. The observatory was located on Söndre Strömfjord at the Arctic Circle on Greenland's west coast.

Hassell was greatly impressed by the description and pictures of the area and reports on the weather he might expect to encounter. He was one of the first aviators to believe that a practical route from America to Europe could cross Greenland.

Early in the spring of 1928 I had sailed ahead of the main party of the second University of Michigan Greenland Expedition. I was to bridge the gap between the departure of the aerologist, who was leaving after a year's work, and the arrival of the main party in the summer.

I left New York on 12 March and sailed from Copenhagen on 1 April for Greenland on the Danish vessel *Disko*. Accompanied by two Eskimos, I traveled overland from Holsteinsborg with dog team, arriving in early May at Söndre Strömfjord. With no radio, I knew nothing of the preparations being made for Hassell's flight until the rest of the expedition arrived two months later. With them came an aviator, Elmer Etes, Hassell's representative, plus 400 gallons of aviation gasoline and some oil.

Etes's job was to locate a satisfactory landing site for Hassell's plane, *Greater Rockford*. After an extensive search, he found a potential airstrip on a raised clay terrace, eight miles from Mount Evans. Even though in places it was gullied and covered with boulders, we were able to lay out a 1,500-foot runway, almost perfectly flat. Hard as cement, it stood at least twenty feet above the highest tide.

On 15 July we made contact for the first time in more than six months with the short-wave station of *The New York Times*. Nine days later startling news from the air plunged our entire camp into activity. Late in the evening we received two radio messages from the managing editor of the *Times:* "Hassell planning to start Wednesday morning [the next day]" and "Hassell ready to start. Asking if landing field ready now or how soon. We tried nightly to communicate with you directly."

But the next day Hassell postponed his flight because of bad weather. Even a day's respite gave us additional time to get the field in shape. Furthermore, we had to haul more than a ton and a half of Hassell's gasoline on our backs those eight long miles to the airstrip.

Then we had word that Hassell and Cramer had crashed five miles from take-off at Rockford, Illinois. Disappointed, we assumed this accident would end any further attempts that summer, and busied ourselves with scientific studies which had been neglected while we were hauling gasoline and preparing the landing strip.

But within three weeks, on the fourteenth of August, the radio alerted us: Hassell and Cramer had repaired their badly damaged plane. Their first stop was at Cochrane, Ontario, where they were delayed for a few days. On the eighteenth of August they left Cochrane at noon, scheduled to arrive at our primitive airstrip in Greenland about midnight, during the few dark hours of the Arctic summer night.

We kept watching for them long after the sun had risen, and through the long northern summer day. When the plane failed to appear by noon of the nineteenth, we knew they were lost. With charts, we tried to imagine where they might be. If they had successfully crossed Davis Strait, we supposed that they had been forced down somewhere to the south of us, in the Sukkertoppen hinterland—a rugged and unexplored wilderness of incised plateau, dotted with lakes and cut by glacial rivers.

There were no planes to hunt for them, nor could we send out search parties into that vast unknown region. We had no way of knowing where they might be on the barren wasteland.

False alarms were radioed from several widely separated areas in Greenland, Labrador, and the Canadian bush country. Here and there people said they had seen the *Greater Rockford* or had heard its motor. Each report proved untrue. Hassell and Cramer were given up for lost.

Two weeks later our summer party was packing up to go home to Michigan. This was during the caribou hunting season, and there were Greenlanders in our camp who had crossed the fjord from the Sukkertoppen hinterland, where they had been hunting, to barter with the college students who were eager to get souvenirs to take home. One of the Greenlanders saw smoke across the fjord; he insisted it could not be from a fire lighted by the hunting party.

We sent over a motorboat to investigate. It brought back Bert Hassell and Shorty Cramer, bearded and grimy, gaunt after fourteen days of near starvation, but grinning happily as they jumped ashore. Just one day later their fire might not have been seen, for the Greenlanders with their keen hunters' eyes would have been gone, and our main expedition would have sailed. The three of us who were to stay at the station would probably have been so busy with our scientific duties that we would not have seen the smoke.

They told us what had happened, after we'd satisfied their hungry bellies. After crossing Davis Strait, they were carried by high winds about two hundred miles off course to the south. Their fuel was almost gone, so they decided to land on the icecap while they could still maneuver. They touched down about ten miles inland and only seventy miles from the airstrip. They covered the engine and started for Mount Evans. They had a rifle, a hatchet, a lump of pemmican, and a map. The map was faulty, and they mistook a nearby lake for an arm of our fjord.

For two weeks they wandered over the icecap and the neighboring barrens. They went around the streams that flowed from the glaciers. They jumped crevasses in the eternal ice. At night they huddled in their coats to keep warm, for they had neither sleeping bags nor blankets, and temperatures on the icecap rarely rise above the freezing point, even during the long summer days. The small piece of pemmican was rationed. Cramer shot two ptarmigan, but they had to eat them raw. There is little wood to be found in the Sukkertoppen hinterland.

Shorty Cramer was undaunted. He was going to try it again. When I first met him at Mount Evans, he was in his early thirties.

We became fast friends. Cramer was from Indiana, and had been flying since World War I, when he was an Air Corps instructor at the age of twenty, at Kelly and Brooks Fields in Texas, and later a test pilot at Scott Field in Illinois. After the war, he went to New York to fly in Mayor Hylan's noted aerial police squadron. Then he took to barnstorming, which gave him rare experience for those days. However, he had no fame as a pilot during an era when the names of the noted barnstormers, racing and stunt pilots were as often on the lips of schoolboys as were the names of great ballplayers. His fame arrived with that 1928 hop to the icecap.

Before leaving Mount Evans, Cramer asked me to prepare for him a summarized report of our meteorological findings. He wanted scientific data to convince the airlines of the possibilities in the northern route. We do not always recognize the significant mileposts in our lives. That simple request from Shorty Cramer was to launch my participation in the great adventure of Arctic aviation during three decades of startling achievement in that field.

During the next year, Shorty Cramer managed to win the interest and the backing of the publisher of the *Chicago Tribune,* Colonel Robert R. McCormick. One of the Colonel's many enthusiasms was the future of commercial aviation. In what seemed no time at all, Cramer was ready to take off for Greenland again, this time in a plane oddly named the *Untin Bowler*. Cramer asked me to join the venture as a technical advisor on Greenland conditions. I provided him with a multiplicity of details, but he was unable to test their veracity on this flight, for it came to a quick end in the Hudson Straits, below Baffin Island. The *Untin Bowler* was blown from its moorings in one of the fearsome storms that churn the seas of those latitudes, and it was wrecked ingloriously among the drifting ice floes.

Far from being discouraged, Shorty worked harder than ever to realize his dream. Success was in the air during the spring of 1931, for there was now official interest in a northern air route. United States Postmaster General Walter Brown was interested, and so informed Vilhjalmur Stefansson and Edwin Thompson of Trans-American Airlines, Inc., who were supporting Cramer. Unhappily, Mr. Brown added that no funds were available for an experimental flight.

President Hoover was also enthusiastic, although he did nothing official to further the plan. The governments of Canada, Great Britain, Denmark, and Germany were interested. By this time, Cramer was launched on a crusade to prove his point, with the support of such polar authorities and scientists as Professor William Herbert Hobbs, my mentor at the University of Michigan, the colorful Peter Freuchen, as well as Stefansson.

In the meantime, I was spending my second year in the Arctic, this time in company with Max Demorest, a young geology student from the University of Michigan. We were isolated on the west coast of Greenland, and our radio, the only possible source of information, was out of commission. I knew nothing of Cramer's detailed planning. Not until I reached Copenhagen, on 1 August 1931, did I learn that throughout the spring and summer he had been trying to reach me in Greenland to tell me my role in his adventure.

Cramer's plan was to start at Detroit. He would fly over Labrador to Greenland. From Holsteinsborg on the west coast, he would fly north along the coast to find me at my study of glacial movement. He would pick me up and then fly back to Holsteinsborg. We would then fly over the icecap to Angmagssalik, where he expected me to spend an additional year making observations of weather on Greenland's rugged east coast. It was typical of Cramer's dedication to his idea that he never for a moment considered that I might have other plans for the next year. In point of fact, he had already sent to Angmagssalik, by the only boat of the year, all the supplies, books, and equipment that I might conceivably find of use. He was probably right too. If I had known what he had in mind, I would have agreed instantly.

However, Max and I were already en route to Copenhagen, completely unaware of Shorty's preparations. In the leisurely fashion which is typical of Greenland travel, we were making our way down the coast to take passage for Denmark.

When I reached Copenhagen, Peter Freuchen lost no time in seeking me out. That was my first meeting with the gigantic, bearded, one-legged Viking whose battered features later became so familiar to countless millions of television viewers, and to the legions of readers of his books about the Arctic. Peter was then a younger Viking, already a veteran of the north country, an expert on Eskimo life, and the possessor of a tremendous enthusiasm for Shorty Cramer's dream. Any idea I may have had to return to the University of Michigan to take up the classes and the academic routine that waited me was ruthlessly brushed aside by Freuchen. He was the Danish representative of Cramer's American sponsors, and he was immediately enlisting me in the crusade. Peter was an artful persuader, but he didn't have to work very hard on me. The plans took shape literally before I unpacked my luggage.

Rapid-fire, in that ferocious growl with which Freuchen was accustomed to speak English, I was told the details. When Cramer reached Copenhagen, I was to fly back with him to Angmagssalik. Three decades later, I can remember how my heart leaped at the idea of flying over the wild seas. When I was safely in Greenland, Cramer would return to Denmark, pick up Freuchen, and fly back over the route to the United States.

We ordered flying clothes and equipment; Freuchen put me to work with a reception committee that would give Cramer a wild greeting when he landed at Copenhagen.

On 6 August, radios and newspapers headlined the news that Cramer had landed at Angmagssalik with an unidentified companion. At that time, public interest was centered on the flight of Charles and Anne Morrow Lindbergh to the Orient. Cramer had quietly taken off from Detroit on 27 July. The sponsor deposited

Copenhagen that very day, was enough for Cramer. He at once tuned up his motor.

Waving good-by to the crowd, Cramer climbed into the Bellanca, roared down the runway, and twice circled the field. A telegraph messenger rushed onto the field at that minute, frantically waving still another message. Apparently taking it as an expression of good will, the flyers waved back and headed east, disappearing over the North Sea. It was the most dramatic moment of the flight. The paper that the messenger so despairingly waved was a storm warning. It had arrived one minute too late. Cramer should have disregarded his backers and followed his own judgment as he had been doing thus far, carefully selecting his weather. Within a few hours a storm broke off the Norwegian coast. In Copenhagen the great crowd grew restless as hour after hour passed with no sign of Cramer. At midnight the field was closed and the disappointed welcomers straggled away.

By the next day the storm was at its height, with a strong gale blowing. Cramer and Pacquette definitely were missing now. It was the fourth time that Cramer had been missing. Remembering his reappearance in 1928 after he had been given up for lost, I felt optimistic; few others did. In his last communication, received by a Norwegian radio station at three o'clock the previous afternoon, an hour and a half before he was due at Copenhagen, Cramer had stated only his destination. The chief of the Danish Naval Squadron, in a mixture of gloom and hope, commented: "I would consider the situation hopeless if the aviator were not Parker Cramer." With an air search impossible, cruisers were ordered out in the rough seas. Two days later, a steamer limped in, hours behind schedule. Its captain reported that Cramer would have flown into the worst storm in years. In his view, a plane never could have lasted.

A small cylinder of wood was picked up the next day off the coast of Jutland, but it could not be definitely established as belonging to Cramer's plane.

$1,000 with the Danish government for possible rescue par

Cramer piloted his Bellanca seaplane over Canada by wa;
Cochrane, Hudson Bay, Great Whales, and Baffin Island to]
steinsborg. Then he pointed her nose eastward over the icecap
had difficulty in making altitude with his heavy load but cle
the coastal ranges and flew with only feet to spare over the in
ice, all the way to Angmagssalik. Emergency supplies, a sled,
and pemmican—carried against a possible forced landing—
jettisoned on the way. Cramer was exultant at his feat in f
over the great white barrier that twice had thwarted him.

On 7 August dispatches which reported Cramer off to Reyk
revealed his companion to be Oliver Pacquette, an expert Can;
radio operator and navigator. At Iceland the following mo
the press had its first opportunity to question him. Cramer's a1
was typical of him: "The explanation is that we don't wish t(
about what we are going to do—only what we have done. B
we had crossed the inland ice, we had nothing worth mentic
Then we flew over a range never passed before, thus adding ;
to the future air route."

En route to the Faeroes, Cramer was forced to alight to re]
plugged oil line. The plane rode the waves easily while C
worked on the line.

Two days later, Cramer was forced by a storm to land ;
Shetland Islands after leaving the Faeroes.

Meanwhile, Denmark had followed the brief reports eagerl
citement rose as the day of arrival drew near. At Kastrup
drome, Copenhagen, a great crowd gathered, growing larger l
hour, overrunning the field. News came of the stop in the She
for better flying conditions. A cable was dispatched promp
Cramer, reporting good weather at Copenhagen and suggestir
he land at Kastrup Airdrome at 4:30 that afternoon. The cab
handed to Cramer as he tinkered with his plane. Word (
weather, plus the proposal that he make a triumphant entr

Cramer and Pacquette never were seen again. But although their flight ended in death, they had proved the practicability of using the northern route. This was the great contribution of Shorty Cramer's stubborn ambition.

CHAPTER III

The Great Icecap

ALTHOUGH Cramer and Pacquette lost their lives in the North Sea, close to the European coast, the greatest of all obstacles to their epochal flight was certainly the vast frozen expanse of Greenland itself, with its tremendous central dome of ice and its coastal barrens.

Known to the western world for a thousand years, although its existence was almost forgotten from the sixteenth to the eighteenth centuries, Greenland has always been considered little more than a huge stationary iceberg, of not much use to anyone, until the middle decades of the twentieth century.

The Norse sailor Gunnbjorn Ulvsson probably sighted Greenland in 974, although earlier Scandinavian and Irish mariners may have viewed its forbidding coasts. Eight years later, Eric the Red sailed past the southern tip, Cape Farewell, and guided his ship northward along the west coast into a large fjord where he built a home for his family near the present town of Julianehaab.

Three years later, Eric returned to Iceland to promote colonization of the new country. Wise in propaganda values, he chose an attractive, if inappropriate, name, "Green Land." He gave his adventurous listeners very persuasive accounts of the deep fjords, rich pastures, and excellent hunting and fishing. His proposals were received enthusiastically, and in 985 he started for Greenland with a flotilla of twenty-five ships. Only fourteen of them reached their destination; some returned to Iceland, others were probably lost at sea. Estimates of the party that reached Greenland vary between two and three hundred men, women, and children.

These colonists settled in two areas known as Osterbygden (Eastern Settlement) and Vesterbygden (Western Settlement) in the great fjord region of southwest Greenland. Ruins of one of the early settlements are found across the fjord from the former Narsarssuak air base.

Despite the inhospitality of the country, they made a living by cattle raising, hunting, and fishing; and, moreover, their sagas testify to continued literary interests. Recent excavations show that the colonists achieved a considerable degree of comfort and maintained a high standard of culture. Among the finds are ruins of a banquet hall which could have accommodated a hundred people. The ultimate total population of this Arctic colony of Europeans is estimated at between three and ten thousand people.

On a voyage to Norway in 999 Leif, son of Eric, came under the influence of the Norse king who induced him to accept Christianity and to introduce it in Greenland. Leif converted his mother, Thjorhild, whereupon—in about 1000—she built a church at Brattahlid. It seems entirely possible that, by the time of Leif's death in 1021, the country was entirely Christianized. From 1152, when the episcopal see of Greenland at Gardar was made subordinate to the Archbishops of Trondhjem, church life flourished.

Another turning point came in 1261, when the colonists, who governed themselves as a republic, submitted to the rule of the Norwegian king, Haakon. This entailed payment of taxes to a distant ruler, a levy which the local legislative body passed voluntarily. All Greenland trade was monopolized by the king's representatives.

Communication with Norway became regular and frequent while the trade monopoly was enforced in the fourteenth century. In the next century, political changes in Norway and the decimation of its population by the Black Death, cut traffic between the two countries. It is even recorded that in 1484 German merchants in Norway killed all who were acquainted with the route to Greenland. The last contact between Norse settlers in Greenland and the mother country was in about 1411.

Historians have several theories to account for disappearance of the Norse colonies. Some scientists say that the colonists were killed off by warlike Eskimos who either came down the west coast from the north or advanced northward after rounding Cape Farewell. Others believe that through marriage the settlers were assimilated by the more numerous and hardier Eskimos. Still another theory emphasizes climatic changes. The true answer probably would include a combination of these and other circumstances, including the breakdown of communication with Europe.

What kind of land was it that engulfed those early colonists, that has harassed the hardy Eskimos who survived them through the succeeding centuries, that has offered so harsh and forbidding an environment for the new pioneers of the air age?

Its 825,000 square miles make Greenland a land mass as large as Mexico, long described by geographers as the earth's greatest island.* Solid ice covers more than four-fifths of its surface along its 1,500-mile length from its southern tip at Cape Farewell to Cape Morris Jesup in the north, and across its broad reaches, 700 miles at its greatest breadth. The assumption that Greenland is a far Arctic land is only partially correct, for Cape Farewell is in the latitude of Oslo and Leningrad and farther south than Anchorage, Alaska. At the other extreme, Greenland's northern tip lies only

---

* Scientists now say that there are actually three islands under the icecap, and recent studies show that the ice may be 14,000 feet thick in some areas where it extends a mile below sea level. The weight of the icecap through the ages has forced the land mass to sink into the plastic mantle of the earth.

400 miles from the North Pole, nearer than any other land mass.

The flat dome of the vast icecap, rising to approximately two miles above sea level at its highest point, dominates the island. Except for a narrow coastal ribbon that varies in width from about 100 miles to virtually no land at all— coastline that is emphatically punctuated with ragged mountains and deep fjords—Greenland is buried under the second largest glacier in the world. The icecap is ranked in size only by the frozen cover of Antarctica.

The outer margin of the icecap, covering an average distance of seventy-five miles away from the coast, is honeycombed with crevasses or fissures, particularly where active outlet glaciers lead to fjords. A crevasse is simply a huge crack in the ice caused by the slow but inexorable forward motion of the sheet of ice over an uneven surface. Some of them are wide enough to swallow a four-engined aircraft without a trace. They seem to be bottomless, extending hundreds of feet deep into the icecap. They are often hidden from the human eye, camouflaged completely by smooth-blown bridges of snow.

The great inland icecap seems stationary, yet it moves constantly to feed the rapidly shifting marginal glaciers that eventually calve into icebergs. Glacier movement in Greenland has long been studied by scientists. A Danish geologist named Ryder declared in 1886–1887 that the Upernivik Glacier, one of the most active, moved an average 102.2 feet in 24 hours at a point near its center. He also said that it traveled 124.2 feet during one particular day, the highest glacier speed ever noted.

My observations of this immense glacier, high on Greenland's west coast, did not support Ryder's findings. The University of Michigan expedition that I headed in 1930–1931 reported velocities only about one-half those determined by Ryder.

How much has the great ice sheet changed since the last glacial period, which was at its peak probably 20,000 years ago? Is enough snow falling annually to preserve it essentially in its present size and shape for many millennia? Or is it melting and evaporating year by year? These are the questions of keenest interest to the scientists who study it.

The Swiss glaciologist DeQuervain said that more ice accumulated annually than was dissipated, strengthening the theory that the icecap hasn't changed much since the days when the glaciers of the most recent Ice Age blanketed vast areas of the Northern Hemisphere. He also reported in 1912 that coastal glaciers seemed generally to be receding.

Conflicting reports from Eskimos indicate that in some places the ice mass has receded strikingly, or remains relatively stable, while one explorer tells of a South Greenland glacier that advanced so rapidly to the coast that, within the memory of living Greenlanders, it buried a group of Norse ruins.

The Jacobshavn Glacier, at 69° N. in West Greenland, moves forward and back with impressive variations. Between 1851 and 1875, it retreated more than 2.48 miles. In four more years, it had swiftly receded 1.24 miles farther east. During the next winter, it reversed its field, traveling .62 miles west in six months. Then it retreated again 1.24 miles in less than a year. Finally, in 1902 it had moved 2.48 miles west of where it had been in 1880.

The Upernivik Glacier has been receding. My measurements in 1931 showed that it had retreated an average of 3,000 feet and, in some parts of its front, as much as 5,000 feet. I also examined the Giesecke Glacier in 1931, and determined that since Ryder had measured it in 1886, it had receded 2,000 feet in its active section.

The icecap is inhumanly cold, and its temperatures rarely rise above the freezing point even when southern Greenland is enjoying a moderate summer day in July or August. Its usual ranges are between + 27° and − 49°, but far lower temperatures are not at all unusual. Precipitation on the inland ice is lower than that of the coastal areas, and it decreases markedly toward the northern parts of the island, as distance grows from the moist air of the Atlantic Ocean.

Both icecap and coastland are visited by sudden and violent gales, known to Alpinists the world over as foehn winds, which blow down the sides of mountains from the peaks. In Greenland these winds blow savagely down the slopes of the great frozen dome.

Travel on the icecap is always limited by the hazards of the marginal zone. Safe and practical routes over this treacherously crevassed region are few in number and not always generally known. Experienced glaciologists can ascend to the icecap over the fissured areas in relative safety, but the novice, such as an airman whose plane is down on the ice, has no choice but to await rescue. Far from being potential highways to the coast, the outlet glaciers are usually active and therefore are heavily crevassed and always difficult to traverse.

Some of the snow bridges across crevasses are strong enough to bear the weight of men, but they will not ordinarily support a mechanized vehicle of any considerable size. Travel is extremely difficult for other reasons. The snow surface changes constantly; a hard, well-packed surface may be replaced in a matter of hours by a thick layer of fresh loose snow. Even with surface temperatures below freezing, strong sunlight may turn the surface into a slushy combination of water, ice, and snow. Frequent winds of high velocity carve the surface into a rough, gullied terrain, or pile the snow into huge drifts.

The interior of Greenland is startlingly similar to a great desert like the Sahara. Each of these vast wastelands supports no life of its own. Each is dominated by the everlasting wind. Intruders are in constant peril from driving snow on the icecap, from driving sand on the desert, from killing cold on the one hand and from terrible heat on the other. Yet each of them, frozen reaches of ice and burning dunes of sand, have lured adventurous spirits since men first crossed their borders.

The first men to look upon the icecap were Eskimos, remote ancestor of today's Greenlanders, who migrated across the frozen expanse of Baffin Bay and its upper channels from their hunting grounds on Baffin Island and Ellesmere Island. There is ample evidence that they lived on the east coast north of Scoresby Sound. It is unlikely that they crossed the icecap to get there. Presumably they went around it to the north.

The Eskimos have awesome folk tales, built upon ancient superstition, about Greenland's interior. They see it as a dread and mysterious region, peopled by ghosts and monsters. The primitive Eskimos believed that magic and charms were vital to hunting success; magical ceremonies attended birth, maturity, marriage, and death. So they viewed the icecap as the terrible barrier from which evil spirits emerged.

Many of the old tales that are still current concern the *quivitut*, "man who went into the mountains." Like the call of the wild or the inclination to leap from high places, the *quivitut's* lure comes without warning, usually during the black winter. When it strikes, it drives a man out into the night toward the massive icecap. A few may return cured; for most, it is a form of suicide. Those who die become *quivituts*, inhabiting the lifeless, frozen interior, seeking to lure others to destruction because they are lonely or because their nature has become essentially evil. Invulnerable to human injury, the *quivituts* are monstrous in size and sometimes take wing. The Eskimos believe that these dark spirits take upon themselves the powers of the devil.

There were other wild spirits on the icecap, according to the folk tales, and so the Eskimo had no reason to venture upon it until white men came along with their drive to conquer its frozen wastes. Of course, there was no game out there. Why should any practical Eskimo have anything to do with it?

The early Norse visitors were probably quite familiar with the character of the icecap, but it is unlikely that they did much traveling on it.

Few really serious attempts were made to explore the icecap until the latter half of the nineteenth century. There were, however, some tentative Danish explorations early in the eighteenth century. Probably the first person to scale the icecap purposefully was Major Clauss Paarss who, in 1728, was sent to Greenland by the Danish King for that purpose. His instructions were to cross the icecap from west to east to seek traces of descendants of the old Norwegians who had disappeared centuries earlier from the west coast and were thought by some to have migrated to the east coast of Greenland.

Paarss also was to examine the nature of the mysterious interior. look for cattle or wild animals, find any suitable fodder and search for precious minerals. Lacking any familiarity with the true nature of the icebound country, he optimistically proposed to ride across it comfortably on horseback. He was not long in being completely disillusioned; his small company, inexperienced in travel on ice, had progressed no more than two hours on the marginal zone of the icecap before it was suddenly halted by a gaping, bottomless crevasse.

Paarss was a man of determination and endurance, however, and this failure was not enough to discourage him. The next year when he again attempted to penetrate the interior, this time by foot, he had somewhat better luck, spending three days becoming better acquainted with the nature of the icecap. Toward the east he could see only more and more snow and ice, interrupted by an occasional nunatak.* The prospects were so forbidding that he acknowledged the impossibility of the task assigned to him and reluctantly turned back.

The next attempt to invade the icecap was made in 1751 by Lars Dalager, an enterprising and inquisitive storekeeper in South Greenland. Having heard exciting Eskimo legends of mountains shrouded in mystery far across the icecap to the east, he grew

* Nunatak is an Eskimo word meaning "island surrounded by ice."

curious and, hoping to establish their existence, organized a small party to seek them.

After ascending the icecap only a short distance, the adventurous storekeeper saw what he thought were the fabled mountains. But the rough, almost impenetrable marginal zone, overspread with crevasses, obstructed him as it had Paarss and he was unable to make any appreciable progress toward them. In a week's time, having traveled ten arduous miles over a slick ice surface, he was forced to return to Frederikshaab. Rather than the legendary mountains, however, what Dalager actually saw were more nunataks (which now bear his name) free of snow in the high summer sun.

Dalager had traveled far enough and spent enough time to bring back a fairly accurate account of the icecap. A man of great courage, determination, and vision, with no fears of the unknown, he certainly would have gone farther had he been able to do so. The eighteenth century expeditions, of which Dalager's was the last recorded, revealed little about the extensive desert of ice.

In the middle of the nineteenth century renewed interest in the icecap was inspired by two men—one of the most accomplished among Swedish explorers and scientists, Baron A. E. Nordenskjöld, and the imaginative and brilliant Danish government official and scientist, Dr. Henry Rink. Although a director of the Greenland Trading Company, a government monopoly, Rink's interest went far beyond the unexciting problems of merchandising. His pioneering studies of the natives of Greenland are classics of their kind, and his descriptions of the country with special emphasis on the icecap marked a new era in Greenland's scientific history that has persisted to this day. He reflected on the geographical significance of the icecap and wrote about it with so much enthusiasm and vigor that he captured the imagination and interest of scientists and explorers all over the world.

Rink argued persuasively that Greenland should become a huge living laboratory for the study of glaciers and glaciation. Among the first to emphasize Greenland as the source of icebergs, he described their importance and menace to transatlantic shipping. Rink hypothesized a relationship between Greenland's icecap and the last Ice Age that once covered the North American continent as far south as the Ohio River. Scientists and explorers of many nations were attracted by Rink's theories and made plans in increasing numbers to explore the ice sheet as a relic of the Pleistocene and to investigate its influence on the climate of the nothern hemisphere.

While Rink was busy writing about his observations and theories, the Hudson's Bay Company official who had distinguished himself in Canadian Arctic exploration, Dr. John Rae, was sent to Greenland to determine the icecap's possibilities as a telegraph cable route from America to Europe. It seemed easier and more logical to follow the northern route with short over-water stretches and to lay a span of the cable over the icecap rather than under great reaches of the Atlantic Ocean. This was the first attempt to use the land areas of the north—Labrador, Greenland, Iceland, the Faroes—on a route to connect North America with Europe. Rae could penetrate only a short distance on the ice in the neighborhood of Narsarssuak in the Julianehaab district. The cable project consequently was abandoned.

Rink's description of Greenland brought the first of a long series of American explorers who sought to solve its mysteries. Dr. Isaac Israel Hayes, who had served as a surgeon on an earlier Arctic expedition led by Dr. Elisha Kent Kane, sailed in 1860 for North Greenland with the avowed purpose of making an attempt to reach the Pole. Hayes made several trips to the surface of the icecap in the vicinity of Cape Alexander, latitude 78° N.

In 1867 the famous Alpinist, Edwin Whymper, ascended the icecap on the west coast, a short distance north of the Arctic Circle. Like so many others who preceded him, he believed that the barren area of ice merely surrounded an interior of thick forest, lush meadows, and abundant animal life. He fully expected to find an interior paradise populated with herds of reindeer that had migrated from the coastal area, presumably over the icecap or along fjords that penetrated deep into the interior.

Whymper had little more success penetrating the interior than his predecessors; however, he did ascend far enough to be overwhelmed by the immense stretches of snow and ice that blocked his path. The vast accumulation led him to conclude that there must be an enormous reservoir of snow for its production, and he concluded that the interior could not be free of snow and ice. He estimated the interior of the inland ice to reach the staggering elevation of 8,000 feet. It was a remarkably good guess.

Real progress in lifting some of the shroud of mystery that always had obscured the icecap was made in 1870. Nordenskjöld and the botanist, S. Berggren, after being deserted by two accompanying Eskimos, reached an elevation of 2,200 feet in an attempt to cross the ice sheet from a point on the west coast at its narrow southern end. Of significance among Nordenskjöld's scientific observations was his description of glacial dust known as cryoconite.* It created world-wide attention among geologists.

Thirteen years elapsed between Nordenskjöld's first and second

* Cryoconite, which Nordenskjöld described for the first time, is a fine grain powder that is found strewn extensively on the surface of the ice. When this dust absorbs the warm rays of the sun, it sinks into the ice, forming perpendicular cylindrical holes. These vary from one to two feet in depth and from two inches to two feet in diameter. They give the surface of the ice the appearance of a huge unsymmetrical sponge. Nordenskjöld first hypothesized that the cryoconite dust was of cosmic origin but later accepted terrestrial origin as a probability. In 1880 Holst made several penetrations of the icecap to examine Nordenskjöld's glacial dust. He concluded that it was of the same substance as the mountains of the coast and was not cosmic but wind-blown.

Professor Wilson of the University of Massachusetts, who made a petrographic study of cryoconite in 1953, also arrived at the conclusion that the cosmic origin hypothesis could not be supported because none of the so-called cosmic minerals were observed. Neither did he find evidence to substantiate Poul Harder's (1908) rather unusual hypothesis that cryoconite is a decomposition product of ptarmigan excrement. Wilson's examination showed a marked similarity between the cryoconite and samples taken from an outwash plane silt near the icecap, thus supporting Holst's findings. Wil-

reconnaissance of the icecap. During the intervening years he focused his efforts on the problem of navigating the Northeast Passage. On his second expedition to Greenland, in 1883, he was determined to travel far enough to find the elusive pasture lands and reindeer which he still believed existed in the desiccated realm of snow and ice. For this important journey he employed two Lapps because they were accustomed to cold weather and to traveling great distances on skis. Although he did not find the rich agricultural land of corn and grass which was his ultimate objective, he did progress farther than in 1870.

In eighteen days—this time from a point within the Arctic Circle—Nordenskjöld's party covered 73 miles and reached an elevation of 4,953 feet, more than twice as high as on his earlier attempt. Soft, wet snow, glacial lakes, and running glacial streams of frigid water, into which both men and sledges repeatedly sank, made further progress laborious, if not impracticable. Their forward movement was so wearisome that Nordenskjöld decided to dispatch the two Lapps into the interior, confident that traveling light on their skis they could reach the long-sought inner valley. As anticipated, they did make excellent mileage and time. They pressed on another 80 miles to reach an elevation over 6,000 feet before returning. But, disappointingly, they brought back no green foliage

---

son writes that during the summer strong winds frequently blow up the fjord, pick up dry silt from the terraces, mud flats, and the hills, and deposit it on the icecap.

The melting effect of cryoconite recalls a recommendation made during the war by a distinguished explorer. He sent the Commanding General, A.A.F., a long, discursive memorandum in which he proposed to melt the Greenland icecap. The reason for undertaking such an unusual venture was never satisfactorily explained except that the explorer wanted to help out in the war effort and, of course, to supervise the project. His recommendation was simplicity itself: he urged that planes used for dusting wheat and cotton crops be used on sunny days in Greenland for spreading lampblack over the icecap. The sun's rays would be absorbed by the lampblack in a manner similar to that of cryoconite, and, after several dustings and with the help of an army of soldiers who would chip away at the glaciers emptying in fjords, he predicted that the icecap would melt and disappear.

from trees, no evidence of plant specimens or animal life, but only word that no land was visible. The expedition had its rewards: in thirty-one days of ice travel, Nordenskjöld and his Lapps had set a new record for penetration of the interior of Greenland.

The years between Nordenskjöld's first and last attempt to cross Greenland were marked by some desultory activity on the icecap. In 1871 Moldrup attempted an exploratory expedition without praiseworthy results. Four years later Amund Helland, a Norwegian geologist, measured the rate of movement of several Greenland glaciers. Helland found incredible glacier movements of from thirty to sixty feet in a day. Other geologists were still inclined to discount some of the reported rates of movement because of the lingering tendency to compare Greenland's glaciers with mountain glaciers which, while notably less active, received more intensive study.

In 1876 Holm, Steenstrup, and Kornerup set out to explore the icecap from the interior of the Julianehaab district, near the present Narsarssuak Air Base. Like others who had attempted to ascend from this neighborhood, they found progress painfully slow over the rough ice and deep crevasses. They were forced to confine themselves to measuring some nearby glaciers.

Two years later Lieutenant Jensen of the Danish Army was sent by a Danish commission to investigate the icecap. With two Danish companions he spent twenty-three days on its surface and returned with some important geographical discoveries. They traveled on foot, each hauling a small sledge loaded with provisions, tracing Dalager's earlier route. They dragged their loads over the badly incised marginal area and finally reached the ice-free rock outcrops, or nunataks, that Dalager had assumed were mountains on the east coast. From the top of one of these nunataks Jensen, looking east across the wasteland of ice, sighted still other snow-free peaks glistening in the sunlight which he, in turn, thought were coastal mountains of the east coast. Determined to investigate these new summits, he later in that year traveled twenty miles beyond the Dalager group of nunataks to those he had sighted. To his bitter dismay, instead of finding himself on the east coast as he had assumed, he had in actuality discovered another group of nunataks faintly coated with earth. These now bear his name.

Jensen and his adventuresome companions, like others who have traveled on the icecap, suffered from the cold, bad traveling conditions, and insufficient food. The hardships they reported were enough to dissuade officialdom from sending out any other exploratory parties to seek the east coast that year.

Three years after Nordenskjöld's last journey on the icecap came the first of a series of Greenland and polar explorations by the most striking figure in Arctic history—Robert E. Peary, who became the most distinguished of American Arctic explorers.

Peary made Greenland his principal area of operations. Almost every year after 1891 he invaded the frozen wastes. The United States Navy Department, in which he was a civil commander, gave him leave of absence, reluctantly on occasion, but he never enjoyed financial aid from the government; he used his own limited private means. For his later expeditions wealthy friends undertook the raising of money, relieving him of financial worries.

In 1886, two years before Nansen crossed Greenland, Peary and a Danish companion named Maigaard, made a survey in the Disko Bay region on the west coast to test Peary's theories of travel on the icecap.

Peary hoped to become the first to cross the icecap. He was determined to find solutions to the vexing problems of the icebound interior. He was sure that crossing Greenland was possible, and he even described the icecap as an "Imperial Highway" to the east coast.

Peary's 23-day reconnaissance took him 100 miles inland and to a record elevation of 7,500 feet. His difficulties on the icecap in this first Arctic venture were invaluable on his future expeditions. He became convinced of the efficiency of a small party as compared to a larger one, and later he invariably was guided by this conviction. Peary also became an expert on snowshoes and skis.

Admiral Peary too often is remembered only as the discoverer of the North Pole. Actually, some of his major discoveries were made over a period of years while exploring the icecap of Greenland and preparing for his final successful dash to the Pole. His discoveries in Greenland are, in many ways, as dramatic as his successful conquest of the Pole—and, from a geographical point of view, more important.

But Peary had to yield the honor of being the first to cross Greenland. The crossing was made in 1888 by Fridtjof Nansen, the audacious Norwegian scientist and explorer, who later also won international distinction as a great humanist. Nansen was the winner of the Nobel Peace Prize in 1923, and was among the first of the international servants that the Scandinavian countries have so well supplied to the world.

All the earlier attempts on the icecap had started from the west coast, which is more heavily populated than the east coast. The unsuccessful explorers, fearful that they would reach no habitation on the eastern shores, turned back to their starting points. Nansen considered this poor strategy; instead of leaving settlements behind him, he intended to start from the unknown with populous villages ahead.

He chose three Norwegians to go with him: Otto Sverdrup, a retired ship's captain; Olaf Dietrichsen, a first lieutenant in the Norwegian infantry; and Kristian Kristiansen Trana, a peasant from northern Norway. Since he had originally planned on taking reindeer, Nansen believed that Lapps would be useful to him. They are a hardy race, and at home in the rigors of the Arctic. He selected two: Balto, age twenty-six, and Radna, age forty-five. Nansen was only twenty-six years old at the time of this expedition. Planning within limited funds gathered in Norway and Denmark, Nansen had to economize wherever possible. He solved the critical problem of sea transportation to the east coast by arranging to be taken from Iceland on a Norwegian sealer that was to spend the summer hunting season along that coast.

Near the middle of July, 1888, Nansen and his party of five excellent skiers left the sealing vessel in their own boats in an attempt to reach the coast only two miles away. Drift ice, currents, storms, and pack ice kept them drifting for fruitless days, farther and farther from the cost. For two weeks they were at sea, consuming badly needed food and strength, fuel, and particularly valuable time. Not until 16 August did they finally begin their ascent of the icecap.

Progress was slow; on the first day they were able to cover only three miles to an elevation of 500 feet. Here they pitched their tent and slept on the icecap. Because of melting snow and ice, at least in the marginal area, daytime travel was difficult. From then on they traveled mostly at night.

At 7,980 feet of altitude they reached a plateau on the inland ice where there was no longer the continuous struggle with slush and bad footing. Travel was much easier. With the changing complexion of the surface they were also able to change from snowshoes to skis, enabling them to move more rapidly. Toward the end of August they reached their highest elevation, 8,250 feet. Now the slope was continually downhill. They were also aided by favorable winds. They lashed tarpaulins to their sleds as sails and took advantage of the friendly surface and helping breeze. On 19 September they sighted nunataks that fringed the west coast and then the west-coast mountains. On the twenty-fifth of September, they left the icecap and set foot on solid land. Their troubles were not over; they had crossed Greenland but still faced sixty miles of arduous travel down the length of the fjord to reach Godthaab. This final leg of the journey took several days of sailing in a boat improvised of willows and covered with sailcloth.

Nansen added greatly to the meager knowledge of the icecap. For the first time, a realistic picture of that desolate region was available. Contrary to earlier opinion, Nansen found a great deal of moisture on the icecap. He experienced rain or snow during half of the 40 days he spent traveling almost 400 miles on the inland ice.

The most important of all Nansen's scientific findings were his meteorological records. It was a study of Nansen's weather observations and especially his description of wind circulation that led William H. Hobbs later to develop his theory of the glacial anticyclone that so stimulated Arctic climatic studies for more than four decades, even though the very scientific work that the theory engendered disproved it finally.

After Nansen's successful crossing, Peary's new goal became the solution of the great geographic mystery of what lay beyond the icecap to the far north. To do so, he learned to live among Eskimos, to adapt himself to their primitive conditions, to subsist on seal meat and walrus blubber, and to endure rigorous hardship.

The northern and northeastern part of Greenland was a blank on the map. Peary went into the white wilderness without knowing exactly where his travels would take him, what he would find, or how long he would take to complete his journey. Some held to the view that Greenland might extend northward even to the Pole itself.

On 1 May 1892, with twenty dogs pulling two sleds, Peary and three companions started on the first of his many great sledge trips in North Greenland, discovering the sea on the east coast and advancing the theory that the great ice mass was an island.

The journey was the first made on the icecap that used dogs for transportation. Peary did not, however, discover an "Imperial Highway" nor did he find the most practicable route to the Pole. His dash to the Pole was from the northern tip of Ellesmere Island. The success of his first North Greenland expedition made him famous.

Three years later Peary and two companions started on a second trans-Greenland trip of over 1,300 miles, this time with an additional sled and forty-two dogs. Taking a slightly different route, Peary headed toward Independence Fjord, which he had discovered on his earlier journey. Frightful storms beset them day after day. Half-starved, and with only nine dogs surviving the ordeal, they were saved by killing musk ox when they reached Independence Fjord.

The return trip across the icecap was made on half rations. With only one of the forty-two dogs still living, the party reached its headquarters after twenty-five days of fatigue and starvation. Only four moldy biscuits were left in their food pouches. Having conquered the icecap, Peary now turned his thoughts toward the goal of all Arctic explorers, the trip to the North Pole.

Now there were many expeditions launched across the inland ice. A large Danish expedition was headed by L. Mylius-Erichsen in 1906. This party proposed to study the icecap scientifically, and to cross the center of the island, but Mylius-Erichsen and two companions died on the icecap while exploring northeast Greenland.

In 1910, Captain Ejnar Mikkelsen and a companion traveled on the icecap to recover the diaries, notes, and sketches of Mylius-Erichsen.

Then followed three crossings of geographical importance. The first was by the towering Danish-Eskimo explorer, Knud Rasmussen, the only other leader to follow Peary's perilous trail by dog team across North Greenland. He was accompanied by the fabulous Freuchen, who did the navigating in spite of a severe and painful attack of snow blindness. With superior mapping, this expedition proved that Pearyland is really part of Greenland. On the return trip, Freuchen almost died from starvation and exhaustion. Only seven dogs survived the journey, and the men had no provisions but tobacco when they reached Thule * in September.

* The large Thule air base, built after World War II, was adjacent to Rasmussen's trading station, established there in 1910. The trading post was recently removed to Kanak, sixty miles north.

Rasmussen took another party across the tough northern section of the icecap in the summer of 1917. Two members of the expedition were lost—one was eaten by wolves; the other, a famous Danish botanist, starving and exhausted, died a few miles from safety.

Another Danish group, led by J. P. Koch, made a very important crossing of the icecap in 1913. Koch was accompanied by the renowned German geologist, Alfred Wegener, who later led expeditions of his own. The Koch party had sixteen horses put ashore on the east coast. They all escaped during the landing operation, and only ten were recaptured. The other six were never seen again.

Koch proposed to cross the broad central dome of the icecap, a journey of 750 miles. His party left its winter quarters on the east coast with five heavily laden sledges, each drawn by a horse. There were only two pleasant days during the first forty days in the interior. Blizzards raged for twelve days. The horses became snow blind. Three of them had to be killed; the remaining two solved their own food problem by eating horsemeat.

As the days lengthened and the sun rose with the approach of summer, every man in the party suffered from peeling skin and festering blisters. In the soft snow, both men and horses wore snowshoes. On 11 June, one of the remaining horses had to be killed, but now the going was easier because they were on the long downhill trek toward the west coast after reaching an elevation of 9,850 feet. Continuing their scientific studies throughout the trip in spite of the terrible conditions, the scientists made many valuable meteorological contributions to the knowledge of Greenland. One of their most surprising discoveries was to find traces of snow sparrows and polar foxes as far as 300 miles from the nearest exposed land, far beyond what had always been considered the limit of life on the icecap.

The last horse gave out on July 4, only seven miles from the coast, but it was the first, last, and only horse to cross Greenland on the hoof.

The icecap continued to be a busy place in the years immediately preceding World War I. An expedition in 1912 was led by the Swiss, DeQuervain, who crossed from Jacobshavn on the west coast to Angmagssalik on the east coast. His expedition was well planned, highly organized for glacialogical and meteorological studies, and ably executed. He had six companions, twenty-nine dogs pulling three sleds, and ten Eskimo porters.

World War I stopped exploration, and for several years the icecap was ignored by explorers, except for Rasmussen's second Thule expedition in 1917.

The first of a number of University of Michigan expeditions led by Professor William H. Hobbs was sent to Greenland in 1926. The University's scientists were in the field between 1926 and 1933. I was aerologist on the 1928 expedition that wintered at Mount Evans on Söndre Strömfjord, near the site of Narsarssuak. In 1930–31 I was leader of the Fourth University of Michigan Greenland Expedition, serving in that capacity as a Fellow of the Scandinavian-American Foundation. The year was spent making glaciological, geological, and meteorological studies near the great, intensely active Upernivik Glacier.

Max Demorest was my only white companion. We had with us a Greenlander family of five. During the same year another University of Michigan student was making meteorological studies in Ivigtut.

The prime object of the University of Michigan Greenland Expeditions was the study of wind over the great icecap, but we also worked in geological, glaciological, botanical, and other scientific areas. The last of the University of Michigan Greenland Expeditions, 1932–33, was co-sponsored by Pan American Airways. They were showing interest in a northern route to Europe. This was the only University of Michigan Expedition that had a party that occupied a station on the icecap for any protracted period of time.

The expeditions of Professor Alfred Wegener, the German scientist, were the most important ones to make glaciological and meteorological studies in Greenland in the period between the two World Wars. The Germans were also concerned with the problem of new air routes. I had met Professor Wegener in Holsteinsborg in June 1929, when he was making surveys to establish a feasible route from the coast to the interior of the icecap. He was also experimenting with new mechanized equipment for over-snow travel and geophysical instruments for measuring the thickness of the ice.

The principal Wegener expedition went into the field in 1930 when I started my studies in the Upernivik District. Wegener established three stations along the seventy-first parallel: one of these was on the east coast, another on the west coast, and the third and most interesting one was located midway between the two coasts on the icecap at an elevation of 9,700 feet. This station Wegener called Eismitte, meaning "middle of the ice." Wegener's expedition was unusual in that it was the first to use propeller sledges successfully on the icecap. Indeed, it was the first time that mechanical means of transportation were used. Earlier J. P. Koch had attempted to get tractors on the icecap but had failed to do so. Perhaps it was from Koch that Wegener, who had been a member of Koch's expedition, got the idea of using mechanical equipment on the ice.

Three summer trips with ten heavily loaded sledges were made from the west-coast base, hauling supplies and equipment to Eismitte. The two scientists who were to be left at Eismitte for the winter months were still fearful that they lacked sufficient provisions until they could be relieved the following spring or summer.

Wegener was also worried about the wintering party and made a special trip to Eismitte to make sure they were all right. He reached Eismitte late in October on his last journey accompanied by a native, Willemsen, and another scientist. It was obvious to him that the supplies were not adequate to provide for the five men who were now at Eismitte. Assessing the situation, Wegener decided that three could see out the winter; he would not jeopardize the lives of his companions, so with Willemsen he left Eismitte for the coast in clear weather on 1 November. He never made it. Lacking radio communications with the station at Eismitte, the west coast station did not know that Wegener had left the icecap post and had perished. They assumed that Wegener, Willemsen, and the three scientists were holed up for the winter.

A relief party reached Eismitte on 6 May 1931, to learn that Wegener and Willemsen had disappeared on their return journey to the base station. They retraced Wegener's probable route to the west coast. At a point 113 miles from his destination they saw a ski standing upright. It belonged to Wegener. Under the snow, carefully wrapped in blankets and dressed in his best furs, lay Wegener's body, perfectly preserved by the icy cold. His meteorological notations and diary had disappeared. Presumably they had been removed by Willemsen, the native, who had accompanied him. Willemsen's body never was found—and he and Wegener became two more of the legendary *quivituts*. From the evidence since made available, it is probable that Wegener died of a heart attack induced by exhaustion. At the time of his last journey he was fifty-one years old, not too old for exploration but not young for the physical exertions required of him. He had spent a long time on his last icecap journey—forty-one days on the trip from the west-coast station to Eismitte. There seems no doubt that his body had been buried by Willemsen, who had set up the ski as a marker.

The last of the large pre-World War II expeditions was the 1930 British Arctic Air Route Expedition to Greenland. I learned a great deal about this important venture in conversations with most of the expedition in Denmark in 1931. It had several objectives. The first was to complete a survey of 200 miles of coast north of Angmagssalik. It was to explore the interior of Greenland and to study the meteorological conditions in the coastal area and the icecap over a period of at least a year. The expedition was exploring a proposed air route to the Western Hemisphere by way of Greenland; it had two De Haviland Moth airplanes for surveying the icecap from the air.

The expedition left England on 6 July 1930 aboard Shackleton's old ship *Quest,* and arrived at Angmagssalik a fortnight later. Forty miles from Angmagssalik, where twelve years later the Air Force was to establish a rescue station, they found a suitable base and from there they set out to establish an icecap station 140 miles inland at an elevation of 8,000 feet, the highest point in the vicinity between the two coasts. The icecap station was built from a double-domed tent with a tunnel entrance. The trail to it from the coastal area was marked with red flags each half mile. The plan was to have the occupants relieved every month. No two men would man the station for a protracted period of time.

The plan did not work quite so readily. The first occupants of the icecap station were Lindsay and Riley. In October they were relieved by Biggam and D'Aeth. At the end of October a party set out to relieve them, but had to return because of poor surface conditions and bad weather marked by continuous blizzards. As winter came, it was apparent that repeated journeys to the icecap station would be impossible. Nevertheless, the expedition was determined that the station, vital to the meteorological survey, should be manned throughout the winter.

When the party to relieve Biggam and D'Aeth finally did reach the station, Courtauld, one of the relievers, volunteered to stay on alone because the supplies were not sufficient for two. Courtauld began his solitary vigil on 6 December. He had a tent 10 feet in diameter, at an elevation of 8,000 feet on an expanse of endless ice and snow. The undertaking caused considerable worry to those at the base, and probably Courtauld himself had moments of regret. It was quite possible that one of the many sweeping blizzards would bury the tent and make it unlikely that a relief party would find Courtauld in his tomb the following spring.

The position of the tent had been astronomically determined. The relief party in the spring, after great difficulty, found Courtauld on 5 May, imprisoned by ice but nevertheless in favorable health and good spirits. From his tent home buried in the ice, there projected only the ventilator and the tops of the meteorological instruments he had used throughout the winter. He had continued his scientific studies throughout the dark winter months and had withstood the loneliness, discomfort, cold, and blizzards exceptionally well, while undergoing an unusual psychological and physical experience. He had held the lonely station alone for five months.

While Courtauld was manning the icecap station, other members of the British Arctic Air Route Expedition were busy making plans at their east-coast base for the crossing of the icecap. Two crossings were made successfully. A party of three (Scott, Stephenson, and Lindsay) left the base on 1 July with twenty-seven dogs and provisions for six weeks. Their plan was to survey the coastal mountain belt where Nansen started his crossing in 1888 and then proceed obliquely to Ivigtut, collecting data on the altitude of the icecap. The highest altitude the travelers reached was approximately 9,000 feet. Like Nansen, they traveled by night, taking advantage of better surface conditions; in one period of four days they traveled the phenomenal distance of 108 miles. On the western slope of the icecap, with a favorable trailing wind, Lindsay rigged sails for their sleds. While crossing the icecap, they had averaged 16.6 miles a day for the full journey.

When they reached the coastal area, they had to kill their dogs. Lindsay wrote: "Then towards midnight came by far the most unpleasant job of all the expedition. In southwest Greenland there are cows and sheep. Huskies and domestic animals cannot live together and we had been told that we must kill our dogs. Our only consolation was that they did not die hungry. Each dog was given ten pounds of pemmican, a sort of prisoner's breakfast."

A second crossing of the icecap by a pair from the BAARE was made by Rymill and Hampton. They left Angmagssalik on 14 August, heading for Holsteinsborg on the west coast. Their travel equipment consisted of two sledges, two kayaks, and twenty well-fed dogs. They took a series of elevations and meteorological observations on the way across. The wisdom of carrying kayaks hundreds of miles across the icecap was debatable. Rymill and Hampton had planned well; they knew that once on the other side their journey was by no means over—they could use the kayaks to descend the entire length of Söndre Strömfjord. They hoped to reach Holsteinsborg from the east coast in about six weeks. In the early stages the going was much worse than they had expected. The crevasses, running water, hummocks, and soft snow made travel difficult, but after they had reached a food depot 15 miles inland the surface condition improved. The next 280 miles over the inland ice were covered in thirty traveling days. They were held up for only two days by high winds and snowdrifts.

As they approached the west coast, surface conditions again steadily deteriorated. Continuous rain, swollen streams on the icecap, and large ice hummocks rising fifty feet high forced them to abandon one sled. Flocks of snow buntings, no strangers to the icecap, came out from the coastal region to greet them, followed by the ubiquitous ravens that were out for an easy meal. Fifty years previously, Nordenskjöld's party had seen ravens whirling around on the icecap less than 100 miles from where Hampton and Rymill saw them. It was the presence of ravens, an occasional fox, and snow buntings that had led Nordenskjöld to suggest the existence of an oasis in the interior of the icecap. The snow buntings gave Rymill and Hampton the same optimism that Nansen had when he, too, was approaching the west-coast mountains after crossing the icecap.

They reached the head of the river that runs from the icecap to the south branch of Söndre Strömfjord on 30 September, still 113 miles from Holsteinsborg. Game seemed abundant, so Rymill and Hampton decided to carry the kayaks for twenty-five miles to the head of the fjord and travel from there by water, hunting seals for food. They reached a lake near the icecap on 5 October and crossed it by kayak. The season was well advanced, and the next night the lake had frozen over completely. Six miles beyond the lake, the river feeding it to Söndre Strömfjord was free of ice, and they continued the journey by kayak.

Their troubles still were not over. While shooting rapids, both Rymill and Hampton capsized in their kayaks and lost their paddles. Although Rymill also lost his kayak under ice, luckily it soon caught against a downward-projecting ledge and was recovered. Sleeping bags, the tent, and every shred of clothing were soaked, and the men spent the rest of the day and most of the night trying to dry clothing with what little fuel they had left.

The October nights were now so cold that the river froze over; kayaks and equipment had to be carried to the fjord which remained open. From the top of a small ridge just across Söndre Strömfjord from Mount Evans, they were excited to see six seals playing in the fjord. On 15 October, after the warmest, dryest, and most satisfying night they had spent for some time, they saw on the far side of the fjord a good-sized fishing boat. They kindled a fire and fired rifle shots and succeeded in attracting the attention of the owner of the boat, a Greenlander, who told them in broken English that he was in charge of a search party sent from Holsteinsborg to look for them since they were about a month overdue. The Greenlanders for five days had searched all the approaches to the icecap on the Mount Evans side of the fjord (where the huge Söndre Strömfjord air base is now located) and were about to start on the southern side.

The rescue of Rymill and Hampton was like the rescue of the American flyers Hassell and Cramer, who also had lighted a fire in almost the exact location across the fjord from Mount Evans when we discovered them in September 1928.

The third surface crossing in 1931 was made by two young Norwegians—Martin Mehren and Arny Höigaard. While the British crossings were from east to west, Mehren and Höigaard followed the opposite pattern. They employed 15 Eskimo porters, who carried their equipment to a height of 3,100 feet on the icecap. From there the two young men took off with their equipment on two sleds drawn by 16 dogs. They reached their maximum altitude of 9,700 feet on 4 August, and from there, with a favorable wind, they were able to speed along by means of sails made of tent cloth. They arrived on the coast fourteen days later.

Again there was a span of several years before the next crossing. In 1934 Martin Lindsay, accompanied by Andrew Croft and Daniel Godfrey, crossed from west to east, starting at Jacobshavn. They traveled over 1,000 miles across and down the inland ice to Angmagssalik. In 80 days of surveying they held to a swift pace of 13.6 miles per day.

Two years later came the last pre-World War II crossing. This was accomplished by the French anthropologist and explorer, Paul-Émile Victor, who with two companions made the journey from Christianshaab to Angmagssalik.

CHAPTER IV

The Search for Landing Sites

THE PANZER divisions began to roll in the spring of 1940. The "phony war" came to an abrupt end in a series of terrible slashing drives by the Wehrmacht. One catastrophe after another made the free world shiver; Norway, Denmark, the Lowlands, France rolled under the crushing tank treads and crumbled before the screaming dives of the Stukas. Italy marched grandiosely into the hostilities. Britain stood alone, facing the bristling continent. German U-boats, perfecting the wolfpack tactics, swarmed in the North Atlantic. Along the Channel coast, landing craft began to pile up along the wharves, ready to take aboard Hitler's victorious legions. Arrogant young paratroopers grinned as they sang, "We are marching against England."

While the European earth was being torn by the Wehrmacht and the Luftwaffe, official American eyes were turning slowly toward the northland, to the northern air route that now was desperately needed.

During the years before the war, the airway had attracted attention. After Cramer had pioneered it, there was continuing activity over Greenland where the icecap was the principal obstacle to the planes of that period. Wolfgang von Gronau crossed the icecap north of Scoresby Sound three times as he flew between Germany and Canada. Farther south, the British Arctic Air Route Expedition used a small amphibian plane for crossing.

Then, in 1933, a Lockheed Sirius seaplane swooped unheralded out of the skies over the west coast of Greenland. It was piloted by Colonel Charles A. Lindbergh, accompanied by his wife. Where Lindy went, the eyes of the world followed. Greenland was in the news.

Lindbergh made numerous flights up and down the coast and over the icecap, surveying the route for Pan American Airways. He searched for possible bases and studied conditions along alternative air routes between America and Europe. His doubts as to the commercial possibilities of the northern airway slowed considerably possible aviation developments in the northland, although in the same year, the Italian Fascist leader and aviator, Italo Balbo, led a mass of Italian planes over Greenland en route from Rome to Chicago.

However, when the northern airway was needed a few years later, Lindbergh's lack of enthusiasm was smothered by two loud and clear voices shouting the possibilities of aviation in the Arctic: Professor William H. Hobbs, the great teacher and Arctic scientist, and the expert aviator and explorer of the north, Bernt Balchen. They repeatedly called attention to Greenland in Balchen's terms, as the "great aircraft carrier of the Arctic." This was during the period when long-range German aircraft were making reconnaissance flights over the icecap.

Hobbs and Balchen deserve the principal credit for American ventures in Greenland. Instead of becoming a Nazi jumping-off place in the Western Hemisphere, it became a major American bastion in the struggle to whip Hitler.

Hobbs, fiery and voluble, battled his way through Washington skepticism in order to win his fight. For two years, the State and

Greenlanders in fragile kayaks, wearing cloth instead of traditional furs, hail a PBY flying boat on the ice-edged summer waters of a fjord. They still live on seals, walrus, bears, and narwhal hunted from these frail craft. Their colony near Thule was moved sixty miles north when noisy, odorous planes and ships drove away the game.

Motorized snow sleds, shown on the Greenland icecap, speed today's travelers across Arctic wastelands. They are superior to dog teams for rescue and exploration as long as fuel and maintenance are at hand. Sleds like these aided attempts to rescue the Flying Fortress crew that was marooned on the icecap for six months in World War II.

Big bombers down on the icecap make only dots upon the vast frozen desert of interior Greenland (700,000 square miles of eternal frost). When planes went down in World War II, the Air Force stopped all operations to rescue crews. Casualties were amazingly low along the great lifeline that supplied fighting planes for European skies.

American and Soviet fliers stand in amity before a symbol of alliance at Fairbanks on the lifeline to Moscow. Hitler's "1,000-year Reich" was about to crumble, and soon U. S. aircraft like this would cease to roar through Arctic skies toward Siberia. This Russian and hundreds like him packed up and went home; the Iron Curtain was about to fall.

5000ᵗʰ AIRPLANE DELIVERED ALSIB ROUTE LADD FIELD ALASKA 10ᵗʰ SEPT 1944

A shark-nosed bomber is readied for polar flight at Ladd Field, great Alaskan base, where cold-weather flying experiments in World War II set up safety measures for the worst Arctic conditions. The lives of twenty-six men of the testing crews were lost in the battle to make polar flying safe. Countless lives have been saved by their sacrifices.

Vital radar watch of trans-polar skies is kept by American and Canadian officers at Combat Operations Center, North American Air Defense Command in Colorado Springs. This scanning post tracks air-borne objects thousands of miles distant. If attack ever came, the men in this room would flash the warning and monitor the battle.

Along the DEW Line at dawn, radar probes the Arctic skies at Tatalina Air Force Station, ready to flash instant warning of hostile aircraft. More than 60 stations stretch 3,000 miles along the 70th parallel from the Aleutians to Greenland. These northern sentinels cost a billion dollars and now supplement the titanic BMEWS network.

Massive sky scanners, longer than football fields and higher than fifteen-story buildings, are BMEWS radar antenna at Thule, Greenland. This station, with others in Alaska and England, searches polar skies to detect instantly the firing of missiles from Soviet launching pads. Each screen uses 1,500 tons of steel and can stand in 185-mile winds.

Delta Daggers on patrol slice across an Arctic fjord between barren, snow-covered coastal mountains. The all-weather interceptors carry air-to-air guided missiles, both heat-seeking and radar. With high altitude and long range, these knifelike fighters (F-102A) are top weapons in NORAD's defense line against air-borne enemy attacks.

Radar platform aloft, a U. S. Navy Constellation, is one of a patrolling fleet that extends the DEW Line off North American coasts, from Newfoundland to mid-ocean and westward from the Aleutians. The crew has thirty-two men who run electronic and radar equipment. Picket ships and Texas Towers also keep the DEW Line vigil far offshore in both oceans.

Mileage marker stands in the polar sea, posted by crewmen on Ice Island T-3 in 1957. Distances to world centers were inexact before the paint was dry, for the ice island is on an ever-circling voyage around the Arctic Ocean, and has traveled more than 15,000 miles since it broke off from an Ellsmere Island glacier many years ago.

Aircraft on a pedestal is perched on Ice Station Bravo (T-3) in the Arctic Ocean. The plane, forced down years ago, was cannibalized and abandoned. The ice beneath it, insulated from the sun and shielded from wind, did not recede seasonally but left the plane high above the island's surface, where it acts as a pilot's check point.

Snow weasel and helpers drag the runway on Bravo to allow take-off of a C-54. Kidney-shaped and yellow-tinted in the view of air observers, the ice island has been watched and manned by the Air Force for a decade. Abandoned in September 1961, when it grounded on the continental shelf, the island has now been occupied once more.

Snow house on T-3 rises swiftly with modern tools wielded by Lieutenant Colonel Joseph O. Fletcher—donor of the island's popular name "Fletcher's Ice Island." Central heating, good meals, and recent movies helped relieve the men's tedium and confinement.

Men on Bravo in the Arctic Ocean crouch before the "Operations Building" on the ice island's runway. Another nearby sign proclaimed the air strip as EUREKA INTERNATIONAL AIRPORT, and suggested that tickets to civilization were available on "luxurious C-54's and C-119's arriving from and leaving for Thule and Resolute Bay—occasionally."

War and Navy Departments were battered by a Hobbsian frontal assault. Serious though the matter was, to me and other advocates of action in Greenland, it was a delight to watch and listen to Hobbs in action, for the professor was an unrelenting antagonist.

One of his principal targets was Colonel Lindbergh. Hobbs had been angered by the Colonel's curt rejection of the professor's suggestions that Lindbergh try some landings on Greenland's great inland ice dome, as well as on Hobbs's field in the ice-free coastal area. In his flights for Pan American in 1933, Lindbergh properly enough used a seaplane and made landings in the fjords. But Mrs. Lindbergh's account of their experiences notes that "we flew over Hobbs's camp." Hobbs logically concluded that "it is evident that the Colonel had looked down on this great plain, miles in length and at least a mile in breadth."

Lindbergh's persistent scorn of Greenland in 1941 just spurred the volatile Hobbs on in his campaign to make the island an Allied stronghold. During 1940 and 1941 he was repeatedly and loudly beleaguering Washington to urge naval and air bases in the north country.

"On my own initiative," wrote Hobbs later, "I visited Washington and, on conferring with Army and Navy officers, I quickly discovered that Lindbergh's counsel had been taken. No bases in Greenland were thought possible.

"I then personally put the facts before the officials of the War Plans division of the State, War and Navy Departments. By displaying photographs of the airfield which I had prepared near my base, I dispelled the Lindbergh view that land planes could not possibly make landings in Greenland because of the climate and rugged topography.

"I made both oral and written reports to Army, Navy, and State officials. When I brought them to the attention of Commander Forrest Sherman (later the Chief of Naval Operations), he replied: 'But we have been given to understand that it is impossible to land a plane anywhere in Greenland.'

"When I showed him the view of my Camp Lloyd * airfield at the head of the *Söndre Strömfjord* (which was to become Bluie West Eight), he became excited."

"And," confirmed Admiral Sherman, "he was the first to guide us to the *Söndre Strömfjord* area."

Sherman's excitement was matched, Hobbs said, in interviews with General L. T. Gerow, Chief of the War Plans Division of the Army, and with Hugh Cummings of the State Department. Hobbs suggested that a flier search for other fields along Greenland's west coastal land ribbon between Disko Island and Cape Farewell. "The Army flier, after his scouting, could report only one other possibility, and that but a few miles from Camp Lloyd. After examination on the ground, this second field was found less desirable and the Camp Lloyd airfield was selected for a principal base.

"From that time," added Hobbs, "events followed in rapid succession to secure bases there."

The principal "event" was the Lend-Lease Act, which increased the need for a northeasterly ferrying route to Great Britain. The demand, of course, multiplied after Pearl Harbor.

Hobbs was aided and abetted by Balchen although his technique was different. Balchen, the Norwegian-American polar flyer who had flown Byrd over the South Pole and who, within six months of his commissioning as an Air Force captain had risen to a colonelcy, was familiar with Greenland and its great potential. Quietly he exerted his tremendous influence in official quarters in Washington and particularly on General H. H. Arnold, commanding general of the Air Force.

There had been some interest before Hobbs and Balchen went to work on official opinion in Washington. The Air Force had in-

---

* Camp Lloyd was the base of the University of Michigan Greenland Expedition at the head of Söndre Strömfjord. The nearby aerological and weather observatory was called Mount Evans for the elevation on which it was built.

vestigated Greenland. In 1939, Major J. K. Lacey had been sent to Greenland to make a survey flight.

A proposal was made that year in the United States Senate that Greenland, which controls approaches from the east, northeast, and north, be purchased from Denmark. With Lacey's survey incomplete, the War Department sought from government agencies an expression of views about Greenland; the response was discouraging. The findings, like those that stopped Greenland's purchase when proposed by Peary in 1916, were that Greenland, largely ice-capped and fog-bound, had no natural facilities suitable for the operation of either air or naval forces and that strategic consideration offered "no justification" for its acquisition.

The purpose of Major Lacey's survey was to add to the meager store of information about Greenland's flying potential. In some respects his findings confirmed pessimistic earlier reports. He found maps inadequate and inaccurate, radios functioning badly, no landing areas and, of course, no facilities for repairs. Furthermore, he added that no reliance could be put on navigation by radio compass. He warned of the need to prepare carefully for flights in low temperatures.

We were not alone in our interest in Greenland. The Germans, who in the twenties and thirties had supported scientific expeditions under Wegener and von Gronau, among others, now acquired the major part of the stock of an Icelandic aviation company. Their aim was to control the Greenland-Iceland airway over the North Atlantic by taking over Iceland, its focal point. Herman Goering was interested in Greenland from a personal point of view. In keeping with his fascination for ancient Teutonic splendors, he schooled himself in the art of falconry. In pre-war days, he favored the savage falcons of the Greenland coasts for his hunting, and he had them imported in considerable numbers.

The Germans were aware of the importance of meteorological data from Greenland for European weather forecasting. Their bombing raids on England relied on forecasts using Greenland weather information. Later, when American and British pounding of German cities was crucial, they were able to forecast the timing of the raids by their observations of suitable flying weather. The Nazis maintained a weather station in Greenland, high on the rugged and inhospitable eastern coast at Sabine Island.

Iceland lies only 400 miles east of Greenland, and a German air attack against that island, in February of 1941, again stressed the importance of American control of the northern air route.

There could be no question of Iceland's strategic role. In enemy hands it would have constituted a grave menace to convoy lanes to England and Murmansk. German occupancy of Iceland would have been a threat even to the North American continent. It was necessary to the allies as a base for protection of shipping lanes and for the ferrying of short-range aircraft, an essential link between Greenland and England. These were the considerations which underscored England's occupancy of Iceland in May of 1940. (Later our government undertook to share British responsibilities there.)

The AAF was building up defenses in the northeastern continental area while the Germans occupied Denmark, Norway, France, launched the battle of Britain, and prowled the North Atlantic. Our State Department was not idle. Weeks after the sailing of an American survey expedition, an agreement relating to the defense of Greenland was executed on 9 April, 1941, in Washington by Henrik de Kauffman, Minister for the Kingdom of Denmark, and U. S. Secretary of State Cordell Hull, permitting the United States to establish bases and other installations in Greenland.

The survey expedition we sent to Greenland reported a promising area for airfield development near the southern tip of the island, at Narsarssuak. In west Greenland a much more satisfactory location for a staging field was found at Söndre Strömfjord, as Hobbs had predicted. The survey party failed to find any site for an airfield on the eastern coast. Construction of the two fields was given top priority. When finished, they were to be used for any necessary ferrying operations to England.

We rushed a task force into Narsarssuak Fjord, established a weather station, and started laying the groundwork for an airstrip.

The site selected at Narsarssuak certainly was not the best for a landing field even though, geographically, it was ideally located midway between Goose Bay and Reykjavik, approximately 775 miles from each. Professor Hobbs knew of the area and is supposed to have recommended it as well as Söndre Strömfjord, although he had never seen the Narsarssuak location. Perhaps the name, Narsarssuak, which in Greenlandic means a "great, flat place," appealed to the 1941 surveyors.

A Major Gorlinski of the Corps of Engineers reported on the site although it is said that, like Hobbs, he never actually visited it. Gorlinski was under the mistaken impression that the area was covered with gravel, but the task force which arrived in July found only glacial till, a mass of large rocks and boulders, which their bulldozers and earth-movers couldn't handle. The contractors who had to build the airstrip over the till referred to the boulders as "Gorlinski gravel." If Gorlinski, Hobbs, or any competent geologist had seen the site, he would have been able to advise the engineers what to expect.

The landing party, however, was totally unprepared for what it found, and the project got off to a poor start, with inadequate equipment, bad terrain, and fickle weather. Everyone lived on shipboard at the beginning, but in early August the men went ashore to live in a tent camp.

Two weeks later the camp was almost destroyed by a sudden gale of hurricane velocity, one of the foehn winds that blow ferociously down from the domed icecap. It scattered tents and equipment all over the site. Barges and ships were buffeted on the shoreline. The storm damage amounted to thousands of dollars.

In spite of the initial handicaps, ground for a runway was broken on 5 August, less than a month after the group's arrival.

The runway was ready for small aircraft early in October, but it was not put into use until some months later, when a Lockheed transport of the Royal Air Force Ferry Command came out of the clouds after circling Narsarssuak several times. The plane made a landing on the new steel mat strip. Because of lack of adequate communications, it arrived without warning and probably would have been shot down, if there had been any antiaircraft artillery at the field. Just a month later, I flew into Narsarssuak on the Liberator piloted by Colonel Arnold, the four-engined aircraft that made the pioneer flight over the northern airway.

Work began on Greenland's second air base in late September of 1941, farther north on the west coast just above the Arctic Circle in the interior of Söndre Strömfjord. This was where the University of Michigan Expedition on which I had served had prepared a landing field for Hassell and Cramer in 1928. Narsarssuak was considered the principal site, with Söndre Strömfjord largely in a standby role.

A landing field on the east coast also was deemed essential, and a suitable site was earnestly sought. Survey flights during 1941 by Captain Elliott Roosevelt and others had produced no results.

So important was the east field considered that serious thought was given an airfield to be constructed in Boston on floats and towed for anchoring in one of the east Greenland fjords. Before this plan had gone very far, Major Frederick Crockett, commander of a small weather station at Angmagssalik, found an area slightly north of that small community which gave promise of a field with a single landing strip. The field, with the misleading code name Optimist, was used occasionally as an alternate in the ferrying operations. Its principal service was as an important base for some rescue missions on the icecap.

While the search for a landing site was going on, research laboratories were busy studying the construction of a huge floating airfield made of ice. It was argued that such airfields would be useful, not only as bases for the ferrying of short-range aircraft through the northern latitudes, but also for air operations against the submarines which were causing such great havoc in the North Atlantic. The project was not completed for three reasons. In the first place, the battle of the Atlantic took an unexpected turn for the better because the submarine patrols from established bases began to take heavy tolls of German U-boats. This, in turn, made it possible to send short-range aircraft by surface vessels to the United Kingdom, thus obviating the necessity for having them flown. Finally, extra gasoline tanks on fighter aircraft enabled them to fly directly from west Greenland to Iceland.

Had the submarine menace not been conquered, the manufactured ice airfield might have become a reality. A kind of ice compound, Pykret, made of wood pulp and water, was devised. Tests indicated that it would not melt readily and would stand up well against bombing and torpedo attacks. The project was quite feasible. Prime Minister Churchill, among other wartime leaders, attached importance to its possibilities.

The route through Söndre Strömfjord was planned as an alternate line of flight for aircraft moving from Goose Bay to Iceland during the periods when bad weather made landings impossible at Narsarssuak or when facilities there were overloaded. Flying weather proved better along the alternate route through Söndre Strömfjord and across the icecap of central Greenland than it was to the south along the route through Narsarssuak.

The route finally selected was a modification of original British and Canadian plans which had contemplated a northern route from Gander Lake, Newfoundland, to a single base in southern Greenland, and thence to Iceland and to Britain. A field in Labrador had not been thought essential. Such a route would have required the construction of only one base in Greenland in addition to those already in use. Several factors made the field at Gander Lake undesirable as a staging point: the volume of traffic flying directly to Scotland had become too heavy for ready accommodations; the field was not well located geographically as an intermediate point on flights to Greenland from Maine; and, finally, weather at Gander Lake was inferior to that in interior Labrador.

After the Lend-Lease Act in 1941, American and Canadian officials began to investigate landing field sites in Labrador. Heavy losses to submarines also made it necessary to find additional suitable bases for anti-submarine aircraft.

The Royal Canadian Air Force and the United States Army Air Force each sent survey missions to Labrador. In June 1941 the first mission, led by Eric Fry of the Dominion Geodetic Survey, explored the eastern coast of Labrador in the vicinity of the North-west River. The party discovered a flat sandy area near the head of Goose Bay, which, although over 100 miles inland, was accessible from the sea through Hamilton Inlet and Lake Melville, and offered excellent advantages as an airport.

During the same month an American party headed by Captain Elliott Roosevelt undertook aerial reconnaissance of Labrador for a similar purpose, and also recommended the Goose Bay area for an American airfield.

Shortly after receipt of Fry's report, the RCAF sent engineers to Goose Bay to lay preliminary plans for the projected air base, and by September the Canadian government had awarded a contract for the building of an airport there. The first ship bearing basic supplies docked on 29 September near the site of the projected base. Two days after Pearl Harbor, the first airplane landed at the field on a temporary snow-packed runway with a gravel base.

In the succeeding months RCAF personnel slowly swelled the original detachment, and in February, a U. S. Air Force officer was sent to Goose Bay to make plans for an American weather station. In the meantime, the United States undertook the task of setting up a ferry service from Moncton, New Brunswick, to Goose Bay.

CHAPTER V

Building the Crystals

WHILE THE route from Presque Isle to Goose Bay, Greenland, Iceland, and Prestwick, Scotland, was in the very early stages of construction, General Arnold conceived the idea of flying short-range fighter aircraft directly from the western United States to Scotland. The route he had in mind would have several advantages. The Great Circle route, which was to be followed, would be shorter and would have superior continental weather. (It is now used by the Scandinavian Airlines System, Pan American, and TWA.) Planes from California factories would be flown to Great Falls, Montana, our great ferrying point on the Alsib route to Alaska. From Great Falls the planes would not be on any established air route, thus avoiding the crowded airways in the United States. Furthermore, this proposed route would avert long overwater hauls, and staging points could be located within the safe distance of 400 miles of each other.

At that time, I had temporarily left the field of geology and was serving as director of admissions and records at the University of Minnesota, although like most Americans I was wondering how I was going to serve my country in the inevitable conflict. I got the answer late on a Saturday afternoon in August of 1941. A telephone call to Minneapolis from Washington told me to be at the Munitions Building in the capital on Monday morning, ready for an important meeting. This was immediately after the Argentia Conference between President Roosevelt and Prime Minister Churchill, held on warships off the Newfoundland coast. They had discussed General Arnold's plans for a northern ferry route and supporting weather stations.

I learned at the meeting that we were going to go to work on airfields and weather posts in northern Labrador, Baffin Island, and the east coast of Greenland. The west and south Greenland fields were already under construction. The conferees, who were Air Force officers and Arctic explorers, pitched into the job of deciding on sites. We had a sense of urgency, because the season was already late for Arctic surveys and construction.

On the basis of the summer reconnaissance flight led by Elliott Roosevelt (the one which had also recommended the Goose Bay area), a site near Fort Chimo in northern Labrador had been selected and was given the AAF code name Crystal I. A second location was approved for Frobisher Bay on Baffin Island. This became Crystal II. A third, Padloping, in northern Baffin Island was called Crystal III.

Although he surveyed Greenland's east coast by air, Captain Roosevelt was not able to find a suitable site. He was pessimistic about the future of the entire route. I was astonished to find, for instance, that he believed he had discovered a 25,000-foot mountain near Scoresby Sound in east Greenland—directly in the line of flight from Söndre Strömfjord in west Greenland to Reykjavik. This was a major geographical discovery, if it were true. It might indicate still other undiscovered mountains of great altitude. I asked Roosevelt to point out the exact spot of the mountains he had seen, and it proved to be directly in the route followed by Lindsay across the icecap in 1936. He had found the highest elevation to be 11,000 feet. Questioning of Roosevelt's pilot made it obvious that the crew of the survey plane had been confused by an Arctic mirage, not at all an unusual occurrence in high altitudes.

All the sites selected on Roosevelt's recommendation were in relatively flat areas and far enough inland so that weather (except at Crystal III) was much less foggy than along the coastline. For short-range fighter aircraft, both climate and shorter hops favored a route through Labrador, Baffin Island, and thence to west Greenland.

The Air Force put me to work right away. I was to participate in planning the stations, buying equipment, recruiting personnel, and the actual establishment of the base in Frobisher Bay. It was unusually late in the season to be organizing expeditions to the Arctic, but we couldn't afford to wait. Fortunately, the U. S. Antarctic Expedition had just returned and many of the experienced explorers were available for Arctic duty.

The project was given top priority. We procured equipment, signed up personnel, leased shipping, and took care of a thousand and one chores ranging from the purchase of Arctic reading material and having shots for overseas duty to instructions on the construction of prefabricated housing. By early September I was aboard a former Danish motorship, the *Sicilien* (built for tropical service), headed for Halifax, Nova Scotia. Trawlers were assigned to the expedition, and on 27 September we sailed from Halifax. Four days later we anchored at Corner Brook, Newfoundland, then moved on for our rallying point at Cape Burwell on the northern tip of Labrador, which was reached on 6 October.

The *Sicilien* carried most of the equipment. Flanked around it were nine trawlers, seven of which were diesel-powered and of steel construction, and two were Norwegian fishing vessels of wood construction reinforced for work in ice. The party to establish Chimo Station left Burwell on 9 October in three trawlers, after receiving supplies from the *Sicilien*. Our remaining contingent then sailed into an uncharted fjord in Frobisher Bay where the party which would establish a base in the interior of the bay departed in three trawlers. The *Sicilien* and the three remaining trawlers then sailed for Padloping to establish Crystal III.

Because of the lateness of the season and lack of charts, the group that I accompanied (the Crystal II party) was unable to reach the site recommended by Roosevelt. However, we discharged cargo on a small island a few miles from the head of the bay, where a weather station was established. In November, I returned to the United States aboard the trawler *Lark* and back to my responsibilities at the University of Minnesota. The following summer construction began on a landing field at the head of the bay, the location originally planned.

Upon my entrance into the Air Force in February 1942, one of my first assignments was to find any likely spots for further airfield construction in the Hudson Bay area. Literature on Southampton Island, which I had never visited, indicated some level areas that probably would be good for airfield construction. I questioned Canadian explorers in Ottawa who told me that a suitable site could be found on Southampton. Because of weather, the Belcher Islands in Hudson Bay were not considered.

I was also interested in the possibilities of Churchill on Hudson's Bay, a town that was the terminus of a railroad line from Winnipeg. I had some knowledge of Churchill, having spent several days there in the early thirties. A geological map of Churchill showed a sizable sand spit that could be easily bulldozed into a landing strip. Both Southampton Island and Churchill, which was founded in 1685 and is one of the oldest communities on the North American continent, were visited by engineers who said they were suitable for construction sites.

An interior field would also be built at the Pas, on the rail line between Winnipeg and Churchill. This was to be the first stop beyond Great Falls, Montana. The route—Great Falls, the Pas, Churchill, Southampton, Crystall II, Söndre Strömfjord, Optimist,

Reykjavik, Prestwick—certainly met the rigid requirements laid down by General Arnold for the ferrying of fighter planes. The staging areas were a short distance from each other, the weather over most of the route turned out to be as good as had been expected, and the route would relieve the concentration of aircraft over airways across the United States. Fields actually were constructed at Crystal I on Ungava Bay, at Crystal II in Frobisher, and at Southampton Island, Churchill, and the Pas.

This interior route, however, was never used for ferrying purposes, and it gradually declined as the war went along, in spite of the initial bursts of energy with which the airports were planned and built. The only importance that these airports had during the war was in providing weather information for the main route from Presque Isle to Goose Bay and across Greenland.

So much of the Hudson Bay route was over wilderness that it undoubtedly looked formidable to inexperienced pilots. Fear of the unknown may have been a factor in the neglect of this interior route. Probably of greater significance, however, was the fact that the range of fighter planes was extended by equipping them with extra fuel tanks. This enabled them to make the longer hops from Goose Bay to Narsarssuak and thence to Iceland. Another deciding factor was the success of our air and surface patrols in making the North Atlantic convoy route secure from enemy submarines. By the time the interior route was in operation, it was safe to ship the short-range fighter planes on fast freighters. This involved less risk than flying them across the northern route.

The weather reports from this northernmost air route determined a great deal of the safety of air operations farther south, and so its installations, built at enormous cost after they were declared vital by our high command in 1941, were not wasted.

CHAPTER VI

"Bolero"

THE PIONEER flight of the Liberator bomber in which I was a passenger early in April 1942 was dispatched to test the new airstrips in Labrador, Greenland, and Iceland, and to check flight conditions and flying time between Presque Isle in Maine and Prestwick in Scotland. Lieutenant Colonel Milton W. Arnold, in command of the plane, also was under orders of the Ferrying Command's general staff to make a survey of the route to find out exactly what the prospects were for successful flying of fighter aircraft to Britain. The flights were scheduled for June. Our findings were not designed to make anybody in headquarters jump for joy.

In the first place, there was action immediately needed at Goose Bay, Labrador, to ease strained relationships between our men and the Canadian troops at that station. The Canadians occupied one side of the runway and the Americans were on the other. Our soldiers were unhappily dependent upon the Canadians for most of their basic needs, because we had not yet built sleeping quarters and dining halls. Everyone, including transients like ourselves, was fed in the Canadian mess hall. There was plenty of food, but it was badly prepared.

Our Liberator crew had been told to bring sleeping bags for any emergencies that might arise. We were lucky to have them, for Goose Bay had no sleeping accommodations for transients, and this was only a few weeks before ferrying operations were to start. I was back in Goose Bay in June and found that some of the poor conditions had been corrected, but they were still bad. Our troops didn't move into their own new quarters until November. When I came through again in December, beds and bedding were still in short supply. There were additional problems created when transient crews piled in and their planes were grounded sometimes for weeks by bad weather.

During our April general survey, Colonel Arnold found operations pretty bad, especially in weather and communications services. Our flight was delayed four days for lack of adequate weather information, and then we left without a reliable forecast.

Our reports must have been listened to in Washington. The entire route erupted in preparations for the beginning of the great ferrying movement that would throw the weight of U. S. air power into battle beside the R.A.F. against the Germans.

Colonel Arnold, surveying again in May, found conditions quite a bit better, but there was still plenty of need for improvement. For one thing, little weather information was being relayed among bases in Iceland, Greenland, and eastern Canada. Colonel Arnold found messages in which forecast data requested by Greenland from Gander and Presque Isle were delayed fifteen days. Another delay was twenty-nine days. This was only a month before the scheduled movement of large numbers of aircraft.

One of Colonel Arnold's recommendations was that a qualified officer fly the route continuously, armed with authority to take whatever action was necessary. Colonel Arnold was selected, but his authority was limited to recommendations. Accompanied by the regional weather and communications officers, he kept the route under constant surveillance during the month or so immediately preceding the projected large-scale movement of planes. He fought hard, and by the end of June better conditions could be seen.

The first large-scale ferrying operation was given the AAF code name Bolero, and it was to supply the initial elements of the Eighth Air Force. The plan called for the ferrying of Lightnings, with Flying Fortresses serving as mother ships, each Flying Fortress convoying a group of four Lightnings.

The Bolero project had jurisdictional headaches. Over the objections of Brigadier General Harold L. George of the Ferrying Command, Brigadier General Frank O'D. Hunter of the VIII Fighter Command had control of the air movements of all Bolero units. General George wanted unified control of all operational facilities and air movements. He won his argument. Control of all aircraft was placed in the Ferrying Command. However, the plan was not put into effect until the first movement had been completed. All succeeding ferrying operations were taken over by the Ferrying Command which, on 20 June 1942, became the Air Transport Command.

The first elements of the Bolero movement, 18 Flying Fortresses, took off from Goose Bay for Greenland on 26 June 1942. It wasn't a good day for the AAF. The seven aircraft which cleared Goose Bay in the morning arrived at Narsarssuak without incident. Eleven cleared in the afternoon; one landed at Söndre Strömfjord, three were forced down along the west coast of Greenland without casualties, and the remaining seven returned to Goose Bay. They failed because of inadequate weather information, poor forecasting, bad communications, and inexperienced flight personnel.

Additional flights proceeded without mishap until 15 July when six Lightnings and two Flying Fortresses came down on the icecap. However, the losses on the Bolero movement were less than anticipated. Though some planes were lost, not a single person was seriously injured.

The difficulties encountered in these early ferrying operations had been foreseen by those who had flown the route. We had accurate information about the enormous difficulties of maintaining a fixed schelule. Some general officers in Washington believed that faultless service from the United States to Prestwick would flow in a few weeks. The optimism was not shared by those along the route.

By the end of August, however, 386 aircraft had crossed to England by the North Atlantic ferry route. These included 164 Lightnings, 119 Flying Fortresses, and 103 Skytrains.

There were 920 planes that tried to cross by the end of that year, and 882 reached their destinations. Approximately 700 belonged to the Eighth Air Force. The anticipated accident rate of 10 per cent actually amounted to 5.2 per cent. Among the 38 planes failing to reach Prestwick, 29 were classified as "wrecked" and nine as "lost."

Particular concern had been felt about twin-engine fighters— the Lightnings. Only seven of 186 failed to reach their destinations in 1942. In addition to the six wrecked in July, only one was subsequently lost. Nearly all the 700 planes delivered to the Eighth Air Force were flown by their own combat crews, young men who had just completed their training.

When the North Atlantic situation suddenly became critical because the Air Force lacked cargo aircraft, General Arnold called on the commercial airlines. A deal was made with American, TWA, and Northeast Airlines to fly transport schedules to Greenland and later to Iceland and Scotland. This was the beginning of contract air cargo operations.

Northeast Airlines opened service to Goose Bay in February and to Greenland in May 1942; in July Northeast was flying as far as Prestwick. American Airlines provided transport service between New York and Iceland. Transcontinental and Western Air, using Stratoliners, opened service directly over the North Atlantic to the United Kingdom. These airlines had flight and maintenance personnel who knew most of the tricks of winterization.

CHAPTER VII

Snow, Rain, Sleet, and Ice

THE ESSENTIALS of a weather service ranging from Maine to Iceland were established by the Air Force between March and December of 1941. This meteorological chain relied heavily upon a number of existing Canadian stations in Quebec, Labrador, and Baffin Island, and Danish stations in the villages in Greenland. While the Goose Bay airfield and the three fields in Greenland were being built, weather and communications men moved in, but weather always remained the deadly enemy.

Our fliers hated Greenland's snow, rain, sleet, fog, wind, and ice. They could see no fertile slopes or grassy meadows browsed by livestock. Their view picked out salt water and jumbled rocks, and then the interior ice. Except for a few dwarfed willows, no trees grew. They saw only a few foxes, ptarmigans, ravens, seals, snow buntings, screeching sea birds and rarely a polar bear. Day and night the wind blew; snow crystals formed in cloudless skies. The base at Narsarssuak went from unlimited visibility to zero-zero and back again in a matter of minutes.

One of the dangers to our fliers was ice fog or cirrus crystals formed at ground level. In more temperate climates these almost never appear below 20,000 feet. Visibility in these ice fogs is poor horizontally, but from an elevation looking down it is good, due to vertical alignment of the crystals. A pilot can see a runway from directly above but cannot have it in sight as he angles for a landing. When temperatures are extremely low and the air is calm, smoke from a barracks or even an airplane's engine exhaust is sufficient to cause ice fog.

Foehns, the furious winds which blow from the icecap to the sea, are common during all seasons along the marginal zone of Greenland. A warm dry wind, similar to the chinooks that descend the Rocky Mountains, the foehn can blow up to hurricane strength and will raise the temperature from far below zero to well above freezing and jeopardize aircraft in flight or at rest. Its effects can be felt for hundreds of miles. The foehn picks up dust and pebbles, sand-blasting the propellers of parked planes, making them dangerous to fly. All induction systems and superchargers become filled with sand and rocks which must be removed before engines can be started. Engine coverings are torn to shreds and de-icer boots are damaged beyond repair. I have experienced foehn winds with velocities up to 120 miles per hour. I have seen a Flying Fortress torn from its moorings by a foehn wind and hurled the length of a football field.

All buildings at the Greenland bases had to be designed to resist high winds, and they had to be anchored with chains. At Narsarssuak I saw buildings lifted from their foundations and carried yards away. Windows on the windward side were screened to prevent shattering by flying pebbles. Sand would blast a perfectly smooth hole into a chipped window.

An air inspector's report tells what can happen to planes in a foehn wind (this one was at Narsarssuak): "All plexiglass windshields were sand-blasted and should be replaced (seventy-one aircraft were on the ground at the time). All bombardier glasses shattered. All aircraft were facing into the wind and paint was sand-blasted from propellers, leading edges of wings, etc. Propellers were nicked by flying sand and rocks. All engine covers were torn to shreds by the high wind."

Another of the great menaces to flying on that rugged island was fog. Sea fogs were the most common. They seemed to persist even in violent winds. They moved in almost with the speed of planes. They came unexpectedly and vanished as quickly.

Icing was a constant menace. On take-off, any dew or frost on the windshield or wing surfaces could make the plane a flying icicle even before it became air-borne. A plane could pass into a cloud and emerge with a ton of ice on its wings, fighting to keep altitude.

Every flier knew the menace of the water. No man could expect to live in that cold, intensely greenish-blue water more than eight minutes, or with protective clothing for more than twenty or thirty minutes. With luck he could come down into the water safely and stay afloat in his Mae West. He might be able to swim a few yards but in about ten minutes he would be numb. There was only a little more chance on a life raft. If a man was lucky, a Catalina might pick him up, if it could find him and if it could get close enough in the swells. Otherwise he would die of exposure.

Greenland's weather should not have surprised the Air Force. Studies of weather were available from many research sources. The University of Michigan Greenland Expeditions on which I served had devoted much effort to understanding the icecap and its effect on weather over the North Atlantic. The Greenland Coast Guard Patrol had meteorological data, and information came from a number of other observation posts in the larger Greenland villages. Published weather data, gathered over the years by expeditions and at official meteorological stations in Greenland, were ready for anyone who cared to use them.

At the three airfields in Greenland, perhaps the best weather was found at Söndre Strömfjord. There we had made aerological observations over a period of years in the late twenties and early thirties and had learned something about forecasting foehns by observing cloud formations. Narsarssuak was not quite so good, and the worst weather was to be found on the east coast at Optimist.

Lieutenant Colonel Milton W. Arnold, with whom I traveled in April 1942, reported to General Arnold: "The Northeast ferrying route is the world's second worst weather route." Presumably he considered the Aleutians the worst.

In contrast to the close fabric of the civilian weather stations covering the United States with observation posts about fifty or sixty miles apart, only one hundred foreign stations operated in the whole area from Central Canada to Iceland. In the Hudson Bay region, for example, weather coverage depended in some cases on trappers who supplied elementary temperature and barometer readings for Hudson's Bay Company fur market forecasts.

In Greenland the same type of observations were made by native observers. Not even strategic new United States Army and Air Force stations were adequate. Gaps of more than six hundred miles lay between some of the outpost stations. The ocean observations formerly reported by transatlantic liners had stopped at the outbreak of the war.

The Eighth Squadron and cooperating AACS groups eventually established a complete weather network along the North Atlantic route. Intricate communication channels were set up to flash weather data from eastern United States, England, and Africa to forecasting stations in Greenland, Iceland, Baffin Island, Labrador, Newfoundland, Bermuda, and the Azores. Besides this basic network, new weather instruments were widely used. Planes equipped with specially designed observation devices were assigned to fly weather patrols over the Atlantic. Their reports while flying were passed on to pilots at briefing sessions. Coast Guard ships in mid-ocean reported otherwise inaccessible observations.

Gander, the most important base in Newfoundland, was forced to close down for operations between 20 and 25 per cent of the time because of fog and low clouds. In Greenland, the Narsarssuak runway at the end of a long narrow fjord, is considered safe for groups of planes only when the ceiling is at least 8,000 feet, meaning about a quarter of the time. The ceiling must also be good forty miles away, at the entrance to the fjord.

Meeks Field in Icland was afflicted from September to May with snow, rain, and high winds. A considerable portion of the customary traffic through Meeks had to be re-routed.

These areas were difficult enough, but winter weather is even worse at the more isolated places, particularly where the additional supporting weather stations were set up in Labrador, Quebec, Baffin Island, the Hudson Bay area, Greenland, and in the Canadian Archipelago. Of all of these, only the stations at Frobisher Bay, Churchill, Southampton Island, and Fort Chimo had air strips. The others were completely isolated from contact with the outside world through most of the year.

The training of weather observers was intensified in the United States, and as more capable men became available, more stations were established. American scientists quickly developed new devices to make ground-to-plane weather communication safe and reliable. When flying the northern route became a routine operation, much of the credit belonged to the weathermen.

CHAPTER VIII

The Weird Winter

IT ISN'T likely that any of the veterans of the winter of 1942–43 along the northern route looks back upon those months with nostalgia. There aren't many men who thrive on hardship and discomfort. Perhaps Bernt Balchen is one; the tougher the job he was offered, the more his round Norse face would blossom.

Conditions were terrible at almost all the bases during those winter months. Barracks were in various stages of construction. Some enlisted men were even living in unwinterized tents. Mess facilities were far from adequate; the food was generally poorly prepared and was usually tasteless and monotonous. Some bases had no trained cooks; those that did could not furnish much food nor the equipment with which to cook it. The kitchen furnishings hadn't arrived.

At times when there was plenty of food, the means of cooking it were so limited that officers and men had to spend hours on the chow line. When a man got his meal, he didn't bother to give it a name—whether breakfast, lunch, or supper, it was almost always something out of a can. The dull menu generally featured sausages, sauerkraut, Spam, or dehydrated foods. Recreation was in the same class as the food, limited or non-existent. The men didn't have much spare time, anyway.

Communications remained poor. In the United States, weather passes between stations and airways traffic control centers along teletype and telephone land lines. On the northern route there were no wires. Radio was the only answer. The equipment was already overburdened, and then the high-frequency signals were often blotted out completely by the violent ionospheric storms of the northern latitudes. During our survey flight of the route, these "blackouts" delayed us for days at a time.

Only long-distance transmission seemed to work well. Both high- and low-frequency equipment was needed in the northern latitudes to insure reliable communications. Bad radio reception ruined the work of the forecaster. When he didn't have vital information, he sometimes drew upon an overly active imagination to fill the gap.

Along the northern ferry route electrical phenomena at times looked suspiciously like enemy interference, and that was one of the reasons why the personal element was so important. First-class operators, as well as good equipment, had to be available. Our survey uncovered frequent complaints of inexperienced personnel, both in the planes and on the ground.

Not all difficulties were attributable to poorly trained personnel. As early as 6 March 1942 an operator at Goose Bay noted that in ten days he had been able to make a feeble contact with Narsarssuak only three times. He was disturbed by high-frequency fade-out. When we stopped at Narsarssuak on 12 April we found the forecaster capable enough, but weather and communication facilities to help him work were almost completely missing. Equipment did not get the high priority it deserved.

Some installations had been erected before topographic study of the terrain. Late in the summer of 1942 it was found that the communication equipment at Narsarssuak was improperly located.

With winter approaching, arrangements had to be made to move to a new site not overshadowed by towering mountain ranges. This task was not completed for several months, and the apparatus was not operational until the following March.

Lack of equipment accentuated the shortcomings of inexperienced personnel. Radio procedure was chaotic. It had not been codified properly. Time and time again information on flights was not received until the hum of airplanes was heard overhead.

There was duplication of effort. At Goose Bay, Gander, and Reykjavik, where Canadians or British had set up what they considered to be superior weather facilities, newly arrived U. S. weathermen found themselves repeating observations or making forecasts already made by our Allies. The effort we made to provide our own weather service was regarded with suspicion. The British saw in it an attempt on our part to prepare for postwar operation along the route. Pilots, however, have much more confidence in the weather forecasts of their own countrymen than in those made by others, an argument for maintaining our own facilities that couldn't be disregarded.

The housing situation in the fall of 1942 along the route was terrible. This was true even at Presque Isle where there were no logistic problems. Elsewhere it was much worse. Aircraft maintenance was also seriously falling behind schedule. As the fall months turned into a sunless winter, an increasing number of planes were stalled along the route by the cold. Maintenance at Presque Isle was in fair shape. There was plenty of help and the weather was not too severe. Goose Bay was much colder and had fewer maintenance men and fewer tools with which to service planes. Northward, temperatures kept dropping and so did the availability of men to work on the planes. It was so serious along most of the route, that a crew either serviced its own aircraft with what was available, or waited its turn and hoped that one of the few hardworking linemen would get around to it before the weather really turned bad. There were just not enough trained men in the Air

Force to satisfy the demands for men and equipment that were constantly arriving from all theaters of war.

It was no help to men in the field to know that Washington was well staffed. There were multitudes of men to do the work in headquarters. They typed, filed, reported, answered, and then forgot requests from the field for men and supplies.

A weather officer in the Air Transport Command started a Routing and Record sheet on its way; he requested the installation of a weather station at a particular locality in Labrador. An R and R sheet was standard procedure. It was circulated for co-ordination and comment among all Air Force agencies involved in a problem. Some months later this request for a station reached me. It was thirty-two pages in length by that time, and contained exhaustive comments prepared by fourteen officers explaining why, because of lack of equipment, personnel, transportation, and so forth, the station could not be established. I addressed it to the originator (who by this time was probably in India) with the notation: "So what?" I knew that the station had been erected and was sending out hourly observations.

During December of 1942 men were trying to service planes with cans of oil but without funnels. Gas trucks were either empty or busy elsewhere. One base was a notable exception: it existed in a land of plenty—plenty of cold, plenty of supplies, plenty of everything except warmth and work. An adequate runway had been completed. The snow that winter was unusually deep and covered tons of equipment that no one had thought of inventorying and storing. Actually, the station was slowly starving in the midst of plenty. Great supplies of 100-octane gasoline in drums were scattered around helter-skelter. Yet the one gas truck that was running would pump only occasionally through its hose that was frozen iron-stiff. Mobile repair shops and crew stands lacked crew chiefs, engineers, and mechanics. For the supply of electrician's kits, aircraft inspector's kits, carpenter's kits, fabric worker's kits, instrument kits, and at least five parachute repairman's kits, there were no fabric workers, parachute repairmen, electricians, or carpenters.

The small AAF detail at this northern post spent most of its time keeping warm and keeping fed. KP continued as usual and there had to be, of course, the office force of cryptographers, stenographers, and clerks. There was usually one man to worry about the airport, including the gas truck which seldom worked and many heaters which refused to operate when the day was really cold. Four officers rotated the duties of airdrome officer and all of them, including the commanding officer, gave a hand with juggling freight. On top of this, the Quartermaster Corps had notified the commanding officer that instruments were authorized for a thirty-five piece band in a post with only thirty-two men.

A limited number of planes could find gasoline and oil at all bases on the northern route. If a transient airplane had to spend the night at Narsarssuak or Söndre Strömfjord, it might not be started the following morning. If temperatures were mild and if not more than two other planes had to be started, it had a fair chance. Great quantities of equipment on hand never seemed to include what was vital; it could be assumed that, if any spare parts or major repair work were required, the plane would have to wait until parts or other assistance could be flown from another base. Planes sat on fields for weeks awaiting repairs.

Development of some bases was seriously retarded by the haphazard selection of key officers. A mess officer in one base had been employed for almost twenty years by a drug manufacturing company as a research scientist. The personnel officer at another base was a man with many years' experience in the manufacture of radio equipment. The engineer officer at one station had majored in history while in college and sold insurance after graduation, and lacked any experience with airplanes.

Thousands of tons of supplies, including building materials, snow-removal equipment, gasoline, food, and aircraft parts were moved in by water transport and sometimes by air. Storage tanks for gasoline had to be transported and constructed. Miners were recruited from iron mines of northern Michigan to drive a tunnel into a mountainside at Narsarssuak for the storage of bombs and dynamite. The tunnel never was used because of heavy moisture content. Any geologist could have warned that it would be dripping wet. Most heavy equipment was sent by ships that had to operate during a limited season, restricted to the months from early June to October at Goose Bay. At Söndre Strömfjord, even though it is above the Arctic Circle, ships could go in for six months.

An Air Force inspector found that at Narsarssuak in 1943 an important project that required hundreds of yards of cotton cloth, thousands of feet of sisal rope, hundreds of gallons of ethylene glycol, and multitudes of hardware items, had been provided exactly 25 cotter pins, 33 screw and 144 brush assemblies. Parts and hardware were then accumulating for a project canceled a year earlier. Washington authorized a supply officer at Narsarssuak to purchase coat hangers locally. He was also instructed by Washington to forward, by rail or truck, certain equipment received at Narsarssuak intended for Söndre Strömfjord, four hundred miles away in a land lacking a single road or train.

One plane arrived with a small package in its cargo that contained a box of resin and three spare G-strings for a bass viol. In January, with temperatures hovering at the zero mark, Narsarssuak received two modern refrigerators by air.

Quantities of Arctic equipment were being manufactured in the United States, but it didn't all find its way north. Mukluks, a type of sealskin boot, and the alpaca-lined "mechanic's overall" were both needed but scarce.

The type of clothing issued had limitations. Ground crews could not work without warmth, but too much attention was devoted to designing and testing of clothing for air crews, while mechanics often were unable to service planes in the open. The mechanics needed warmth without undue bulk. Instead, he was furnished with huge parkas, lead-heavy boots, and elbow-length mittens of wolverine fur.

The cold of the first winter was exceptional. Glyco, a fluid antifreeze used in airplane cooling systems, was kept near stoves, and yet congealed. At night the men would climb into their sleeping bags, leaving just their faces out; in the morning they would scrape away a layer of frost around the opening. Metal frames of eyeglasses froze to faces. Ink in pens was always frozen. Typewriters always had to be thawed out on a pot-bellied stove before use.

Some plane repairs were done indoors at Presque Isle, but for the most part they were made in nose hangars outdoors. Mechanics ran in and out of heated tents in 20-minute relays. Bare-handed, they lost fingers; with hampering gloves, they fumbled two hours to change a spark plug.

North of Presque Isle all maintenance was done under nose hangars. One mechanic's first job was changing a hydraulic pump on a Lightning. It was assigned to him because he had worked for the pump manufacturer. "You couldn't work with your gloves on," he said, "so you took them off, took a half-turn on a nut, then shoved your hand down a heater hose." The job took all day; normally it would have taken only an hour and a half. With the temperature well below zero, putting on one small nut in the back of the engine required nearly an hour. First the nut was warmed at a heater so that it wouldn't stick to fingers. Then a mechanic put it between the first two fingers of his bare hand and climbed up the ladder. By the time he got the nut in place, his fingers were too stiff to turn it. Down he went, to warm his fingers and then try again. As many as eighteen times he would patiently go through that procedure before he was able to get the nut started on the bolt so that a wrench could take hold of it.

Engines were sometimes started by a rope tied to a prop blade, wound around the hub, and hitched to a truck. Truck motors, left running all the time, lasted only a few months and then had to be replaced. Each morning the wheels of vehicles were frozen solidly.

The pioneering in Greenland of aircraft maintenance was not helped by continuing confusion in authority. For a long time it was undecided whether Air Transport Command personnel were under the Greenland Base Command. At one base the layout of buildings, operational areas, repair shops, and other facilities was not controlled by the Air Force even though the Air Force was charged with operating and maintaining an air base there. It took many months to solve these administrative problems.

CHAPTER IX

Beleaguered by the Icecap

O NE OF THE great command decisions along the northern route had to be made by Colonel B. F. Giles when he took over the North Atlantic Wing of the Air Transport Command. Which course should be taken when a plane went down on the icecap? Maintain the steady flow of airplanes and cargo to Great Britain? Halt the stream of traffic while everyone pitched in to search for downed airmen?

It was difficult at all times to brake the flights to the battle fronts, but whenever it was necessary, it was done. The policy of the Army Air Force was always based upon the fact that no man is expendable if effort, risk, and expense can save him.

Search and rescue were enormously important to the air crews who flew above the desolate wastes of Greenland, Baffin Island, and Labrador, who crossed seas dotted with icebergs and endless miles of snow and ice in weather that often kept the sea gulls grounded.

Following some bitter early experiences, search and rescue became a carefully planned operation. It was vital to morale that it did. Pilots needed the assurance that they would not be left stranded if they went down. Time is usually the most important factor in Arctic rescue. The winter winds and frosts and icy waters of the northland are swift killers. Lacking the experience it gained quickly enough in later months, the Air Transport Command was at first poorly prepared to meet the rescue problems. A few planes and pilots disappeared without a trace, and they never have been found.

Search and rescue weren't neglected in the beginning; there were too many qualified Arctic experts in Greenland who knew just how to go about the job. The most highly qualified and experienced of all these men was the fabulous Bernt Balchen, who was selected as commanding officer at Söndre Strömfjord. He went vigorously to work planning to solve the problems of Arctic survival. When I visited his station in April and in June of 1942, I found that he knew thoroughly the capabilities and weaknesses of every man in his command. He had introduced a series of lessons about the nature of the country, with emphasis on survival procedures. He recruited lecturers from travelers like myself who had specialized knowledge of Greenland. He was an expert skier, a lifelong hobby that had started when he was a boy in Norway; he gave skiing lessons to boys who never had seen snow.

Colonel Balchen's reputation as an Arctic expert was known to air crews who traveled the route, and they were well aware that when a plane went down, Bernt Balchen went into action. Several of the many rescues that he led were sensational.

The first of these was the rescue of the crew of one of the Flying Fortresses of the 97th Bombardment Group which took off from Goose Bay for Söndre Strömfjord and Narsarssuak on 26 June 1942. Three of the Fortresses were lost. Nine reached their destination, and six returned to Goose Bay. Of the missing three, one was forced down on the heavily crevassed areas of the Sukkertoppen arm of the icecap, an outcropping of the main body of ice on the south side of Söndre Strömfjord. Here surface travelers cannot climb to the icecap. I learned this when I attempted it with two Eskimos in 1931 while searching for the plane abandoned by Hassell and Cramer.

Colonel Balchen first surveyed the edge of the icecap by air. He thought an approach by foot would take weeks. Aerial drops of food and other equipment were then made to the crew of the plane.

On his second survey trip Balchen discovered a lake forming on the ice, a dozen miles from the wrecked Flying Fortress. Balchen decided to land on it with a Navy Catalina. In one of the most daring rescue operations on record, Lieutenant Aram Y. Parunak, USN (pilot), accompanied by Colonel Balchen, set the amphibian on the lake that had formed on the icecap at an elevation of 4,215 feet. The Catalina then took off for Söndre Strömfjord. Balchen, together with Sergeant Hendrick Dolleman and Sergeant Joseph D. Healy, paddled a rubber raft through ice-encrusted water to a beach of blue ice. They camped and awoke the next morning, the Fourth of July, in a sleet and snow storm. The weather cleared, and Balchen and Healy started for the wrecked plane, leaving Dolleman at the camp.

Swollen glacial streams and fog stopped them, and they returned to their camp and changed to dry clothing. They reached the wreck the next day. The thirteen men in the Fortress put on the snowshoes and polar clothing that had been dropped to them. Balchen warned them to leave behind everything except a sleeping bag and a day's rations, but they didn't listen. Their trail, after a few miles, was littered with a wide variety of expendables, including cameras, dress shoes, electric razors, toiletries, and letters. Finally they reached the lake. The Catalina shortly made a second landing to remove the whole party to Söndre Strömfjord.

Minutes after the rescue plane was air-borne, the water of the lake suddenly drained into a wide crevasse that had opened with a roar. The water cascaded into the depths of the icecap.

Colonel Balchen also was active in the next rescue, that of

Colonel Robert W. C. Wimsatt, commanding officer at Narsarssuak. Wimsatt's small single-engine plane, in which he was cruising around the margin of the icecap putting in flying time, was forced down on a gravel moraine some 25 miles northeast of Narsarssuak. Again a Catalina, piloted by Lieutenant Parunak with Colonel Balchen as copilot, was landed on a lake 2,100 feet in elevation and some 12 miles from Wimsatt's wrecked airplane. Colonel Balchen and Major "Mac" McBride of the Medical Corps hiked over the rugged terrain and rescued the injured Wimsatt and Sergeant Grenard who had accompanied him.

A squadron of two Flying Fortresses and six Lightnings had set out from Narsarssuak on 17 July 1942, for Iceland with a forecast of excellent weather ahead. About halfway between Greenland and Iceland, the leader of the squadron received orders to turn around and proceed to Söndre Strömfjord in West Greenland because a low ceiling at Iceland would prohibit a landing. Postwar examination of German records indicates that these orders originated from the German radio station then operating at Sabine Island, Greenland. The squadron leader believed that he was hearing orders from the commander of the Greenland Base Command. The squadron turned around and, when near Söndre Strömfjord, heard orders to proceed again to Iceland.

The planes once more reversed direction and flew eastward. The radioed explanation was that the weather had closed in at Söndre Strömfjord, and at Narsarssuak. With all the flying to and fro across Greenland, the planes ran out of gasoline. Still hundreds of miles from a landing field, they had no choice but to land on the icecap. They chose a spot near the east coast about 160 miles from Angmagssalik and 20 miles within the interior of the icecap.

The first plane to go in, a Lightning, landed with its wheels down. As the plane neared the end of its run, its nose wheel hit a soft spot and the plane nosed over. The pilot escaped with minor scratches. The other planes made belly landings with their wheels up.

A Navy squadron, led by Lieutenant George Atterbury, USN, located the planes and dropped supplies. Major Frederick Crockett, U. S. Army, an Antarctic veteran serving as commanding officer of the weather station established in Angmagssalik the year before, was transported in the Coast Guard cutter *Northland* to the nearest fjord with dogs and sleds. Signals from planes guided him over the heavily crevassed coastal area. He reached the downed planes just five days after they had left Narsarssuak. Weather was good during the entire operation. With emergency rations dropped from the air, the twenty-five men were able to make themselves safe. The planes, it was later learned, had carried no rations or survival equipment; these had been left behind in favor of toiletries and other sundries such as nylons, which the crews had expected to trade for romance in Iceland and England. Had weather delayed the rescue, the men could have suffered severely. Thereafter, survival equipment was carefully inspected on all planes at every station.

None of these early rescues could be called major operations, because the planes went down near the margin of the icecap and the weather was good during the search and rescue period.

A lot was learned from them, however. For one thing, the crews of the downed planes were badly prepared for survival in such emergencies. That was part of my job, to prepare manuals, techniques, and instructions that would give the men a good chance when they lived through an icecap landing.

There wasn't much stir in Washington, however. One other matter held priority—the consistent but unconfirmed reports of Nazi air activity over Greenland. This was during the period when a German weather station was in operation at Sabine Island, high on the east coast; it was later eliminated by combined action of the Air Force and Coast Guard, and one of its staff captured. Aircraft warning systems were deemed more important in the late spring of 1942 than concentration on icecap rescue methods. Major General Dwight Eisenhower made the request of General

Arnold, commanding the Air Force, that "consideration be given to the possibility of locating one or two aircraft warning stations on the Greenland icecap. . . ."

A subsequent memorandum suggested radio weather-reporting and rescue stations on the icecap, although it made no mention of aircraft-warning stations. It was recommended that these stations be placed under my command, but Brigadier General Anderson, of the Plans Division was unwilling to let me go to such permanent duty, so I was ordered to proceed only with the organization of the stations. I selected two men for the expedition who were well qualified. They were Max Demorest, my companion of many months on a Greenland expedition, and Captain Alan Innes-Taylor, who had considerable experience in the Northwest Territories with the Royal Canadian Northwest Mounted Police, with a private air line in Alaska, and in the Antarctic, where he had been a member of two of Byrd's expeditions.

I also signed up William House, who had climbed in the Himalayas, and Dr. John W. Marr, a civilian scientist with a record of much time spent in the Hudson Bay area. We were given the code name, Task Force 4998-A.

After all these years, it is still painful to recall the indifferent co-operation and lack of understanding that we were faced with, even though the venture had the blessing of President Roosevelt.

It was thirty-five days after the memorandum directing the station's construction before I received orders on the eighth of July. The orders stated succinctly that all supplies, equipment, and personnel should be at the Boston port of embarkation in four days. We had anticipated the orders, so we were at least partially ready. In actual time, we had only nineteen days in which to organize, equip, and embark on an expedition of more importance than any previous civilian expedition to Greenland. When the Germans and the British each established one icecap station in 1930 and 1931, they went into the field after a year of careful planning. The Air Force told us to accomplish more work and to do so with less than three weeks' time to get ready. Our venture never had a chance.

We had no control over the enlisted men assigned to us. Seven of them who reported to the task force had not been tested or screened for rugged Arctic duty. None had experience in the north; none was qualified to maintain and service the mechanized snow-traveling equipment. They didn't do badly, in spite of the haphazard selection. One of them, Private Don Tetley, who was listed as a cook, had been a motorcycle racer in Texas, and he could handle the motorcycle engines that powered our six experimental motor toboggans. These machines had never been tried on the ice and snow of the Greenland interior. We gambled that they would work. We had no hope of getting sledge dogs in Greenland. Our clothing, rations, and camp equipment, so hastily assembled, were mostly unfit for the job.

My original plan called for establishment of the stations by parachute drops from planes based at Narsarssuak. Captain James Chapman, who had piloted the Liberator in which I flew to England a few months earlier, was assigned to the project, but his orders were rescinded without explanation. The Air Transport Command was requested to transport all supplies and equipment by air, but ATC failed to furnish any transportation for the initial party. A lieutenant named Mitchell, another pilot eager to participate in the project, was assigned to accompany the ground exploratory party and assist in locating a suitable landing site, but his orders were canceled, again without explanation. The situation then boiled down to this: The mission, planned by the AAF and to be carried out with active air transport and air support, found that air transport and even the services of a qualified officer to aid in selection of a landing area were denied to it. The task force then was left to carry on exclusively as a ground party with insufficient personnel, untried over-snow vehicles, and inadequate equipment. A search by Demorest for dogs on the west coast and in Angmagssalik turned up only six scrawny beasts. On 18 August when the task force arrived at the beachhead selected on the east coast, the only transportation available for icecap operations were six motor toboggans, six dogs, and a sled designed by the French explorer, Paul-Émile Victor, and built by the explorer and Arctic supplier, Anthony Fiala. We thought it was a marvel that anything at all was accomplished.

The Beachhead Station, a 20′ by 20′ prefabricated house, was erected in three days with the help of the crew of the Coast Guard cutter *Comanche*. Demorest then transported supplies for the erection of a second station, this one on the icecap, sixteen miles from the Beachhead Station. A third weather station, later called Atterbury Dome, was erected on a nearby coastal ridge.

We got some good help on the nineteenth of September. Johan Johansen, a Norwegian civilian fairly familiar with Arctic travel and fortunately the owner of twenty-one sled dogs and trail equipment, arrived on the trawler *Nanok*. Then the Air Force sent along a junior officer, trained for duty in the tropics, who had probably never before seen snow and who certainly had no knowledge of Arctic conditions or operations. Unforeseen events later placed him in command, a possibility that apparently never was considered.

In October capable Captain Innes-Taylor, who was to command the Beachhead Station, left for the States to organize a new detachment and prepare for the following year. Lieutenant Demorest was left in charge, but he had to operate a station in the interior on the icecap. House and Dr. Marr had left for Narsarssuak on 28 September aboard the *Nanok* on its last call. With Demorest at the icecap station, the Beachhead Station was left with one untrained officer, one civilian, six inexperienced enlisted men, and twenty-seven howling dogs.

CHAPTER X

The Suspenseful Rescue

A TWIN-ENGINE cargo plane, en route from Narsarssuak to Iceland, was reported lost on the east coast on 5 November, 1942. A search began immediately with all available aircraft from Narsarssuak. At Beachhead Station, Task Force 4998-A began a continuous radio watch. Lights that were thought to be flares in the area turned out to be aurora borealis. The search failed; nothing ever was heard or found of the plane and its crew of five.

One search plane, a Flying Fortress being ferried to its combat destination, was diverted to assist. During its third mission, on 9 November, it crashed on an active glacier at the head of Koji Bay on the east coast. Its position was about thirty miles from the icecap weather and rescue station manned by Lieutenant Demorest and Private Tetley. Making a turn at what the pilot thought a safe altitude of 1,500 feet above the ice, the Fortress' left wing struck a snowdrift. Sliding along the heavily crevassed ice for several hundred feet, the plane finally broke neatly in two with the tail section suspended precariously over a crevasse.

The reason for the crash was not unusual. The plane had flown in a "white-out," a condition like flying through milk. Lack of depth perception is a common phenomenon on the inland ice. Even a person traveling by foot, in the absence of a horizon or any other point of reference, will lose his sense of balance until at last he may be unable to stand. The icecap has no familiar objects like trees on which to fix attention.

The occupants of the Fortress were Captain Armand L. Monteverde, pilot; Lieutenant Harry E. Spencer, copilot; Lieutenant William F. O'Hara, navigator; Corporal Loren E. Howarth, radioman; Private Paul J. Spina, engineer; Private First Class Alexander Tucciarone, assistant engineer; Technical Sergeant Alfred C. Best, Staff Sergeant Lloyd Puryear, and Private Clarence Wadel. The last three were passengers.

The officers on the flight deck received no injuries. Best, in the bombardier's seat, had been thrown through the plexiglass nose and suffered lacerations. Puryear had been injured only slightly. The four other enlisted men had been in the radio room. Two had been thrown through the hatch. Spina suffered a broken right wrist, and Wadel sustained a black eye and bruises. The plane's radio was smashed, but not beyond repair.

The plane carried a half box of "C" or field rations that would last for two weeks with strict economy. The men had no Arctic survival kit, no sleeping bags, no extra clothing, no cooking utensils, and no stove. Their first day on the icecap, the tenth of November, was windy. Everyone huddled for warmth in the bottom turret of the plane. Though they had covered the open end of the broken aircraft with a tarpaulin, fine snow drifted in. For three days the wind blew. When it finally calmed, the men ventured outside.

Lieutenant Spencer thought he saw open water to the east that he could reach by walking. He ventured from the plane cautiously, but when only a short distance from it he fell into a crevasse through the snow bridge that concealed it. He landed on a narrow ledge only a few feet from the surface. A rope made of parachute shroud lines was lowered to him. By this time one of his hands was frozen. That night Lieutenant O'Hara reported frostbitten feet.

Then the men discovered that the tail of the fuselage, where they were sleeping, was settling slowly into a crevasse. They evacuated the plane, dug a room in the ice under the right wing, and stretched the tarpaulin across the opening.

After ten days Corporal Howarth got the radio operating and began sending distress signals.

The emergency rations were about exhausted five days later when the plane was located by Colonel Balchen from a Skymaster, a TWA contract plane. He dropped emergency supplies, including food, sleeping bags, and clothing. Most of the supplies were lost among the crevasses, but enough were recovered to give the men some comfort. Gangrene now attacked Lieutenant O'Hara's frozen feet, and he was unable to walk.

Rescue operations involved the icecap station. Lieutenant Demorest made plans for rescue. On the nineteenth day after the crash, he and Tetley started on motor toboggans, each towing a sled with emergency camping equipment and rations. Colonel Balchen flew overhead, and when Demorest and Tetley were about ten miles out, he gave them the correct course to the shattered plane.

Demorest and Tetley were slowed by soft, drifting snow and engine trouble with the motor sled. They saw a light at the Flying Fortress three miles away, but were stopped by a 30-foot crevasse three-quarters of a mile from the plane. They abandoned the motor sleds and skirted the crevasse on skis. They reached the plane at 3:00 A.M. on 29 November.

Demorest and Tetley found the entire crew in good spirits in spite of the injuries and O'Hara's frostbitten feet. The day before Lieutenant John A. Pritchard, USCG, flying a Grumman Duck from the cutter *Northland,* had landed successfully on his pontoons on the icecap a mile away. Two men, Sergeant Puryear and Private

Tucciarone, had been evacuated. Pritchard was expected to fly others out that same day.

Demorest noted that the men were all in good health except Lieutenant O'Hara, whose feet were now in bad condition, and Private Spina, suffering considerable pain in his wrist. Demorest dressed O'Hara's feet, checked Spina's arm, and then returned with Tetley on skis to their toboggans less than a mile away. There they spent the few remaining hours of the night in their sleeping bags.

At dawn they pointed their loaded toboggans toward the plane. Demorest, leading the way on skis to break trail, probed the snow covering with his ski poles for safe bridges over crevasses. Tetley relayed the sleds, first driving one, then returning for the other. With little more than two hundred yards to go, Demorest believed they were out of the crevassed zone. He left his skis and took over the driving of his own sled. Tetley followed fifty feet behind. Only a hundred yards from the Fortress, Demorest and his sled suddenly fell soundlessly and without warning through a thinly snow-bridged crevasse. Tetley was able to stop his speeding sled. He ran to the edge of the crevasse, shouting for help. Lieutenant Spencer ran up with rope. They were able to see dimly in the dark crevasse the track assembly of the motor sled. It was about 150 feet down, wedged across the hole in the ice. They saw no sign of Demorest.

Without able-bodied men to attempt a search of the crevasse by rope, Tetley spent hours at its mouth watching for some sign of life. He received no answer to his shouts. He knew Demorest was dead, but he was determined systematically to explore the crevasse for Demorest's body. However, instructions were received from the cutter *Northland,* anchored nearby in Comanche Bay, to make no attempt to recover the body.

Lieutenant Pritchard then made a second remarkable landing on the icecap in his Duck. Corporal Howarth was sent by Captain Monteverde to the Duck to warn Pritchard that fog was rolling in and that for his own safety he should leave before it settled too thickly. Pritchard and his radioman, B. A. Bottoms, took off immediately with Howarth as a passenger. They were too late. Fog closed in, and the Duck crashed into a mountainside nearby. When the Duck was located by a search plane a week later, on the first anniversary of Pearl Harbor, Pritchard, Bottoms, and Howarth were found to have been killed instantly.

At this point, a month after the Flying Fortress had crashed, there were two men rescued and four dead. Still on the icecap were three officers and four enlisted men awaiting rescue. Tetley was a stranded rescuer.

The Beachhead Station listened for radio reports of events so close in miles but days away in travel time. The civilian Johansen and Sergeant Howes, driving two dog teams, reached the Icecap Station where Demorest had started on his journey five days before. They left for the plane the next day. After several hours they saw a light in the direction of the Icecap Station; they returned to investigate, under the mistaken impression that Tetley must have returned. Johansen and Howes probably had been confused by a bright star on the horizon.

They started again, and in two days covered twenty miles before Demorest's tracks disappeared. With dog food running low, the dogs in unsatisfactory condition, and the trail gear in bad shape, they were forced to return to the Icecap Station. They reached it on the fifth day of their journey, during which they lost three dogs.

Fairly well supplied by aerial drops, except for twenty-two days in January when rescue planes were grounded by foul weather, the men at the plane did worry about their only source of light in the long Arctic winter night. Their candles were always running low. An old model Coleman kerosene stove, dropped to them for heating and cooking, did not burn leaded gasoline of the type on hand in the plane's tanks. Fuel for the stove had to be dropped, and much of it was lost in the crevasses and deep snow.

Lieutenant O'Hara's condition got worse. The crew decided to transport him in easy stages to the Icecap Station and then to the Beachhead Station on the remaining motor sled.

O'Hara, Spencer, Tetley, and Wadel set out on the eighth of December. Lieutenant Spencer led the party on snowshoes, probing his way carefully over the honeycombed fissures. O'Hara was bundled in a tow sled pulled by the motor toboggan. About a mile from the plane, thinking they had safely crossed the danger area, Spencer decided to relax by riding the motor sled. A bridge of snow collapsed over a hidden crevasse which the sled straddled. Wadel had no chance to grab the tow sled. He plunged to his death, the fifth man to die in the prolonged rescue.

Spencer, Tetley and O'Hara decided to go on, and they covered another five miles before the sled's motor quit. They hastily pitched a tent while Tetley went to work. It took him four days to get the obstinate motor to run. Then the weather kept them from traveling.

Lieutenant O'Hara continued to get worse. Now he couldn't stand any more travel stresses. The three men decided that they had to wait for a rescue, either by plane or by dog team, from the Beachhead Station.

They dug quarters in the icecap, a hole six feet by nine, and only three feet in depth. Days passed into weeks, and weeks into months; the sun began to appear over the horizon, the days slowly grew longer. Supplies were dropped to them whenever the weather permitted. The dog team from the Beachhead Station never did arrive.

Lieutenant O'Hara suffered nausea and diarrhea, was unable to hold solid foods, and was in constant pain. He subsisted on soup for a month. Gangrene was rotting away the flesh of both his feet.

A Flying Fortress, piloted by Captain Kenneth H. (Pappy) Turner, was diverted from the ferrying route to aid in the rescue. It was based at Optimist in order to drop supplies whenever the weather permitted.

In December I flew to Greenland to check the rescue operations. I found that everything possible was being done, now that Colonel

Bernt Balchen was placed in full charge of all attempts to get the marooned men off the icecap. I returned to Washington to find the authorities gravely concerned. A daily report was made to General Arnold on progress.

The Navy offered the use of two Catalinas and their crews, with Lieutenant B. W. Dunlop commanding. A dog team with Captain Harry L. Strong, an experienced Alaskan explorer, and Sergeants Healy and Dolleman, Antarctic veterans, accompanied Balchen from Söndre Strömfjord to Narsarssuak, the main base of rescue operations. A Barkley-Grow airplane that could be fitted with skis was rented from Maritime Central Airways and was flown to Greenland by its owner, Jimmie Wade, with an AAF officer, Captain J. G. Moe, as navigator. Skis would be fitted to the plane at Optimist for rescue landings on the icecap. The Barkley-Grow ran into a snow squall and was wrecked in a fjord near Angmagssalik. Wade and Moe finally were picked up a week later by Eskimos.

Lieutenant O'Hara was approaching the end of his remarkable endurance. Then Colonel Balchen proposed to land a Catalina on its floats on the snow and ice surface of the icecap. The Navy gave its permission for the daring experiment, and two Catalinas were assigned to the project. The first objective was to land as close as possible to the snow sled party. It was imperative to remove O'Hara.

Both Catalinas and Captain Turner's Flying Fortress flew an exploratory trip near the motor sled, but attempted no landing. Captain Turner dropped a walkie-talkie so that surface conditions could be reported to him. Two days later, a Catalina, with Lieutenant Bernard W. Dunlop as pilot, and carrying Colonel Balchen and Captain P. W. Sweetzer, the base surgeon, landed on the icecap. O'Hara, Spencer, and Tetley were evacuated. Flown first to Optimist, they were removed to the hospital at Narsarssuak and then to the United States.

Meanwhile at the wrecked plane, Monteverde, Best, and Spina

awaited the return of the Catalina, but another 22-day stretch of wretched weather set in. Because of the crevasses, the Catalina obviously could not land near the wreck. A trail party could walk the survivors to where the Catalina could land, whence they could be flown out. But who would compose the trail party? Men at the Beachhead Station had tried repeatedly to reach the downed Fortress. Experienced icecap travelers had to be flown in.

Because of high winds and heavy snow more than a month passed between the first landing by the Catalina and its second. At last the weather broke, and on 17 March three experienced Arctic travelers, Captain Strong, Master Sergeant Healy, Sergeant Dolleman, and nine dogs were landed near the abandoned motor-sled camp that had been occupied by O'Hara, Spencer, and Tetley. The next day, 129 days after the Fortress had crashed, Strong and his companions approached the wrecked plane. The snow surface, sastrugi (which are waves in the snow caused by wind), and crevasses were so bad that the rescuers pitched a camp a quarter-mile away and walked to the plane roped together. They found Monteverde, Spina, and Best in poor health and low spirits. They walked the six miles from their cave under the plane's wing to the motor-sled camp.

Another spell of wailing winds and shifting snow set in. Finally, on 5 April, a clear bright day, the Catalina made its third landing, stripped of all excess weight and carrying the minimum amount of gasoline. All hands, including dogs, were loaded aboard.

But now the weather was *too* good. Without any head wind at their elevation, the plane could not clear the snow.

After five attempts at take-off, one of the overworked engines caught fire. It damaged the fuel pressure-gauge line and cowling. Though the engine would run, the flyers decided to await a favorable wind before making further attempts.

To lighten the load, the trail party of Strong, Dolleman, and Healy was put off the plane to find its way to the Beachhead Station; Balchen elected to accompany them. At noon the following day a wind picked up, and on its third attempt the plane rose sluggishly from the snow surface. An hour and a half later, with gas tank indicators registering zero, it staggered into Optimist.

The battle with the icecap had lasted nearly six months, from 5 November 1942 to 18 April 1943. Five men were dead and one disabled for life.

CHAPTER XI

They Didn't Come Back

A MITCHELL BOMBER made an emergency belly landing on December 10, 1942, on a flat stretch of snow along the raw, icy Labrador coast. The heavy plane bumped over the rough terrain, ripping open the bomb bay. A propeller blade, torn from the engine, flew through the fuselage, barely missing the pilot. Nobody was hurt in the crash.

The crew had seventeen blankets, a comforter, and a bed roll. Their food count read like a holiday shopping list: three cans of peanuts, eight cans of chicken à la king, two cans of pineapple, three cans of fruit cocktail, two cans of date-nut roll, a can of brown bread, three boxes of chocolates, twenty-eight Hershey bars, four packages of dates, a pound of soda crackers, another pound of cheese crackers, four boxes of fig bars, a case of Coca-Cola, two cans of salmon, three pounds of coffee, twenty packages of caramels, and odds and ends of rations. The only item which was very military in nature was seven cans of Spam.

The navigator, taking a shot at the stars, accurately decided they had made the forced landing about 300 miles north of Goose

Bay. No member of the crew was worried or felt alarm; search planes would be in the air immediately upon notification of a missing aircraft. The navigator's diary recorded their experience.

Seeing a fox on a nearby ridge and about fifty seals in a neighboring fjord was a good omen, a source of food if they were not found quickly. They constructed a lean-to out of tarpaulins. This was better than sleeping in the plane where they had been cold and cramped. Sleeping individually they had been chilled, so they combined all their covers and slept huddled together in the lean-to.

On the third day the navigator continued to take shots of the stars and, after computing them and studying his map, decided they were quite close to the Labrador coastal town of Hebron. They had sighted no search planes and were beginning to realize that there might be a delay in their rescue. They rationed their supply of food.

On 15 December breakfast for the whole crew consisted of nine cups of coffee and a package of fig bars.

Not a single search plane had been sighted or heard. They discussed leaving their plane for help, a step they had been advised against during briefing sessions. Agreement was reached to permit three of the seven men to take a rubber emergency boat and on the first clear day sail south for help. The boat was launched two days before Christmas, the thirteenth day after their forced landing. The three occupants of the life raft seemed to be making good headway in the choppy waters of the fjord. That was the last ever seen of them.

Christmas Eve came two weeks after the forced landing. For Christmas dinner the men decided to splurge. The meal consisted of a sardine-sized can of kippered herring with crackers, a spoonful of peanuts apiece, a black cough drop and a caramel apiece, a cup of bouillon, a cup of grape drink, and plenty of coffee. Coffee was a highly diluted substitute; they were using the same coffee grounds over and over again.

By now every conversation recorded in the diary was mostly

about food. The New Year's Day meal consisted of a half box of frozen chocolates carefully doled out.

Four weeks after their landing they caught a small bird, boiled it for several hours and made a stew by adding bouillon powder. One man, deciding to look for the village of Hebron, which they knew could not be far away, made no progress in the soft snow that had been falling for days. Another man, with less resilience of spirit than his companions, remained in his cramped lean-to for thirteen days without leaving it.

Confident that he knew the direction to Hebron, the pilot set out a few days later. After a short struggle in hip-deep snow, he found himself growing too weak to continue and returned to the plane.

Preoccupation with food went on unabated. They felt that if they didn't live to eat all the things they talked about, surely they would have mentally eaten some of the best meals in the world. A note of pessimism began to creep into the diary in early January. For the first time they were beginning to question seriously whether they would get out.

They ate their last bit of food, two chocolates apiece, on 16 January, and were left with one bouillon powder and two sticks of chewing gum. Their companions had been gone for a month on 23 January. Three days later all were feeling nausea. The next entry, the last one, was 3 February, almost two months after the forced landing. It was a notation that they had spent a solid week in bed but were still hopeful of lasting out several more days.

Early in March natives found the bodies of the men only ninety minutes walking distance from the village of Hebron.

In Greenland, there were at least sixteen planes that came down on the icecap from 1940 through 1945. The actual figure may be higher because several planes that were never found may have crashed on the icecap. The total does not include those that disappeared elsewhere over the northern route or came down in

Labrador, Quebec, and the coastal area of Greenland. The planes that can be accounted for on the icecap include four Flying Fortresses, one Texan, six Lightnings, one Havoc, one Catalina, one Mitchell, one Navigator, and one Skytrain. Only eight men were killed in the sixteen crashes. Seven of the eight (five officers and two enlisted men) were in one plane, the Navigator that was wrecked on 28 November 1943. The eighth to die was the pilot of a Skytrain which went down on 7 October 1944. A seventeenth aircraft, the Grumman Duck, attempting a rescue from the wrecked Flying Fortress on the east coast, crashed during a snow storm with its pilot and two enlisted men as casualties. Two rescuers, Lieutenant Demorest and Private Wadel, were lost in icecap crevasses.

CHAPTER XII

Sweating It Out

MANY OF THE men who manned airfields in the north and who operated the small weather and communication stations lived in the tradition of Peary, Amundsen, Freuchen, Shackleton, and other great explorers. The life was one of loneliness, hardship, and suffering. Individual reactions to the Arctic's rigors varied with the men who experienced them. Some hated the place, others didn't mind it, a few really liked it. Some found it adventurous and exciting, others thought it dull, dreary, and unbearably monotonous. A few simply couldn't take it.

At Söndre Strömfjord the command officer, Colonel Balchen, provided off-hours orientation in Arctic living and Arctic sports for his men. Balchen's foresight had acquired for the base a large selection of books, many on the Arctic. An athlete himself, he went to Greenland well supplied with skis, snowshoes, hunting equipment, boxing gloves, and footballs. Games and puzzles, as well as a dozen artificial Christmas trees, went in an early shipment to Söndre Strömfjord.

Balchen recognized that many newcomers to Greenland had one

immediate response to their environment—the prospects for hunting and fishing. The angler, seeing the fjords for the first time, visualizes them teeming with fish; the hunter dreams of stalking the land and sea animals—the caribou, polar bear, walrus, seal, and blue fox. But the hunting and fishing are not always good because of seasonal migrations. Early summer is the only time capelin, the small herring-like fish of the fjords, can be caught in any numbers. They come up the fjords in enormous schools to spawn in shallow waters, followed by their enemies—the seal, Arctic char, and cod. Cod and capelin can then be caught in shallow waters with dip nets at the spawning places. Capelin are caught in enormous quantities by Greenlanders who eat them raw during the winter.

Another seasonal migration involves the Arctic char which ascend the fjords to fresh-water streams to spawn. Char is caught by net or by spearing during the upstream movement which begins late in July; the meat is fat and tasty then. Many good fish are found in Greenland waters, including halibut, haddock, herring, and catfish.

Hunters found only limited numbers of animals and game birds around the bases. Some game, particularly the highly prized caribou, are protected by game laws. Caribou, rapidly becoming extinct, can be hunted only in August when the natives migrate to the interior hunting grounds for the month. Ptarmigan and a few Arctic hare were shot near the bases, and some of the soldiers successfully trapped the elusive foxes. Seals, walruses, whales, the rare musk ox (found only in the far north), and most of the bird life went unmolested. A thousand-pound polar bear appeared on the ice of the fjord of Narsarssuak in January 1944. It probably had traveled with the east-coast pack ice, which skirts Cape Farewell and is carried a short distance up the west coast. The provost marshal pursued the huge beast in a jeep over the ice, but it was shot by superior marksmen among the Greenlanders from the settlement across the fjord.

Incoming personnel were conditioned before ever setting foot on Greenland; they expected the worst and looked for it. As planes began going through in large numbers in June 1942, however, matters improved. The transient and cargo planes made the men feel less out of the world, and they could see purpose in what they were doing. Morale at Goose Bay, Narsarssuak, and Söndre Strömfjord was dependent upon the amount of traffic, no matter what artificial stimuli were applied. The most difficult periods came in the winter when weather curtailed operations. The airfields were closed in for long periods, and the ferrying operations were carried on in fits and starts because of bad weather and poor forecasting. In December of 1942, even though my travel orders authorized only one week for my journey to Greenland to review the icecap rescue operations, weather stranded me and I spent three weeks at Narsarssuak before I could catch a plane going south.

Every Arctic explorer, trader, and trapper knows how monotonous life can be in the dead of the northern winter. And a man doesn't have to go to the Arctic to learn how tiresome the mannerisms of companions can become. The chap who gnaws on a pencil, chews his fingernails, whistles through his teeth when he says *s*, sniffles instead of blowing his nose, or cracks his knuckles just for the hell of it, may seem harmless enough, but if there's no escape from it meal after meal, day in and day out, it gets to be pretty terrible.

A medical officer who diagnosed the morale problem at one base concluded his report with this statement: "Service in this area has produced psychiatric problems of first importance. These are caused mainly by a combination of frustrations. The problems are less those of a number of psychiatric entities seen in individuals than the widespread personality disturbances manifested by loss of efficiency, lack of personal initiative, irritability, depression, and other emotional symptoms. It is not known how much of these disturbances is the basis for permanent psychiatric scarring."

The doctor's professional verbiage says that from the standpoint of getting the work done, such individual symptoms as despondency were not important compared with mass disturbances brought about by such external causes as bad news and rumors. The mass disorders, spreading quickly, caused general unhappiness and effected serious loss of time and energy.

For the individual, however, a toothache remains a toothache. What if the work wasn't being done on time? What if the whole outfit did get put behind bars? What if they all stretched out and died? What difference would it make?

The "combinations of frustrations" the doctor mentioned had to do frequently with sex. In fact, according to most reports, sex frustration headed the list of enemies of good morale. Usually the list went something like this: (1) sex, (2) isolation, (3) bad weather, (4) boredom, and lack of orientation, and (5) indeterminate length of service. Frustration rarely was traceable to a single cause. Whatever brought it on was aided by poor food, uncomfortable barracks, failure of mails, news of the death of comrades, and rumors.

Men at the small weather stations were most dependent on mail. They felt forgotten or ignored. A small outfit on the east coast of Greenland had a mail delivery by ship on 17 October 1943; not for another sixty-eight days was there another delivery, this time by air drop. This was on Christmas Eve when a special effort was made to get mail to all outposts. The next delivery was almost three months later, 13 March. Sixty-seven days then went by before another delivery on 20 May. In the seven months between 17 October 1943, and 20 May 1944, two deliveries reached that post.

Sooner or later most men fought off the spells of despondency with whatever weapons were available. Some found the movies diverting, others didn't. Some men shook melancholy by beard-growing contests, collecting pop-bottle caps, whittling wooden utensils, or drawing obscene pictures. One such drawing was capped with an unflattering portrait of a member of the artist's draft board.

Favorite occupations included the building of model airplanes, excavating old ruins, taming wild fowl, and making nets for catching capelin. At Söndre Strömfjord several men who requested the first six-day passes granted there spent the entire time hiking to Russell Glacier and camping. At another northern base, four GI's organized a barber shop quartet which was so good they were sent on a tour of the route. At one northern base the GI's wrote, directed, and produced a melodrama entitled "Flower of Virtue," which packed a Quonset hut with the same happy audience night after night. In one scene the distressed heroine asked: "What shall I do?" The audience shouted: "See the Chaplain!" In another scene she asked, "Shall I sell my body to save our little cottage?"

The building shook with the roar: "Hell, yes!"

At most large bases the movies were well attended and any old film was popular. At one post they asked that the films be run upside down for novelty. At another the hall they had to use was so long and narrow that the only way to accommodate the crowd was to arrange it behind as well as in front of the semi-transparent screen. Those on the far side saw the action in reverse.

Everywhere in Greenland pets were tremendously popular. One enlisted man at Söndre Strömfjord discovered in the base library a book on falconry, and managed to train several of the rare peregrine falcons that Goering had had shipped to him before the war. At one northern base there was a caribou named Bubbles, a blue fox named Dinah Shore, and a black rabbit named Fay. If movies and card playing became tiresome, Eskimo camp grounds and kitchen middens could be visited, a man could go fishing in the fjords at Narsarssuak, or explore the ancient Norse ruins. Several archaeological discoveries were made by young scientists at Söndre Strömfjord.

Food in the messes improved steadily as the installations grew. One of the best steak dinners I have had anywhere was at Optimist in the summer of 1943, prepared by a chef who was one of the thousands in the armed forces who supposedly studied under Oscar of the Waldorf. Whether he had or not didn't matter; the dinner was wonderful.

CHAPTER XIII

Snow Man, Mint Julep,
La Station Centrale, and Northice

THE PEAK of eastbound traffic over the northern route came in the summer of 1944. An all-time record of 130 aircraft landings at Narsarssuak was established on July 4. The planes included Havocs, Invaders, Marauders, Skytrains, Skymasters, and, for the first time, two Spitfires.

A seasonal schedule was keyed to weather. Ferrying of twin-engine aircraft was rushed during the summer period. Four-engine planes with longer range had the route pretty much to themselves in the winter. Parking facilities were extended, servicing of aircraft was improved, better accommodations were provided transient personnel, and forced landings were reduced almost to the vanishing point. The record for safety was phenomenal: the 10 per cent loss anticipated during the early days of the war turned out to be one tenth of 1 per cent.

Germany capitulated, and eastbound traffic came to a virtual halt. Preparations were made to reverse the flow of traffic. On

23 May 1945 began the "White Movement," the flow of aircraft from east to west. It was the first large group of aircraft being deployed from Europe to the Pacific Theater; sixty-three four-engine planes landed at Narsarssuak that day. The westward flow of traffic continued until the latter part of December 1945 when aircraft movement again was coming to a standstill; our men in Greenland were on their way home. From October 1945 to June 1946 only 199 transients arrived in Greenland from airplanes. For the next three years, 1946–49, the Greenland bases for the most part were operated by the Danish Government.

Then the Soviet Union began to threaten the security of western civilization, and again our attention was focused on the Arctic and its aerial approaches. In June 1947, two Air Force officers, Major General William H. Tunner and Major General Earle E. Partridge, on an inspection in Greenland, flew over the Greenland icecap. General Tunner asked the pilot to fly as close to the surface as he deemed safe. He was impressed with flat areas he saw and, as his pilot buzzed the surface, he began to wonder why the icecap would not offer ideal sites for landing strips. When he landed at Narsarssuak, General Tunner raised questions about the possibility of landing aircraft on the surface of the icecap.

This was the start of a plan which AAF named Project Snowman. An eight-man team was organized to make a thirty-day exploration of a fifty-mile area of the icecap. The expedition was to be flown from Söndre Strömfjord in a ski-equipped Skytrain; it would not attempt surface transportation, but would rely on supplies dropped by air. Denmark granted permission for the exploration.

For three weeks the expedition's major activity was aerial reconnaissance to seek suitable sites where ski-equipped planes could land on the icecap and a camp could be set up for surface exploration. Since landings on the icecap were hazardous in any circumstance, a route back to Söndre Strömfjord was considered essential should the plane not be able to take off from the icecap. Efforts were made to see if the sham, fragile bridges of snow over crevasses could be detected from the air. Repeated flights by the reconnaissance plane revealed only that within 100 miles north or south of Söndre Strömfjord there was no route suitable for mechanized equipment through the rough ice.

Need for a land evacuation route was important, also, in order to determine how far to the east of Söndre Strömfjord the icecap station should be. What appeared to be a suitable area was spotted about 100 miles east of Söndre Strömfjord and some 40 miles to the west of a frozen lake on the icecap. The best surface evacuation route ran west from the campsite to a lake, and then farther west to an area near the marginal ice. Mindful of Balchen's wartime experience when he landed a Catalina on a lake on the icecap, the Snowman party was glad to see several large bodies of water on which a seaplane could land.

One of the two Skytrains assigned to the expedition took off on 21 August from Söndre Strömfjord with the necessary men and equipment to establish a camp on the icecap. Making a run dangerously close to the surface of the snow, the pilot observed a discouraging pattern of sastrugi. The surface was rough, but he decided to chance it nevertheless. The plane made a turn and touched down on the icecap two hours after the take-off from Söndre Strömfjord. Considering the wind-blown, crusted surface, the landing was surprisingly smooth. Passengers and equipment were quickly discharged, and within five hours the plane turned into the wind to attempt a take-off. This proved tougher than the landing. The skis were frozen solidly to the snow. Mechanical power couldn't break them loose; the plane remained glued to the snow surface. After two hours of hard work, the job was done by the insertion of strips of aluminum pierced-plank matting under the wheels, which projected into the snow, and then clearing the snow from under the skis. The icecap is always a stubborn antagonist; another problem now cropped up. The plane was put into motion, but the soft deep snow that stretched for miles in every direction kept it from getting up enough ground speed to take off. After a long run, it finally shuddered and slowly rose into a zero overcast.

This experience showed two take-off problems: first, the elevation of the campsite, 7,000 feet; and, two, power generated in the rarefield atmosphere was too limited to overcome the resistance of snow surface to skis. On days when high temperatures softened the snow and there was little or no wind, the plane, even with a light load and full engine power, could get up speeds of only fifty to fifty-five miles an hour. When JATO (Jet-assisted Take-off) bottles were used for additional power, speed was slightly increased but not enough for the skis to break loose from the snow. Only the expertness of the pilot in his careful maneuvering of the controls could get the aircraft off the icecap.

The expedition explored the icecap for twenty-six days. Supporting planes made seven round trips from Söndre Strömfjord to the site selected for exploration. On six of these trips the planes landed and took off from the unprepared snow surface. On the seventh, only drops were made.

The flights proved that ski-equipped aircraft could land and take off from the unprepared snow surface of the icecap. Further studies showed that at least one of the frozen lakes that dotted the western fringe of the smooth ice area was suitable for landings by wheeled aircraft of considerable size. However, no landings were attempted.

The members of the Snowman expedition reached the conclusion, known to many of us who were familiar with Greenland, that it was possible to construct semi-permanent air bases on the icecap. Their comments were qualified, however, by the need for more information on weather, the structure of the snow, surface features, and the effects of the warm season upon the icecap.

The second aim of the Project Snowman was also carried out— to test equipment appropriate for the area and to improve upon search and rescue procedures. Before further study of the icecap and its suitability for the landing of aircraft could be undertaken, approval of the Danish government was necessary. The United States, Canada, and ten European countries, including Denmark, signed the North Atlantic Treaty, and in the spring of 1951 negotiations between Denmark and the United States were completed, leading to an agreement replacing the earlier one of 1941.

Under the terms of the new agreement, the United States obtained permission from the Danish government to operate such bases in Greenland as approved by that government. The agreement also made provision for technical and engineering surveys in selecting defense areas. Signing of the agreement resulted in the construction of the Thule air base on a site approved by the Danes.

Approval also was granted for the 1953 expedition of the Air Force under the code name Project Mint Julep. This party established itself at the frozen lake area some ninety miles southeast of Söndre Strömfjord and forty miles west of the earlier Project Snowman site. Through the summer of 1953, a twelve-man team of specialists made a series of scientific tests on the frozen lakes on the surface of the icecap. They discovered some ready-made landing strips for any size of aircraft. The area also had superior weather and in every way was advantageous for air bases. Cautious, as scientists always are, they recommended further weather observation and more experimentation with air-rescue operations. They concluded, however, that in the event of war the frozen lake areas of the Greenland Icecap presented airfield possibilities that were hard to overestimate. As staging bases or as alternate landing fields for the sake of dispersal or even as emergency landing areas, these airstrips on the icecap offered a wide range of possibilities.

Establishing bases and operating them in the vast interior is a matter of transportation. How could sizable loads of freight and personnel be transported to the interior from coastal bases without having to develop aircraft for this express purpose? Air drop is one solution, but it can be costly, for delicate instruments may be damaged and supplies lost in crevasses or by burial in snow. Men, too, can be dropped by parachute, but then there is the problem of getting them off the icecap, in case of emergency, to the safety of the ice-free coastal margin.

Accessibility by air lift, then, was the only practicable way if air bases were to be constructed on the icecap. The smooth frozen lakes in the marginal zone of the icecap seemed to offer the best prospects for this purpose. They could be used as landing fields with minimum maintenance. The depth of the snow in these areas varied but could be shallow enough at some sites to allow aircraft landings without any surface preparation.

Finally, these smooth ice areas were as permanent as the icecap itself. They were hard and durable surfaces which remained from year to year with little or no modification. My own observations of these areas from the air told me that it was entirely feasible to fly over the rough marginal ice belt and land on selected points on the icecap. The smooth ice area that I saw near the Mint Julep site, at an altitude of between five and six thousand feet, was at least ten miles in width and considerably more in length. Although I did not have the opportunity to study the full length of the smooth ice area, I was told that it extended along the fringe of the rough ice area on Greenland's west coast for hundreds of miles to the south and north. The exposed glacial ice of the smooth areas almost surely could be used as a landing field in all seasons.

The French were very active on the icecap after the war. Their expeditions were led by Paul-Émile Victor, a French government official and noted anthropologist, who had evaded capture when the Nazis overran his country. He then made his way to the French Island of Martinique and from there to New York. He had explored in Greenland, was one of the few living explorers who had crossed the icecap, and was eager to make his services available to our military forces as a cold-weather expert. Victor went to see Vilhjalmur Stefansson to ask his advice about serving in our armed forces, and Stefansson referred him to me for whatever help I could give him. The Air Force seemed myopic on the question of commissioning a French national whose specialty was the Arctic. This did not discourage Victor. He enlisted as a private, went to Officers Candidate School, was commissioned, took a parachute-jumping course to prepare himself better for rescue work, and then served during the war as a Search and Rescue officer on the Alaskan route to Siberia. From there he was transferred to his former haunts in Greenland.

Immediately after peace came, he began to make plans for French expeditions to Greenland and Antarctica. Victor's expedition (*Expeditions Polaires Françaises*) sailed with nine tons of equipment from Rouen, France, and on 1 June 1948, dropped anchor near Christianshaab, north of the Arctic Circle, on the west coast of Greenland. This was a reconnaissance for expeditions that developed into some of the most extensive, best equipped, and most productive that ever have gone to Greenland for scientific purposes. After establishing four camps, the last on the icecap itself, the expedition made a seven-day exploratory trip on the icecap but devoted most of the time to testing and winterizing equipment for the advance party due there the following year.

Victor's main expedition established a weather station near Eismitte, the spot where Wegener and his party had wintered in 1931. The whole French expedition was conducted in a grand manner which, years earlier, lack of suitable equipment would have made impossible. From the west coast a convoy of twenty-two men with five weasels, two trailer laboratories, and seven sledges traveled to the icecap. They were supplied by air drops from an Iceland-based Liberator which dropped fifteen tons of food and twenty-five tons of fuel in thirteen flights.

The icecap party burrowed into the ice, digging out living quarters, store rooms, and laboratories for a winter party of eighteen, the largest that had ever spent a year in the frozen interior. *La Station Centrale* reported a —86° F. reading in December 1949. A third summer expedition of twenty-seven scientists relieved *Centrale* icecap station personnel on 1 July 1950, having transported its matériel across the border zone in record time. Groups of scientists began glaciological and other research at various points on the icecap. Parachute drops of supplies were continued. Eight fresh members of the *Expeditions Polaires Françaises* continued to operate the *Centrale* station until the fourth summer group relieved it in 1951.

The final large non-military postwar expedition was the British North Greenland Expedition led by Commander C. J. W. Simpson. It spent two years (1952–1954) in Greenland.

In planning his own researches, Simpson was influenced by the original method used by the *Expeditions Polaires Françaises*. The unusual feature about Victor's *Centrale* station was that it had been established and maintained almost entirely by air. The more Simpson studied the more he realized that, in addition to the exploration of Dronnigan Louise Land on the east coast where his main base was established, much important information could be learned about the icecap, and success would depend upon aerial support. Simpson was particularly interested in icecap problems related to geophysics, glaciology, and meteorology as well as military application of knowledge about aircraft and surface operation in a hostile climate.

Simpson knew that on that vast snow desert the surface transport problem is the most critical one. The distance to be covered and the weights to be carried by any large-scale expedition are too great for dog sledges, and special over-snow vehicles are necessary. Such large surface operations also require aerial assistance. The British Air Ministry was an enthusiastic collaborator, providing air-lift and air-drop assistance.

One task of the British North Greenland Expedition was to try to calculate the depth of the icecap with modern seismic equipment. This, of course, had been done earlier by Wegener and by the

Victor expedition farther south. The British were hopeful of adding further evidence to the theory, also espoused by the French, that the great weight of millions of tons of ice had compressed the earth's surface below Greenland into a huge U-shaped basin whose bottom might well be 12,000 or 13,000 feet below the top of the ice and several thousand feet below sea level. The seismic survey didn't go well, and the results were only partially successful.

For more protracted observation, a station called Northice was established on the icecap by a group headed by Simpson, 250 miles from the base on the east coast and a little north of the 78th parallel of latitude. The surface party which established the station dug into the ice and, once settled, sent a radio message to the waiting aircraft at Thule giving its approximate position for air drops on which they were dependent.

After several successful drops the supply plane, a Hastings, crashed without warning on the icecap a mile from Northice. As the plane hit the frozen surface of snow and ice, it skidded for nearly a mile, bumping violently and throwing about the surprised members of the crew who, busy dropping cargo, had not been able to take any preparatory measures. When the plane finally halted, the crew and passengers, twelve men, were ordered by the pilot, Flight Lieutenant Mike Clancy, to climb out through the astro hatch. As a fire did not seem likely, the crew returned to the plane for shelter from the biting wind. The fuselage was quite intact and windproof, so they decided to try to insulate it rather than to start digging snow shelters.

Only three men were seriously injured and had to be treated as casualties: Captain Charles W. Stover, a USAF liaison officer aboard as an observer, had chest and back injuries causing him a good deal of pain; Major D. S. Barker-Simson had a broken ankle; and the radio operator, Flight Sergeant F. Burke, had a deep scalp wound and was suffering from severe concussion. Although they had averted any immediate danger of fire, large quantities of gasoline in the wing tanks constituted a source of possible danger.

Lights were not allowed for the time being. Hot drinks, prepared at Northice, were carried out to the wrecked plane in Thermos flasks. The crew set to work to make the plane habitable.

Pilot Clancy, reporting on the crack-up, said that on completing a final free-drop, his plane flew into a patch of mist which caused a complete "white-out." Not long before, an American pilot flying over the icecap had suddenly felt his plane absorbing an unexpected jar. Putting on full power, he was able to climb away. He had no idea he was anywhere near the surface of the snow. "White-out" had deceived him. On at least two occasions during the war planes had made unexpected landings on the icecap when pilots lost their natural horizons. A pilot's only remedy is to rely on his instrument panel for elevation and on the keel of his plane. Having experienced a white-out when on foot, I know how easy it is to lose visual horizon and fall over the smallest snowdrift and how difficult it is to walk upright.

It would require the greatest skill to land a rescue plane on the icecap to bring the marooned men out. The plane would have to become air-borne again at an altitude of more than a mile and a half. No airplane ever had attempted to a take-off from such an altitude in Greenland. Several factors besides elevation had to be considered. The downed plane was 480 miles from Thule, the station from which the rescue attempt would be made. While a rescue plane was en route to Northice, the weather at Thule might close in, and no alternate field existed. Navigation was complicated by the fact that the wrecked plane was only a dot in a vast sea of white unrelieved by any landmarks. The rescue aircraft would not have fuel for an extended search for Northice; it would have to fly directly to it. Because of the distance involved, it must fly from Thule and return in a line as nearly straight as possible; there could be no gas-consuming detours. This meant that a homing aircraft had to be stationed along the route to give the rescue pilot radio navigation assistance.

The rescue was being planned by some of the Air Force's most experienced Arctic experts at Thule. They devoted all their time and energy to it for nearly a week. The veteran who had participated in so many spectacular rescues on the icecap, Colonel Balchen favored awaiting a ski-equipped Skytrain from Söndre Strömfjord for the rescue attempt. However, it was decided to send out immediately an available Grumman Albatross to evacuate the injured, and only a week after the crash the amphibian was on its way to Northice.

A 600-yard runway was marked out on the snow with colored parachutes and long panels of pink fluorescent material. A Skymaster and a Flying Fortress escorted the short-range Grumman to Northice in an overcast and hazy sky. The Albatross' pilot made three dry-runs along the improvised runway and touched down. The plane settled on its hull in the soft snow, just as had the Grumman Duck on the great icecap rescue mission a decade earlier. For a short time the plane was obscured by a whirling snowcloud, and then it taxied across the snow toward the wrecked airplane. When the injured men were loaded, two JATO bottles were fastened to the exterior of the fuselage, a job that took an hour with the temperature at 30° below freezing. When the Albatross was ready to go, the hull was found to be frozen firmly to the snow surface. The plane was rocked from side to side by men on the wing-tip floats. The hull finally broke loose and the plane moved forward. The pilot fired his JATO, and the Albatross was air-borne and climbing steadily toward the sunset. The plane reached Thule safely where the three injured men were hospitalized.

The remaining nine members of the marooned air crew had only two days to wait until a ski-equipped Dakota arrived from Thule. It was also guided to Northice by supporting aircraft spaced out along the route to Thule for homing purposes. The pilot landed on his first attempt and taxied near the camp. Attaching the cumbersome JATO bottles to brackets near the hatch doors was made more difficult than usual because the pilot dared not shut off his engines. The temperature was now 67° below freezing and the blast of the slipstream from the idling motors whipped snow into the men's faces. At an altitude of 8,000 feet even normal exertion is exhausting, but after an hour and a half they completed the job. The pilot opened up his engines, a loud crack sounded as the JATO bottles went into action, and the Dakota rose out of the flurry of snow.

The British expedition itself brought back much that was of scientific interest. Members of the party gained valuable experience in living and traveling in the far north. One group crossed the icecap to Thule, others made seismic soundings along with the usual work of gathering meteorological, geological, and glaciological data.

CHAPTER XIV

Greenland Today

GREENLAND'S MODERN history begins in 1721 with the landing of a Norwegian missionary, Hans Egede, a short distance north of the mouth of Godthaab Fjord in southwest Greenland. For thirteen years the clergyman had urged the establishment of a Greenland mission, but he finally went as representative of a commercial company that he and several merchants had organized. Greenland was then a Danish Crown Colony.

Hans Egede's contribution to the existence of Greenland as we know it now was tremendous. He worked indefatigably for fifteen years as a missionary, leader, colonizer, and explorer. He found the sites of the earlier colonies, and died believing that the descendants of the old Norsemen still lived in Greenland.

The island's economy, after fifty years of private enterprise, was taken over by the state as a monopoly in 1774. The instructions regulating this trade, especially on humane provisions for the care of the natives, stand as milestones of wise colonial administration.

Despite the many excellent features of the trade provisions, the total effect was to support the authority of the Europeans. Greenland's natives were decreasing in numbers, becoming ever poorer, and were losing initiative and enterprise. No one was more conscious of this decline than Dr. H. J. Rink, a mid-nineteenth century director of the Greenland Trade Company. Prior to his appointment in 1868, he had spent sixteen winters and twenty-one summers in Greenland in various capacities, and his writing stimulated the scientific world into a study of the icecap.

His directorship marked another era in the history of Greenland. He made great progress in carrying out his plans to help the natives, develop their country, and stabilize their economic life.

Early trading in Greenland was carried on by a system of barter which still exists in the more primitive areas. Most of the country, however, uses a currency negotiable only in Greenland. Employing it as the medium of exchange, the Trading Company purchases the fish, blubber, skins or whatever other products the natives have to sell.

A commission was appointed in 1948 to study the government's monopolistic activities. Its report resulted in at least one major change: in principle, trade monopoly was abolished. In actual practice, the process of abolition still must extend over several years.

The preponderance of commercial and productive activities remains under the charge of the Royal Greenland Trade Department, the successor to the Trading Company. The government still operates 80 per cent of the business activity; 10 per cent is by private businessmen in Greenland; the final 10 per cent by businessmen living in Denmark.

Greenland's natural conditions limit its precarious economy. Hunting and fishing remain the principal means of subsistence, considering the inhospitable climate, the infertile country, and the abundance of sea mammals and fish. Climatic changes have affected the nature of the sea life and complete social and economic change has resulted.

The seal served for generations as the staff of life to the Greenlander who never could have penetrated north of the timberline without the seal's oil for light and heat, its meat to eat, its fur to keep him warm. His income was almost exclusively derived from sealing, and as seasons changed he depended upon the presence of different species. The native lived so close to the limits of minimal existence that seasonal weather was vital to him. When the weather and ice conditions were good, then his sealing ventures were prosperous. The seals that he killed covered his needs for food, clothing, light, and heat. In bad seasons, when the seals did not appear, near famine among Greenlanders was common.

In this century, Greenland's warming climate and disappearance of seals mean a new economy based upon the store. A community of hunters is becoming one of fishermen. An economy geared so closely to an abundance of seals and whales was bound to change. Not only the warming seas but systematic killing have materially reduced the numbers of both.

The slaughter of seals by Europeans and Americans has profoundly altered the Greenlander's economic life. (Seal oil is an important ingredient of margarine.) Annual killing by Norwegians of 300,000 baby seals at their breeding grounds on the east coast has a serious effect on the seal population of the west coast to which they migrate.

The decline of seals is keyed to the change of climate, a rather recent development. The quantities of pack ice are smaller. A beneficial result is new migration of cod into northerly waters. Cod fishing now is the chief means of subsistence for South Greenlanders. Until a century ago, no one was interested in encroaching upon the Greenlander's economic areas. The northward migration of cod changed all this. Fishing vessels from Spain, Portugal, and France carry on extensive fishing operations in Davis Strait.

Halibut fishing is falling off seriously, and Greenland faces the risk that the stock may not bear up against excessive fishing. Catfish, a new catch for Greenland fishermen, are in demand. Half of our catfish market is supplied from Greenland. Salmon, occurring in quantities only occasionally, are too scattered to assume economic importance.

Some relatively slight crab canning eventually led to the catching of shrimp; now the emphasis is on shrimp. A substantial shrimp cannery operates at Christianshaab, and there are smaller plants in Narsarssuak and Jacobshavn, where shrimp occur in abundant quantities. The catch goes on at all seasons when ice and cold weather do not prevent trawling. The tender, small males are the most highly prized. Greenland exports a million tins of shrimp annually to forty countries ranging from New Zealand, South Africa, and the Far East, to Sweden and the United States.

About 2,000 men fish for cod. In the early decades of this century the kayak, umiak, and the rowing boat provided the principal transportation to the fishing banks. In recent years privately owned motorboats replaced them. The tendency now is to abandon open motorboats for larger, full deck boats capable of fishing farther at sea.

Wolf fish are sought for their tough skins, an excellent substitute for alligator hides. Queen Elizabeth of Great Britain and Queen Ingrid of Denmark have shoes of wolf fish skin in their wardrobes.

Fish are processed at the fishery station and at quick-freeze stations and dry fish plants of the Royal Greenland Trade Department. Salt fish comprise one half the total, chiefly for the large salt fish market in Brazil. The frozen fish industry, with a major market in the United States, is being developed rapidly. Sales of fish to Mediterranean countries, beginning in the 1920's, today form the main source of revenue.

Although fishing is by far the most important source of income for Greenland, other economic prospects exist: 18,000 tons of coal are mined annually in Kutdlisatt, the Greenland coal mines, reducing the need for imports. The coal consumption in all of Greenland is 40,000 tons. The cost of Greenland coal in Greenland is now less than imported coal, although Kutdlisatt's lack of a natural harbor complicates transportation. The quality of native coal equals ordinary English home-heating coal. American coal with its high BTU content supplies heat too intense for Greenland ovens.

Exploration for uranium has better prospects than the search for oil. Professor Nils Bohr, the atomic physicist who is chairman of the Danish Atomic Energy Commission, visited Greenland a few summers ago to survey the mineral-bearing area of South Greenland for uranium in promising quantities. He returned to Copenhagen with rock samples that seemed to have a higher content of uranium than the known deposits in Sweden which have not proved to be economic. Experiments in extracting pure uranium are being intensified.

Commercial mining of lead on the east coast began in 1956, a year after the first mine was opened by a company which was supported 40 per cent by the Danish government, 20 per cent by private investors, 20 per cent by Canadians, and 20 per cent by Swedish investors. Lead is exported to Europe during the abbreviated navigation season.

The Danes fear exhaustion of the cryolite deposits in Ivigtut. Current estimates give the mine, which has already yielded great quantities, another 25 years at the present rate of depletion.

Other products include 30,000 seal skins a year, 5,000 blue and white fox, and 6,200 bear skins. At public auction 300,000 hair seal skins are sold annually.

Sheep raising, started fifty years ago, is successful. For years the Greenlander, primarily a hunter, could not understand the value of keeping sheep, but as he surrendered his nomadic existence, his attitudes changed.

Because the indigenous caribou is almost extinct, reindeer are being introduced experimentally to improve the meat supply. To stimulate the growth of herds, three Laplander herdsmen have been brought to the Godthaab district, center of the experiment. The present herds number 800 head, all developing well; last year's slaughter was 150, all for local markets.

Because reindeer are migratory, raising them creates problems not experienced in sheep raising. The sheep raiser can settle down, but the reindeer herder must be transient, which is displeasing to him since he no longer is nomadic as is the Laplander. Greenlanders used to be footloose as hunters, but with the transition to fishing they wish to be more settled.

Hunting and fishing, however, still remain the chief occupations. The women sew and care for boots, tents, clothes, and sleeping bags. The men handle sledges, kayaks, umiaks, and most wood boats, and look after their hunting equipment. Every town has at least one extremely competent man who can make boat frames. Sledges, likewise, are built locally.

In summer women and children gather berries and game birds' eggs. There is no cultivating of the barren soil. Trade in fish and meat to Danes has been diminishing.

Godthaab, capital city of Greenland, has slightly more than 2,000 persons, more than half of whom are Danes, and has doubled its population since 1950. Although the population of entire Greenland is growing, it still could be squeezed into the Glass Bowl of The University of Toledo.

The natives have a Mongolian appearance. They also bear a resemblance to American Indians and to Siberian Asiatics. Scientists generally agree on their origin in Siberia with a migration through northern Alaska and the Arctic coast of Canada to Greenland, sometime during the ninth century.

For centuries before the pyramids of Egypt were built, ancestors of present Greenlanders probably fished and hunted, as many still do, isolated from the rest of the civilized world. For three hundred years the majority of native Greenland stock has been mixed with European blood; only a few genuine Eskimos exist today in the northernmost part of the country.

Widely scattered settlements along the coast were suitable and necessary so long as hunting was the major occupation of the people. Now that fishing predominates, the smaller villages are slowly disappearing. Efforts are being made to induce the inhabitants to concentrate in fewer and larger towns.

With hunting his prime concern for countless generations, the native used to drop everything else to grab his harpoon. Now the Greenlander is getting lazy. Softening touches of civilization now send him out to hunt only when he must. He does not hunt for the week after next if he has plently of meat today.

The nomadic Eskimos are still well adjusted to the old ways, and are more content than the Greenlanders. The cycle of the hunt affords a seasonal change of diet and occupation, as well as travel between hunting grounds. In summer, the northern Eskimo longs for the colder days of autumn which bring the narwhal with its spiraled tusk and the white whale on their southward migrations. Winter provides good weather for sledging and fox trapping, catching seals in nets, ice fishing, and the supreme sport, the bear hunt, until the long night puts an end to all unnecessary activity.

Spring is welcomed as the season for stalking basking seals. A few weeks later, sea birds, narwhal, and white whale return from the south. The dog sled now is dismantled and the kayak made watertight for the new season. Summer warmth brings open-fishing and kayak parties to hunt seal. In August the Eskimo undertakes the long migration to the great caribou grazing areas at the edge of the inland ice. The Eskimo always faces a stimulating prospect of change, and always lives in the present.

The stranger to Greenland's towns quickly notes the absence of kamiks (skin boots). Women in high-heeled red shoes or flats struggle along a gravel road, boys in colorful bow ties ride motor bikes and bicycles. Greenland girls who greet incoming ships wear rouge and lipstick, nylons, and inexpensive cotton dresses—invariably in bad taste—in sharp contrast to the few who still dress in their bright and appropriate native costumes. Licorice sticks, bubble gum, and cigarettes are prominent; these are the articles most commonly begged by children.

Men and boys wear more functional clothes. The hooded cotton blouses known as anoraks, in varying hues, predominate; they are worn with dark blue wool trousers and rubber boots which replace sealskin knee boots.

On the modern dock in Godthaab, one is impressed by the Greenlander's dexterity in handling machinery. The Danes perform the heavy manual labor which once was reserved for women. The cargo seems to consist exclusively of beer in green and red cases. Typical of Greenland, many crates marked "this side up" were stacked upside down.

The local taxi, a weather-beaten station wagon, carries passengers from the dock to the town. In all of Greenland there are reported to be forty cars, exclusive of those on our military bases. They are used only within a few of the major communities that have suitable roads. The visitor's first impression is of modernistic, functional, and attractive architecture. Houses, government offices, stores, apartment buildings, and schools are built of timber that must be imported from Denmark. Not a single sod house remains in Godthaab. Danes and Greenlanders naturally prefer the frame houses which are more healthful, warmer, and easier to build. The dwellings are painted in bright yellow, green, or red, and almost all have greenhouse flowers blooming in picture windows. Public buildings are painted with more subdued colors.

Godthaab has dial telephones, street lighting, and a master plan of public works. A modern sewage system is planned to replace septic tanks. Surveyors are busy even on holidays plotting new streets, building sites, lighting, and water works. Until civic planning and building are completed, mosquitoes and flies will thrive in rubbish heaps and stagnant water. Insect repellents are effective enough that the visitor no longer needs to wear a broad-brimmed hat with netting, gloves, and tightly-laced, high-top boots.

The private stores in Godthaab have a great variety of merchandise. There are also a photo-radio shop, two barber shops, and two restaurants (where dishes other than fish are served, too), a hot dog stand where you can also buy ice cream cones and hot chocolate, a bakery with home delivery, and a fish house near the dock which gives the Greenlander his purchase in a plastic bag.

A small shop, ostensibly catering to infrequent tourists, features souvenirs which actually are sold almost exclusively to residents for mailing to friends and relatives in Denmark. In 1956 a total of twenty so-called tourists visited Godthaab; they were Canadians engaged in Labrador's iron-ore industry.

What Godthaab lacks most of all is trees. The kayak, so familiar a sight a few years ago, is hard to find either in the water or on shore. Only a few dogs, identified as pets, are seen. Sledge dogs, which can be vicious, are not permitted because they disturb the freely grazing sheep.

Godthaab's church has special pews fitted with hearing aids. Church services, which are held not only on Sunday but several times during the week, are punctuated with a great deal of coughing and indiscriminate spitting even though signs about spitting are posted conspicuously.

Godthaab has the equivalent of a community technical college which accommodates resident as well as local students. Its curriculum is devoted largely to secretarial studies to provide for the needs of government, booming Godthaab's only industry.

Greenland is administered by a special government agency, the Greenland Department, located in Denmark under the direct supervision of the Prime Minister. Also under his supervision is the Royal Greenland Trade Department.

Greenland was not represented in the Danish parliament until 1953, and was not self-governing territory. Political action by Greenlanders has given the Greenland citizen the same status as the residents of Denmark.

The Godthaab radio broadcasts can be heard by Eskimos across Davis Strait in Baffin Island. Several Greenlanders were sent to Baffin Island several years ago to see how Eskimos live there, to compare their mode of life with existence in Greenland. They came back convinced that Greenlanders are much better off, and agreed to beam broadcasts toward Baffin Island. Besides news, these broadcasts include recitals, quizzes, children's hours, music, and church services.

Greenland's major newspaper, the bilingual *Atuagagdliutit-Gronlands Posten,* is published fortnightly in Godthaab. Carrying news of the outside world as well as local items, it is illustrated by Greenlanders and now and then publishes Greenland legends. It receives money from both the government and the Greenland treasury. Another paper, *Avangnamioq,* is printed in Godhavn and appears only in Eskimo. A privately operated bilingual weekly, *Kamikken,* is published in Godthaab.

The press publishes several technical and fictional works in the Greenlandic language each year, as well as the Bible (a best seller), language and other textbooks, and Eskimo primers.

Greenland's earlier written literature, limited in content and variety, was long dependent upon Danish culture, but now is assuming a national character. The first books, which were the Bible and other religious texts, were later supplemented by translations of Danish and foreign literature. As the populace improved in reading proficiency, a demand grew for national subjects.

The real literature of the country is found in the innumerable tales and legends with which the Greenlanders pass the long night. When the sealers returned from the hunt, the kayakers from the fjords, and the sledgers from their journeys after meat, and after matak was eaten, then would come the hours for storytelling. In the dim light of blubber lamps, the Greenlanders would revive the old tales. Some old man or woman who had an ability for reciting legends and had become the bard of the village, would tell the stories in a singsong, almost monotonous tone. The listeners have heard these legends many times, but repetition seems only to add to their appreciation. The Greenlander does not expect surprise or suspense, for the only variations are in details and ornamentation. Plot and dialogue remain always the same. The interest of the story lies in the thrill of recognition.

Greenlanders write well; the most noted authors include Nicolai Rossing; Frederick Nielsen, the Greenlander broadcaster in Godthaab; and Pavia Petersen, a poet and composer, whose novels are published principally in Eskimo. One of Petersen's novels, *A Greenlander's Dream,* translated into Danish, describes social problems with Petersen's advanced views on Greenland's logical development. Both Greenland representatives in the Danish Parliament are writers.

Greenland finds the closing of our base at Narsarssuak disturbing, for the Danes have found it useful as a base for their own commercial operations. Greenlanders are further concerned that long-range aircraft will end the use of Greenland as a transit stop on flights between the United States and Europe. This seems likely, since Scandinavian Airlines System, which had scheduled daily stops at Söndre Strömfjord, now limits them to twice weekly. TWA and Pan American Airways have decided to develop the former air base, Crystal II, at Frobisher Bay, Baffin Island, in preference to Söndre Strömfjord.

Travel by sea is necessary to reach Sukkertoppen, the next sizable community north of Godthaab. No roads exist except within individual towns, and virtually all transportation between settlements in Greenland is by sea.

Sukkertoppen straggles for almost a mile along a rocky shoreline facing the sea to the south and west. To the north and east it is protected from Arctic storms by a row of high hills. Ships cannot tie up to docks in Sukkertoppen, and everything must be lightered to shore. Boxes, barrels, lumber, and furniture are swung overboard from the Copenhagen steamer, stowed roughly, and taken to land.

Sukkertoppen has a powerhouse for electricity; the town also has a well-constructed and cheerful school, an old church, a modern store plentifully stocked, a hot dog stand, and a modern hospital. The water supply is purified and piped from small glacier lakes.

There are attractive, modern apartment houses in Sukkertoppen; they include two floors and basement. They lack bathrooms but do have toilet facilities; they have a kitchen with a breakfast nook, living room, and two small bedrooms. These are part of a slum clearance project.

At a ski run in Godthaab and a ski jump in Sukkertoppen, the season lasts from the beginning of January until late in May, somewhat similar to the period in Vermont. Greenlanders love to ski and have recently organized their own ski clubs. They like both slalom and jumping. Ski clubs now are associated with similar clubs in Denmark, and it is their hope that their champions will compete with clubs there and in Norway. Several Greenlanders are excellent skiers though none has appeared in the Olympics.

A recently completed sanatorium in Godthaab with beds for tuberculosis patients and construction of a hospital in Sukkertoppen underscore the emphasis on health problems.

Tuberculosis remains the most prevalent disease, as it does among other northern peoples. In so dry and crisp a climate, the mortality from respiratory ills presumably should be exceptionally low. However, Greenlanders in the northern part of the country live in damp sod houses. Women, being so much indoors, suffer more. Tuberculosis is so commonplace that, when informed that he has it, the patient usually is indifferent, although assurance that he is as yet unaffected may cause a Greenlander to wring a doctor's hand with joy.

A concerted effort to combat tuberculosis includes comprehensive examination and vaccination at all age levels. During the postwar years a number of patients have been sent to Denmark for treatment. The sanatoriums in Greenland, where more than 350 tuberculosis patients are admitted annually, still are insufficient to take care of all those who require hospitalization.

Greenland's educational structure traces back to the seventeenth century. Until 1950 the schools were church related and were held accountable to the Ministry of Ecclesiastical and Educational Affairs. The highest educational authority was an archdeacon at Godthaab who also was the head of the clergy. The church, throughout this period, was responsible for maintaining a certain level of literacy. Everyone was required to be able to read, chiefly in religious texts.

Upon the separation of school and church, a board of education was established with a new official—Director of Education—in charge. This school board consists of the Governor of Greenland, a representative of the church, and a Director of Schools appointed by the King.

Attendance in the "children's schools" is compulsory beginning at age seven, for a seven-year period. Enrollment has soared, having increased by one-third since World War II, and is now nearly 5,000. The aim of all education is to make the Greenlander self-sufficient; all school programs are offered free, and this is extended to books, lunches, and medical care.

After a child has spent seven years in the children's school, he may go on to a postgraduate school for those 14–16 years of age. Three of these schools (one each in Julianehaab, Godthaab, and Egedesminde) enroll a total of 130 pupils. This two-year program makes up deficiencies of the children's school and prepares the pupils for the more advanced training in the high school. The high school, which accepts students between sixteen and twenty years, is in Godthaab. Its course of study is comparable to that in a Danish high school. Pupils who successfully pass the final examination may go on to the seminary, also in Godthaab. The seminary provides a three-year program for those between twenty and twenty-three and concludes with a catechist-teacher's examination entitling the candidate to a position in the school and church service.

Recently many young Greenlanders have enrolled in Danish seminaries, and about a score are there now. Greenland has no university; young people qualified for higher education must go to Denmark.

Alcohol poses a serious problem for Greenland. For many years the Danish government sold only barley malt for sweet beer. Sale of liquor in the stores was opened by request of the Greenland Council. Seventy-five per cent of crime in the country is attributed to liquor; some towns now have their first policemen, a necessity only since the introduction of liquor. The Greenlanders, being an improvident people, buy liquor instead of food. Prices are kept high to discourage purchase.

The most important punishments for crime are admonition, fines, confinement to a specified area, or prohibition from entering other specified areas. To these may be added compulsory labor, institutional treatment, internment, and other restrictions on the liberty of action. A man accused of such a serious crime as rape is penalized by being moved to a distant community. He will be obliged to live with a hunter or a fisherman to learn those skills.

What, then, can be suggested as the result of the inroads of European culture which have brought nylons as well as liquor, mails as well as jets, diseases as well as health measures? At least some competent observers contend that these contacts with the outside world are proving of doubtful advantage. The introduction of an unassimilable culture deprives many a Greenlander of more than he can possibly gain. It is certain that the old museum philosophy of keeping Greenland for Greenlanders is gone. Technical progress, especially aviation, renders irresistible the advance of European culture.

Because of the icecap and despite advances of recent years,

Greenland—the northern lifeline to Europe—remains to most
Americans a geographical dead end. Most of us look upon it as
a windswept, frozen wasteland, a quaint and useless land of
Eskimos, igloos, polar bears, glaciers, and howling sledge dogs.

PART II

Lifeline to Moscow

CHAPTER XV

Northward to Nome

WHEN THE Japanese planes struck Pearl Harbor on December 7, 1941, America was instantly involved in a war that literally covered the world. In succeeding years, this nation had to divide its resources precisely and judiciously—so much matériel and manpower to overwhelm the Germans, sufficient men and equipment to stem the flood of Japanese conquests and to turn them back to their island empire.

Theaters of war were quite logically divided. Troops were committed to one or the other. An aircraft built on Long Island or in the sprawling suburbs of Los Angeles was ticketed for Europe or for the Pacific before it began to take shape on the assembly line. Soldiers' and sailors' battle ribbons were geographical signposts, telling which of the two wars they had seen. Supply officers of all the services worked their nerves to the breaking point, trying to make the right decisions about countless millions of items of war matériel: how much to the European front, how much to the Pacific?

Few of the military operations outside the mainland United

States were strategically mounted against the Axis as a whole. They were aimed at either Germans or Japanese, not at both. The air route to Alaska was one of the exceptions.

Early in the war, when disaster topped disaster in the Pacific, there was no proper limit to speculation on Japanese strikes. Would they attack the Aleutians? (They did, holding Kiska and Attu for a time.) Could they ever land on the mainland of Alaska? Would they return to invade Hawaii? Would they eventually storm ashore on the Pacific Coast of the United States itself? Would their early naval triumphs permit them easily to control the sea lanes from the Pacific ports to strategic Alaska? Would their carrier-based aircraft throttle the coast airways that linked Seattle and Nome? Or, turning northward, would they deal Vladivostock in Siberia the kind of blow that crushed the Philippines and Singapore? These and a myriad other contingencies had to be plotted and countered.

On the other hand, there were the Germans with almost all of Europe at their feet, a stranglehold on North Africa, and their submarines prowling in wolfpacks along the Atlantic approaches. The Wehrmacht, ground to a standstill perhaps in the bitter Russian winter, nonetheless promised to crush its way to Moscow and Stalingrad and on across European Russia just as soon as the warm spring sun melted the ice and snow and dried the mud so that the panzers could roll again. Once the Soviet Union collapsed, would the Germans roll across Southwest Asia to clasp hands with the Japanese in India? Would the Luftwaffe burn the Soviet Air Force out of the skies? While America and Britain raced preparations to launch a second front against Hitler in the west, could the battered Soviet army hold the Nazi juggernaut in the east?

There was one certainty among all the harried speculation. Alaska was the jumping-off point against these possible Japanese moves in the Pacific, and Alaska was helpless without aircraft and the means to keep them flying. Moreover, with German subs ready to slash ferociously at the convoys to Murmansk in the

Soviet Arctic, there was only one safe route for American aircraft to travel to the eastern front. There had to be another northern airway, this one leading from the great aircraft factories of continental United States, across the rugged wilderness of British Columbia and the Yukon to Alaska, thence across the Bering Strait to Siberia and safe transport to the Russian front.

All the Japanese threats did not materialize, nor was Alaska ever seriously endangered, but the lifeline to Moscow was vital and remained so until Hitler's broken legions rolled backward to the original borders of the Third Reich. It is a vital lifeline today, when Alaska is the largest state of the United States, and an enemy infinitely more powerful than Hitler lies just fifty-six miles across the Bering Strait.

The problem of an inland air route to Alaska immediately posed one of the toughest logistic questions ever to face military and air engineers—the vast expanse of almost unbroken wilderness that stretched from Dawson Creek in British Columbia to White Horse in the Yukon and thence to Fairbanks in Alaska. There had to be at least three airports, and everybody knew where they ought to be located: one at Fort Nelson in the muskeg badlands near the foothills of the Canadian Rockies, where a trading post, a British Columbia Police station, and an Indian village clustered lonesomely on the banks of the Nelson River; at Watson Lake in the Yukon wilderness, high in the upper stretches of the Rockies, and at the old Klondike mining town of Whitehorse in the Yukon.

Modern military airports, however, cannot be constructed without either heavy machinery or an army of laborers. There was no road of any kind through the seventeen hundred miles of wilderness; there were scarcely any trails, since Indians, trappers, and Mounties traveled by boat on the countless streams that traverse the Canadian northwest.

Build a road, then—hadn't there long been plans for one?

It would take too long.

Bulldoze a path, and then use the bulldozers to build the landing strips.

It would take too long.

Somebody must have said jokingly, "Why don't we do it all at once, road and landing strips and communications, all together?"

Somebody else must have taken him seriously. That's what the Air Force and the U. S. Engineers and the Public Roads Administration and civilian contractors proceeded to do.

While great airports suddenly mushroomed in the trackless forest and the rugged mountains, a twisting ribbon of gravel literally jumped, at an average eight miles a day, south from Fairbanks and north from Dawson Creek to link the airports in a long chain that led to the eastern front in the Soviet Union.

The air route to Alaska, however, did not leap into being from charts on conference tables in the winter of 1941–1942. It was a tremendous engineering job when it was undertaken, but it had its conception two decades earlier in the laconic report submitted to his superiors by Captain Bill Streett of the U. S. Army Air Corps, who had just completed, in 1920, a military expedition by military aircraft from the United States to Nome, Alaska.

"The air route to Alaska," said Streett, "is not feasible until air fields are made along the route."

The fragile planes of Streett's expedition were battered and buffeted when they made take-offs and landings at primitive landing sites, and they were kept airworthy only by the mechanical aptitudes of Second Lieutenant Eric "Swede" Nelson. He proved himself invaluable again in 1924, when he was a member of the Army's "Round-the-World Fliers" as they risked Alaska's perilous landing strips.

Ten years after Streett's flight, a squadron of Martin B-10 bombers, the first bombing plane to exceed 200 miles per hour, made the hazardous Alaska hop. The squadron's commanding officer was Lieutenant Colonel H. H. Arnold. The flight roster, in later years, pinned almost enough stars on its shoulders to fill the field on an American flag:

Lieutenant Colonel Arnold, Flight Commander and leader of one of the three elements; Major Hugh J. Knerr, Flight Commander second element; Major Ralph Royce, Flight Commander third element; Captain Harold M. McClelland, Wichita, Kan.; Captain Westside T. Larson, Vallejo, Calif.; Captain John D. Corkill, Chicago; First Lieutenant Hez McClellan, Baton Rouge, La.; First Lieutenant Charles H. Howard, Ashland, Ore.; First Lieutenant Lawrence J. Carr, Chicago, Ill.; First Lieutenant John S. Griffith, San Antonio, Calif.; First Lieutenant Ralph A. Snavely, Long Beach, Calif.; Second Lieutenant L. F. Harman, Boise, Idaho; Captain Ray A. Dunn, Long Beach, Calif.; Major Malcolm C. Grau, Philadelphia, Pa.; plus sixteen enlisted men.

Scarcely a month before Pearl Harbor, Colonel Edmund W. Hill of the Air Corps submitted a report on his just-completed inspection flight over the embryonic Northwest inside route which was undertaken with "the aim in view of adding to the meager store of information now at hand for AAF personnel engaged in making the flight through Canada to stations in Alaska."

The same difficulties experienced on the North Atlantic route were found on the route to Alaska. Among other things, Colonel Hill stated that maps were almost useless because of inaccuracies; service radios, when they functioned, did so badly; intermediate landing areas and facilities for repairs were completely lacking, as they had been during Streett's flight twenty years earlier. Colonel Hill added that no reliance should be placed on navigation by radio compass and that most fields were not suitable for heavy aircraft. He warned of the necessity of making careful preparation for flights in winter, recommended the inside route as preferable to the one in operation along the coast from Seattle to Juneau, and added this ominous bit of advice:

"Should trouble . . . develop in the uninhabited stretch north of Edmonton which necessitates a decision between bailing out

. . . or making a crash landing, the latter choice should be made. The advantage of this selection will become obvious after flying over the desolation."

Contradictory as it may seem, in the years following Captain Streett's first exploratory flight, aviation had made great strides *in*—even though not *to*—Alaska.

Bush pilots were the pioneers; they started the first mail, passenger, and cargo routes within the 49th state. Pan American Airways entered the picture in 1932, as much to learn about cold-weather flying as for any other reason. Even then, Pan American had global plans and ambitions in connection with which first-hand knowledge of flying conditions in Alaska would be useful. In advancing their vision of the air future of the Arctic, they supported meteorological as well as aerial surveys in Greenland as well as in Alaska.

The Canadian portion of the air route to Alaska had been surveyed by the Canadian Department of Transport in 1935. An air-minded explorer named Grant MacConachie opened the inside route, developing his crude bush flying service into the Yukon Southern Airlines, which operated air services between Whitehorse and Edmonton, and wherever else in the Canadian north anyone wished to go. MacConachie's equipment was far from what the Army classifies as "heavy" and the fields which he developed were primitive. Later the Yukon Southern Airlines was purchased by the Canadian Pacific Railway Company Airlines, which took over the plane service between Edmonton and Whitehorse. In those days there was much discussion of a highway that would someday be built along the same route.

In the spring of 1939 Canada made an appropriation for preliminary work along MacConachie's route. In 1940 this project was given further impetus by appointment of the Canada-U. S. Permanent Joint Board of Defense. The Canadian Government decided that the development of this airway should be in accordance with Canadian requirements and at its sole expense.

The main airfields along the route were to be constructed at Grand Prairie in Alberta, Fort St. John and Fort Nelson in British Columbia, and at Watson Lake and Whitehorse in the Yukon Territory. Grand Prairie had surface transportation, the Northern Alberta Railway, a single track line manned by conductors who always informed their passengers that they were riding the farthest-north railway in North America. Fort St. John was connected by road to the Northern Alberta's end-of-steel at Dawson Creek. Whitehorse, at the other end of the route, was connected with Skagway by the legendary White Pass & Yukon of Gold Rush fame.

Fort Nelson and Watson Lake, however, were deep in the heart of the northern wilderness, and only trail-breaking bull-dozers could make them accessible for air-route purposes.

It was not long after the initial survey that it became apparent there was a difference of opinion between what the Canadian Government and the United States Army considered an adequate airway. With the European war raging furiously, the Air Corps experts were thinking in terms of heavy bombers, lightning-fast fighters, and navigation aids that would enable any sort of craft to negotiate the route safely, regardless of terrain and weather. The Canadians obviously had in mind something less than that.

Within the borders of Alaska itself efforts to hurry along construction of an airway were a bit more advanced. After years of pleading, the Civil Aeronautics Administration finally had an appropriation to construct airfields. Early in 1941, while the snow in Alaska lay many feet deep and blizzards still were howling, CAA engineers and experts ranged far and wide making surveys, selecting sites, and gathering useful information. They had waited a long time for their chance.

The Alaskan construction season lasts only from May to October. Before the river ice jams had broken, thousands of tons of earth-moving equipment, housing, and other supplies were hauled over the snow and muskeg in the wake of giant D-8 caterpillars. One veteran bush pilot flew every item except large tractors into one camp—houses, radio towers, feed, tools, pipe, Diesel generators, and workmen.

Army men freely predicted the CAA and its contractors would not be able to complete their ambitious program, but they did. Two months before Pearl Harbor, every CAA field in the schedule was in condition to be used by military aircraft, a remarkable achievement that may well have saved vulnerable Alaska and the Pacific Northwest from Japanese invasion.

It was only a matter of days after the hysteria created by Pearl Harbor that things really began to happen. High staff officers in Washington immediately realized that the situation was critical. On 4 February 1942 General Arnold asked that the Canadian government grant permission to Northwest Airlines and Western Air Express to operate in the Dominion, and for Pan American to augment its operations between Seattle and Southern Alaska, which touched on British Columbia and Yukon Territory. General Arnold's memorandum concluded:

"In view of the ultimate necessity for conducting operations on a grand scale against Japan from Siberian air bases it is vitally important that preparations be laid immediately to support the extraordinarily heavy air traffic through Alaska to these Siberian bases, on which operations must necessarily depend."

It is interesting to note that in view at that time was the optimistic hope that American planes might soon be winging against Japan from Soviet bases rather than that the route would be utilized to ferry planes to the Russians for use on the eastern front.

Northwest Airlines dispatched that company's first survey flight over the interior route on 27 February, and a similar Army party flew over the inside route early in March. The main development effort would be made here rather than along Pan American's coastal course from Seattle to Juneau. Telegraphic reports which streamed back to Washington confirmed earlier misgivings: crude fields; poor communications; inadequate housing, equipment, and fuel supplies. No ground facilities meant no airway.

In order to make the route serviceable for major operations, enormous quantities of heavy equipment and thousands of men would have to be moved in to remote points, many of which could only be reached by dog team and pack train. The long-range plan was for a daily capacity of forty to fifty combat planes and seven to ten transports. The job looked impossible.

Someday, of course, ground communications would be provided by the Alaska Highway, but in March of 1942, that project was also just getting under way. Construction units were bulldozing the road north from Fort St. John, north and south from Fort Nelson, north and south from Whitehorse, and south from Fairbanks. In the far north, working seasons were shorter, and some bulldozers that were brought in by plane did not begin to walk down the endless miles of timber until June of 1942.

There was a lot of work ahead for thousands of men before full-scale air traffic could flow between Great Falls, Montana, and Fairbanks, Alaska.

CHAPTER XVI

The Battle of Northwest Airlines

GENERAL ARNOLD issued orders that shaped the Alaskan air route. The stretch between Great Falls and Fairbanks would serve, in summary, as the handle of a two-pronged pitchfork that would prod the Axis. The tines forked at Fairbanks—one curving up to Nome, the other to Anchorage and the Aleutians. The Nome route would take planes to the Soviet Union; the Anchorage leg would provide a defense line for the Aleutians and southern Alaska.

There were a great many cooks, however, and some of the broth threatened to spoil. The Canadians seemed in no hurry to get started. They were committed to furnish and install radio ranges, furnish and operate traffic control, construct all buildings on the air route, and supply and operate the necessary additional power units, submitting a schedule of charges for payment. The Ferrying Command of the U. S. Air Force would provide radio. Everybody promised to get right at it. That was on 10 April 1942.

Three weeks later, with the Japanese expected any day in the

Aleutians, there were no signs of Canadian activity. Nobody had any authority, and nobody had any a month later, either.

The agreement with Canada provided that the Canadian government would pay for the construction of new airfields and other works of permanent character, but that the United States would pay for all extensions and improvements that exceeded Canadian postwar requirements. It was a generous arrangement on the part of the United States, but the Canadians had never shown any desire to make unjustified profits out of joint efforts, and further, the criterion of the Canadian share of the cost was her modest need for postwar air service in the desolate northern bush. After some of the red tape was cut by conferences and directives, Canadian efforts began to make themselves known.

Lack of accurate information about the country, the weather, personnel problems, and general foul-ups resulted in an amusing aura of optimism in Washington. This was reflected in General Robert Old's advice to the Air Service Command that spring, that "probably no delivery can be made over this route for the next thirty days." Thirty weeks turned out to be more like it.

The fact that no airway existed did not prevent a considerable number of planes from flying the route from Edmonton to Fairbanks. There was no choice; the flights were necessary.

As over the North Atlantic route, a commercial carrier was called in to assist in the trying situation created by the lack of aircraft and flyers trained in cold-weather operations. In this case it was Northwest Airlines.

While the selection of Northwest Airlines was a happy choice, it resulted eventually in somewhat unhappy complications. Probably no commercial airline in the nation was more fitted for the job. Its peacetime schedules had been flown over the coldest sections of the United States. Well organized and experienced, Northwest knew most of the tricks of winterization. It already was operating across the Canadian border with a routine schedule to Winnipeg. Northwest was winter-minded.

The airline jumped at the opportunity to work the route. Patriotic motives and outstanding services aside, it would be naïve to deny that all contract airlines cast a calculating eye toward the best business potential in the postwar future. It would be a natural development for Northwest to extend its operations to Alaska since this would be an opportunity to establish a firm toe hold, even against the understandable disapproval of the Canadian Government.

Northwest wasted no time getting started. During the first five weeks of piecemeal flying it carried 45 tons of cargo and 200 passengers, a mere dribble compared to what was to come later, but in those early months every pound of freight and every passenger were important. On 29 April a regular daily schedule out of Edmonton was inaugurated. Northwest had moved in with determination, set up shop—if a few men with a few tools and spare parts can be called "shop"—and was operating.

It was immediately apparent not only to the airline but to the AAF as well that aggressive action would have to be taken to solve the communication problems along the route. Again as over the North Atlantic area, lack of land lines was the principal obstacle. Between Edmonton and Fairbanks there were only 345 miles of old, rusty wire. Most of it was in Alaska. In the Canadian sector radio was the quickest way to establish communication. But the meager wireless facilities were strained to capacity and the familiar ionospheric storms of the north plagued all reception.

The period was one of considerable confusion mixed up in cross purposes on communications. Washington failed to issue clear-cut authority and directions. The AAF, Signal Corps, CAA, and other government services were each working as though the others didn't exist. Pan American, Northwest Airlines, Canadian, and civilian communication agencies were also in the act, anxious to maintain and expand their holdings and authority. This was a time of bidding for new markets. Even with a war on, all concerned seemed to be looking into the future.

The immediate result of the confusion was that Northwest Airlines was directed to install and operate radio stations at six Canadian locations on the route to Fairbanks. It was a logical decision. Northwest had the know-how, the men for the job, and the initiative to do it quickly. But having communications along the route in the hands of commercial operators with postwar designs was not acceptable to the Canadians.

The ensuing effort to switch from civilian to military operation came to be known to the Army Airways Communication System men along the route as "The Battle of Northwest Airlines."

The first two AACS officers assigned to the route were Second Lieutenants W. R. Hilbrink and S. H. Dobrzensky. When briefed in Washington, they were told what they might expect. The briefing probably ran as follows:

"The AAF has an air route through the Northwest to Alaska which is in the process of being set up by a commercial airline under contract with the government. It was felt that since the AAF is a tactical agency and not an air-route operator the best plan would be to employ someone experienced in the particular type of operation desired. Northwest Airlines has already pioneered this route from Minneapolis through to Fairbanks. It has installed and is now operating a string of six radio stations along the route.

"These stations are going to be our primary concern. The Canadian Government has required that these stations be militarized at the earliest possible date due in part to its reluctance to continue, or increase, its dissemination of classified weather information to the American civilian personnel. Apparently the Canadians prefer that the setup be military, and possibly they fear the intrusion of civilian airline personnel.

"This coincides with our original plan—that civilians be hired to pioneer the operations, then turn them over to the Army in the same way a contractor turns over buildings.

"Therefore our plan is this—we are going to send six communications officers, one to each of these stations, and give them thirty to sixty days in which to familiarize themselves with the setup and personnel, and then we will send selected enlisted men, one at a time, to each station to be broken in and then to displace the civilians.

"It is imperative that the utmost tact and diplomacy be employed because the civilians may resent the Army taking over after they have endured the hardships of pioneering. It is desirable that no friction whatever be permitted to develop, and the taking over must be adjudged to fit such a policy at each station."

Four additional officers, Lieutenants Jones, Holst, Gubitz, and Ferrabee were added to the project, and after a few days at Great Falls they proceeded to their various stations. The untenable situation quickly came to a head.

Lieutenant Dobrzensky's experiences may be taken as typical. He arrived at Whitehorse to discover that an AACS station was already in operation. The Commanding Officer of the 11th Weather Region at Anchorage had sent up four enlisted men to provide a link between Whitehorse and Fairbanks for the dissemination of weather, using Royal Canadian Communication System facilities. No mention of this station had been made during the preliminary briefing.

The new officer introduced himself to Gene Folkstad, the NWA station manager. The NWA had had no official information or instructions as to the Army taking over. Folkstad believed that Lieutenant Dobrzensky was simply there as "window dressing" because the Canadians had insisted that the setup be militarized.

According to D. J. King, divisional superintendent of Northwest Airlines, reporting on his firm's effort later in the war, the original understanding of the airline was that it was to operate communications for at least the duration of the war.

"Our contract," King said, "called for us to *build and establish* an air route to Alaska as fast as possible, including communications, navigational aids, hangars, runways, gas installations, and so on."

"When we started out, there was virtually nothing along this route. We had to pioneer the job under difficult conditions. When we started there was no clause in our contract nor any understanding that we were to turn over the communications stations to the Army."

King said Northwest Airlines was loathe to relinquish the radio stations for three main reasons:

1. "We had a paternal interest in the route. We had undergone the hardships of setting it up and we felt that the job of operating it, once it was completed, belonged to us.

2. "We were afraid of the inexperience of the Army personnel that was to take over the route. We hesitated to lose the communications system which worked to give us operational safety. We were unwilling to send aircraft out without adequate radio guard. We felt, and still feel, that such expert radio guard was essential to the successful operation of our aircraft.

3. "The *esprit de corps* of our employees accounted for a part of the conflict. An airline is like any other organization. An Army unit, the Marine Corps, and so on, depend on the *esprit de corps* of their men. We would not want men around who did not have the interest of the company at heart. And we were not satisfied at that time that the Army could come in and do the job that we had done. Our men on the job in many cases resented some pipsqueak of an officer, with little experience, who could come into a station and begin to issue orders and try to run things."

A fourth reason, not mentioned by King at this point but later alluded to by him, was what is known as the "profit motive"— which, however, cannot be held against Northwest. They were in business, doing a good job, and their men were enduring hardships side by side with the soldiers, although at much higher rates of pay and allowances.

Practically all of the difficulty could have been avoided. The problems that arose can be attributed to the ambiguity of the basic agreement under which the airline went to work for the Army. Unfortunately, nothing in the contract made specific provision for assumption of the radio by the Army, once the route had been set up. It was, therefore, quite understandable that for operational and profit reasons Northwest should try to cling to its stations.

The company did not regard this in any way as an unpatriotic act or as opposed to the best interests of the Army, King asserted. "The Army," he said, "is mostly made up of civilians—civilians in uniform. And though we are a civilian organization, we are working for the best interests of the country. We are, after all, Allies too. We thought we were best qualified by experience and past successes to do the job."

King then mentioned several instances of military contributions by his company during the early period, such as ferrying a flight of B-17's out to the Aleutians when they were vitally needed, although no Northwest pilot had previously flown a four-motored aircraft.

However, with the faulty basic agreement not placing them under any clear compulsion, Northwest "assumed" the inevitable inefficiency of Army operation before a fair test could be made; assumed the bossiness of Army officers before these officers had been on the scene more than a few minutes, and were seeking reasons to justify their refusal to turn over the radio stations.

AACS, anticipating the hostility of these civilian pioneers, stressed the importance of tact and diplomacy in relations with the company personnel.

At headquarters relations between the Army and NWA seemed outwardly excellent, but at the stations up the line relations were far less amicable. Lieutenant Dobrzensky wrote:

"A very great amount of credit should be given to the enlisted men of the AACS. They put up with extremely difficult working conditions that grew out of hostility and continuous opposition from the civilian operators. In effect, we had two crews of operators and two officers in charge. The Army men had instructions to 'keep peace in the family'; meanwhile, the civilians made no bones about their opposition to Army control and dislike of Army personnel.

"Whenever a poor operator was heard on the circuit, the civilians could be expected to say, 'That's an Army op.' Whenever there was an apparent delay caused by administrative requirements, the cry of 'red tape' went up, and they continuously referred to the 'efficiency of their company setup' as opposed to the alleged confusion, red tape, and delays of the Army.

"It was a commonly expressed opinion within our own group that Northwest was after a postwar airline; and it appeared to us that they were loyal to their company beyond reason in trying in their own way to further this end by keeping out the Army. From my observations at Whitehorse, and from meeting various of Northwest's supervisory personnel, this feeling existed throughout the region.

"It is again emphasized that the fact that no more than minor clashes took place is due solely to the self-control and discipline of this initial group of radio operators. They bore the brunt of it and did a good job."

As the year and tempers grew shorter, conflict between soldiers and civilians continued. There can be no doubt that NWA was protected by contract in its assumption that it was entitled to continue operation of the radio stations along the route. They were not willing to surrender this function without a final struggle.

On Christmas Day in 1942 the Commanding Officer of the 16th AACS, Major Ulrick, found it necessary to inform officers in charge at AACS stations that "... contrary to our expectations, the AACS has been unable to assume control of the facilities and services installed and at present operated by Northwest Airlines. Due to technicalities in the contract with Northwest, neither AACS nor Northwest Airlines are in a position to assume full supervision and responsibility. The situation is being considered in conference and a decision is expected in a few weeks.

"Meanwhile it will be necessary for the route to continue operation with present equipment and personnel and with a minimum of friction. AACS personnel are assigned to each station for training and to help, under the direct supervision of the Officer in Charge, in the establishment and successful operation of communications services to flying personnel. It is not desired that AACS personnel work under the supervision of Northwest employees. It further will not be necessary for Northwest employees to work under the direction of AACS personnel. Any matters requiring the co-operation of both our personnel and theirs are to be worked out between the officer and the Northwest station manager, each of whom will be expected to supervise his own personnel. Any matter which cannot be settled amicably at the station will be referred to his office and to the Edmonton office of Northwest. All concerned are urged to settle the smaller details locally without reference to higher authority whenever possible. Small differences of opinion and personalities should not be allowed to interfere with our general purpose: to furnish the best possible service to flying personnel. Officers in charge are reminded that the situation is delicate and are requested to display as much tact and courtesy as possible to promote harmony until supervision of the route has been assigned."

It must have seemed pretty obvious to everyone that in the midst of a war for survival this was a ridiculous situation which would, sooner or later, wind up with a loud explosion.

Colonel Tom L. Mosley, Commanding Officer of the Alaskan Wing of the Air Transport Command, brought it to a sudden end on 18 January 1943 in a precise directive that gave AACS complete control of all fixed communications in connection with movement of aircraft along the route to Alaska. Colonel Mosley's decision declared:

1. Effective this date, all fixed communications of the Alaskan Wing in connection with the movement of combat, cargo or any other aircraft over routes under the jurisdiction of the Alaskan Wing will be controlled by Regional Communications Control Officer, 16th Airways Communication Squadron, who is responsible to the Director of Communications for all matters pertaining to communications of the Alaskan Wing.

2. Under the supervision of the Regional Control Officer, military personnel will be used on CW operations. Contract cargo communications personnel will be used on voice operations and will by direction of the Army officer in charge at each station cooperate in the training of Army personnel for phone circuit operation.

3. This directive demands without any leeway whatsoever the positive control of all fixed communications in the Alaskan Wing by the Regional Control Officer assigned to this Wing for that person. Any person not wishing to comply with the above may complain direct to the Commanding Officer, Alaskan Wing.

4. The militarization of the Communications System of the Alaskan Wing, including communications personnel of fixed communications will become effective 15 February 1943. Any civilian operator so desiring to remain in his present position as a military operator may do so by submitting a request to the Regional Communications Control Officer, 16th Airways Communications Squadron, Edmonton, Alberta, whereupon he will be informed as to proper procedure to follow for voluntary induction in the Army. Upon induction he will be given a grade and rating commensurate to his present rate of pay. The Regional Communications Control Officer will assist them in every way possible.

At higher headquarters of Northwest Airlines Colonel Mosley's decision was accepted as final and no further resistance was offered.

The battle was over.

King, in advising all his Northern Division radio operators and station managers of Colonel Mosley's directive, said: "We regret this change of policy. However, it is not for us to question but for us to comply whole-heartedly with the intent of Colonel Mosley's directive. It is well that I assure all of you that this change was not necessitated by the inadequacy of Northwest's ability to operate an efficient radio circuit.

"For your guidance, Northwest Airlines had no desire to influence you in determining the position in which you might best serve the all-out war effort. Should you, or should you not, elect to become a member of the armed forces, your seniority and standing with the airlines will remain the status quo.

"Between the present date and 15 February I will expect each man in every possible way to assist and instruct Army personnel in the operation of the Communications System."

When asked what finally induced Northwest to give up the struggle, King said: "There was really nothing else we could do. We were informed that after 15 February we would receive no further reimbursement for operation of the radio stations.

"However, I wish to state very definitely that I regard the Army's taking over of these stations as a natural development. With the sort of job that had to be done, it was necessary for the Army to handle communications along the route."

King stated that considerable political pressure had been exerted initially by the Canadian Government to keep Northwest Airlines, as an American commercial operator, out of permanent operation on Canadian soil. He was of the opinion, however, that the Canadian Government had since tempered its earlier view because of the desirability after the war of "Freedom of the Air" for all airlines—American, Canadian, and others—if any of them were to prosper. "It now appears," King said, "that the principle of 'innocent passage' will be in force."

When Northwest abandoned its stations, King said, no provision was made for resumption of operation by NWA of these stations after the war. "Who gets in after the Army pulls out is still being contested. We have nothing to hide. We make no secret of our desire to handle this route. However, no one knows what the outcome will be."

It is doubtful if this squabble shortened or prolonged the war by a single second, and there is no evidence that operations on the Alaskan route were affected. But the conclusions are fairly obvious and not entirely unimportant. When the conflict started, the Army Air Force, if only through lack of numbers, was not equipped to inaugurate and maintain an essential military operation. A civilian commercial organization was. But within a surprisingly short time the American men in uniform, and their machines, were qualified to take over the job.

CHAPTER XVII

Life in the Bush Country

A FRENCH CANADIAN workman along the Alaska Highway tried in 1942 to explain to a friend of mine why there were so many mosquitoes, gnats, yellowjackets and other insects to plague the men in every construction camp from Dawson Creek to Fairbanks. He had trouble making his point in English. "Bugs, bugs," he said excitedly. "Like rabbits. From one comes a hundred." The history of the Air Force weather service brings that story to mind; every difficulty was bound to engender a hundred others.

When the Alaska airway was decided upon, there was no Air Force weather service in Canada. The Canadian Department of Transport was growing in western Canada, serving the pioneer airlines, which had their own limited weather installations here and there. Air Force pilots, already flying planes along the Northwest route, relied on these meager sources and the advice of bush pilots for weather information.

Most of the time the pilots had little to go on, and often that wasn't worth much. At Watson Lake, where the weather was generally socked in, the distraught weatherman wasn't allowed to forecast for fear of giving valuable data to the Japanese in the Aleutians. He would read the sequence, which was often garbled beyond meaning after decoding, and then he would give the Edmonton forecast. Edmonton was a thousand miles away, and the forecast was already old and useless for his district, where the weather changed in the time it took him to read his instruments.

The service was much better in Alaska. The 11th Weather Region, the U. S. Weather Bureau, and the commercial airlines could give information that was usually reliable.

Then the 16th Weather Region was set up for Canada, on 1 September 1942. The weather reporters were quite a crew: trappers, Indians, Eskimos, missionaries, Mounties, and Hudson Bay factors. Their reports were far from reliable, but at least they were reports.

Survey parties were sent out to find out about suggested stations in the Canadian wilderness, to be manned by the meteorologists who were being assembled in the States for the 16th Weather Region. The problems began to sprout. Maps were mostly incorrect and often useless. Lakes and rivers were shown where none existed. Mountain and lowland elevations were all wrong. Some stations were located by swivel-chair planners in spots so wild and inaccessible that even the Indians and Eskimos thought the white men were crazy.

The stations were built, however, and manned by soldiers who had to be rugged to survive. Temperatures ranged from a low of 75° below zero to a high of 90° above. Winter readings stayed at sixty below for days at a time.

During the hot and windless days of summer the men were plagued by swarms of every kind of winged insect in the northland: blackflies, sandflies, deerflies, horseflies, caribou flies, gadflies, mooseflies, buffalo gnats. There were mosquitoes by the trillions, and hornets of a dozen varieties. "Bulldogs" were blood-greedy insects that could fly upwind. "No-see-ums" were known as "creeping fire," and the man who was allergic to their bite often had to be packed up and sent back to the States, because he was constantly in agony and swollen to gross proportions.

The men at Watson Lake declared that the only way there could be more mosquitoes at that Rocky Mountain post was to make them smaller. An engineer at Fort Nelson smacked a comrade's sweaty back, and then started to count the dead mosquitoes. He'd killed more than thirty with one blow.

There were vicious winds and icy freezes in the wilderness and on the open tundra along the coast line. Men froze their cheeks, ears, extremities, and even their lungs. They didn't have the proper clothing, and they hadn't been trained for the rigors of Arctic living. They were lonely in the long winter nights, and their food was bad, and the mail never seemed to arrive. Floods in the spring and ice in the winter made deliveries impossible for weeks at a time. When they were isolated, their only touch with the rest of the world was by radio.

In their isolation and loneliness, however, the men of the weather service used ingenuity and resources they probably didn't know they had, to make their lives more comfortable and the monotony easier to bear. They didn't get what they needed, so they built huts, cabins, furniture, bunks, chimneys, and anything else that could be fashioned with hand tools.

At Fish Lake, the men built a boat with a wooden frame covered with canvas and waterproofed with pine pitch. They launched it and crossed the lake to hunt. They came back with a thousand pounds of moose meat.

They had "beef sessions" at Fish Lake, where any man with a complaint had the right to air it.

A letter written in January of 1943 from the Norman Wells Station by Sergeant Leo V. Corbett tells about some conditions at northern stations:

"The temperature has been below zero since we arrived and today the wind was so strong we were unable to work out of doors. The tent which will be our weather station is not completed. For a barometer base we were trying to drill a hole in the ground with bits that the Imperial Oil Co. has here. It is next to impossible to make a hole five feet deep to sink a four-inch pipe. (Because of the frozen subsoil.)

"We eat two meals a day, at 9 A.M. and 5 P.M. In a wind like today's it takes us an hour to walk the two miles to the station. We had rabbit last night—they were snowshoe rabbits killed by the cook who throws cans of C rations at them. He killed fifteen in one day that way.

"Things are conveniently located. The radio station is three miles from the landing field, the barracks two miles from the field, the field is eight miles from the Army Camp. Our barracks are slightly crowded—fifteen men to a 16- x 28-foot cabin.

"These boots are no blinkety-blank good. Instead of issuing those things they ought to give us an extra pencil. At least we could use the pencil. The boots may be all right in the summer and spring but the only things for the feet during the winter are mukluks or moccasins. Felt boots are also good."

In another letter, Sergeant Corbett told of the difficulty in traveling in a storm:

"In the blizzard today it took us quite some time to walk the two miles from our cabin to the landing strip and when we got there our eyelashes were frozen and a bottle of mouth wash in Corporal Chewning's pocket was frozen solid."

Accidents and personal injuries in the weather service were few, and most could be attributed to the weather rather than to carelessness by the men themselves.

Fire, hazard of any isolated camp, was a constant threat. At Hay River, Northwest Territories, a muskeg fire destoyed buildings and equipment. At the Pas an explosion of hydrogen, used to fill observation balloons, tore the hydrogen shed to splinters. Eventually the dangerous hydrogen generators were replaced with cylinders. Another hydrogen explosion was caused by static electricity at Providence, N. W. T. In that accident Corporal William W. McCrannahan suffered painful burns. As a result, the balloon ascensions at all stations using similar equipment were stopped until a device was found to reduce static electricity to a minimum. All hydrogen generators were grounded, and operators were required to wear metal bracelets connected by wire to grounded rods.

One of the common troubles was the fact that buildings fell apart when spring thaws revealed that the foundations were constructed on frozen subsoil or perma-frost.

The spring floods were always dangerous. One of the worst swept down on the meteorological station at Galena, Alaska, in May 1944. The river ice broke on 13 May and piled up for miles, forming a huge dam. Four days later the rising river waters broke across the road which separated the camp area from low land in the river valley. The men raced to move equipment and supplies to higher ground. The rushing water rose two feet in a matter of a few minutes. An hour or so later six feet of muddy water covered the weather station floor. It remained for several days, while observations were made as usual from high ground.

The weather men handled dozens of odd chores. They helped care for sled dogs, ministered to sick and indigent natives, refueled planes, kept landing strips in fair repair, shoveled snow, and unloaded barges. They had to use tact in dealing with the Canadians, particularly the native Indians and Eskimos who visited the station.

At Aishihik, one of the weather stations, a few Indians persisted in unwanted conviviality day after day. They were a vagrant group, indolent and beggars, but not seriously troublesome. Their personal cleanliness left much to be desired, especially in a warm room. They were repeatedly told that strict Army regulations forbade having them as semi-permanent visitors. The Indians didn't understand. Two of the men finally staged a mock quarrel that to the astonished Indians looked like the real thing. The Indians first saw the two quarrelers exchanging verbal insults. Knives were suddenly pulled. There was a Mack Sennett chase from one building to another, with a detour through the cookhouse where catsup was liberally spread on a hand, arm, and neck. The victim returned to the Indians and collapsed at their feet. The Indians vanished.

Most Indians and Eskimos were respectful, thoughtful, and generous and showed their admiration for the white soldier by looking to him for advice. Their particular hero at one weather station was Sergeant Myron E. Smith. An Indian woman, whose husband was away on a caribou hunting trip, was taken sick. She appealed to Sergeant Smith for help. Canadians told Smith he was wasting his time; Indians wouldn't take white men's medicine. The Sergeant produced a bottle of medicine he knew could do her no harm and might do some good, and convinced her she should try a dose. Then by promising to replenish her firewood supply, he persuaded her to take the balance of the bottle. In a short time she had made a complete recovery; Sergeant Smith was not at all sure why. The tribe affectionately named Smith "Snookum" which seems to mean strong or powerful.

Sergeant Eugene J. Coghlan wrote interesting tales of life at the isolated meteorological station at Kokrines. Here are some excerpts:

"We lacked proper mitts, footgear and fatigue gloves. We bought our own mittens and canvas gloves. We hired a native woman to make us moccasins and boots with moose-hide bottoms and caribou skin tops. G.I. mukluks are okay if they can be had. . . .

"Green men don't seem to recognize the danger signals preceding frost-bite. One AACS man froze his ear solid; but perhaps it's better to learn the hard way. Advice on this score is usually scoffed at. . . .

"Young men seem to suffer more from mental depression than the older ones. Girl friends marrying somebody else is the greatest morale wrecker. Homesickness is bad at the beginning, but usually eases off after a few months. Mail is great for morale, of course, but too few men realize that to get mail they must write letters. Special services sent us an electric phonograph and records. One of our men was content, even happy, while playing the phonograph but the minute he shut the machine off he seemed more depressed than ever. . . .

"Cabin fever is a serious malady. The victims are not aware of it but a newcomer sees it right away. It usually starts with the men talking about one another behind backs. Externally, everyone is all smiles—but thoughts are daggers. The cure is simple enough. Just say it to a guy's face and he'll probably blow up and sound off right back at you. But after the smoke has cleared away the tension is gone and relations show a definite improvement. The main bug in this sounding-off cure for cabin fever lies in the average guy's unwillingness to say it to the other man's face. It takes practice and a certain amount of boldness. . . .

"Another angle which has to do with morale is this: it's about women, native girls in this instance. When one soldier woos a girl away from another soldier and both soldiers are living under the same roof, there is trouble. If the loser for the girl's favor happens to outrank the winner, the plot thickens. And if the loser pulls rank on the winner, watch out!"

Life at the Nome station, back in civilization, wasn't much better. It was established in February of 1942 under Staff Sergeant Perry J. Emmert. The men lived in Quonset huts that had been set in an area of gumbo-like mud. The men suffered for eighteen months before the quarters were moved to an area known as "the Hollow," where there wasn't much mud, just plenty of standing water in a natural drainage basin.

The men out in the bush might not have considered that they had much for recreation, but they at least were in wilderness where strange sights could meet the eye at any time, where grizzlies and moose and wolves gave excitement to their days. In Nome, most recreational facilities were pretty drab. The day room was confined to one end of a drafty Quonset hut, with a bar, pool table, several wooden chairs, a dart board, a Ping-pong table, and a collection of about one hundred well-thumbed books. Most of them had been written by authors long forgotten, and they usually bore such titles as *Lord Timothy's Return*. The ragged magazines were all years old.

Apart from the few base recreational activities, including the post movie theater, there was always Nome, referred to as the City. The favorite hangout among the enlisted men was a movie theater, THE DREAM, named because the films shown were so old that the spectator wondered if he were living in another world. Another favorite spot was May's—a square, whitewashed building in a land of log cabins, but painted on the inside to look like a log cabin. Its other distinction was that a nine ounce glass of beer cost thirty cents.

I visited Nome in January 1943, when living conditions were primitive, and again early in 1945. By then the men were enjoying solid comforts. There was a new service club and "Klootch" or game room housed in one steam-heated, insulated building. The library was stocked with most of the special Armed Forces editions for the taking, and an excellent selection of current novels and non-fiction. The club had an expansive lounge with a public address system of high-fidelity, baffle type speakers, and a control room where a selection of classical and dance records had been assembled. This system was connected with the mess hall so there was music during meals; sometimes the local army radio station would rebroadcast; at other times there were records requested by the men themselves. On the staff was a Russian speaking officer from the faculty of the University of Chicago who had a limited reputation as a concert pianist. He was called on regularly as a highly appreciated entertainer. The "Klootch" room had two pool tables and two Ping-pong tables, with enough room so that players at one table did not interfere with those at another. The lounge area of the club had a phonograph, a very elegant crapboard, numerous board games, popular current magazines and free cigarettes. The club was by 1945 providing recently released feature movies two and three times a week. Music hours, card evenings, and bingo games were popular. There was plenty of sports equipment.

The Red Cross in Nome had had its face lifted. There was a

popular sandwich bar in a Quonset hut; the whole place had been tastefully redecorated and furnished with gaily colored tables and chairs, a selection of books and magazines, and an excellent radio. Before the Red Cross arrived, a meal in town would cost at least $1.25 (two eggs and a piece of ham). When eggs were available, the Red Cross sold egg sandwiches for ten cents. The sandwich bar had cheese, hamburger, steak, and tuna fish sandwiches for ten and fifteen cents. Fruit juices cost a nickel a glass; the coffee always was free.

The 16th Weather Region in which the men worked was so extensive that when it was organized it covered eight time zones; so sparsely settled that its inhabitants averaged approximately one person per square mile. It stretched from the western shores of Hudson Bay, about 3,500 miles to Attu in the Aleutians, and included the entire Canadian Arctic Archipelago, the North Pole, and the North Magnetic Pole. The weather in this vast area was always changing, and it ranged in season from cold and stormy to warm, placid, and clear. Much of the area was treeless and colorless. All of the land was monotonous, and the rugged duty was sometimes unbearably lonesome.

CHAPTER XVIII

Confusion Along the Alaskan Route

During the summer of 1942 Northwest Airlines operated thirteen Skytrains over the route to Alaska, and fourteen additional Skytrains were moving a 250,000 pound backlog of priority equipment from Edmonton to Fairbanks. These temporary aircraft, the military C-47, were operated by United Airlines, Chicago and Southern Airlines, TWA, and Western Airlines. Northwest Airlines had established its main base of operations at Edmonton and was making hasty preparations for winter operations. Due to lack of priorities for essential equipment, however, it had been unable to complete winterization of its aircraft.

As the fall months turned into winter, the same problems that vexed the men on the North Atlantic run prevailed along the Alaska route. Housing was unsatisfactory at Edmonton; at other stations it was critical. Men would have to live in tents during the following winter when temperatures would fall to 60° below zero. Winterization of planes on both routes, the North Atlantic and the Alaskan, became a matter of urgency as more and more planes were unable to leave the ground because they had not been prepared for cold-weather operation.

Early in December, Lieutenant Colonel E. M. Gavin and a crew of six men left Wright Field, Dayton, Ohio, in a Mitchell airplane with orders to proceed to Ladd Field, Fairbanks, Alaska, the home of the Cold Weather Test Detachment, and to such other places as they felt necessary in order to determine absolute minimum winterization requirements for aircraft that were expected to fly the route.

Colonel Gavin reported that practically the entire time of the six men in his crew was devoted to maintaining and operating their own airplane. In an unusually blunt report he concluded that much of the Arctic lore was fiction. He wrote, for instance:

"Tales of suffering and breath-taking escape, which rival in magnitude the chronicles of all the ancient explorers, are the regular and natural talk of men who work up north, whether they pilot airplanes or swing axes along the Alaska Highway." This, he explained, was natural, for "lonely men in barren lands with little or nothing in the way of recreation have for ages given themselves to story-telling." A personal hardship "grows with the recounting into a Trojan struggle; a man who comes through some tight spot is eventually projected as a new-day Paul Bunyan."

Colonel Gavin found that "what is fundamentally an interesting and truthful, though frequently inconsequential anecdote, more often than not becomes a moral for the uninitiated, a saga of hardship, a warning to the stranger of dangers which surround the story-teller's life. This kind of word-of-mouth epic is the literature of the campfire. It has existed since the beginning and will exist as long as men are far from home and are alone, whether on pounding seas, a burning beach or a windless sweep of ice."

Colonel Gavin believed that so far as winter operation of aircraft was concerned, much could be learned from listening to all types of stories from all kinds of men in the North Country, *provided* they were analyzed and the romance separated from the fact.

"Men who work in the Yukon and in Alaska, men who have lived there, men who have flown airplanes there for fifteen years, men who have experienced almost all the discomfort that nature can give—from these one can learn much about winter clothing, winter hygiene, emergency operations on the ground and in the air that will not be found too readily in books." He warned that the natural tendency to pull the long bow must always be remembered, and airplane crewmen particularly must not be cowed by imaginative stories which they would inevitably hear as they got farther away from civilization. This, he repeated, was most important and should be classified as the principal item in any winterization program.

The unknown is always mysterious and fearful; it is quite understandable that the talk of old-timers might drive a pilot unfamiliar with the north to one of two extremes. Either he will become reckless in an attempt to live up to the romance or he will be secretly afraid to follow the sound principles of his thorough training as a pilot. He will begin to see things that are not there; he will fail to use the remedies he has been taught to apply, and in an emergency he will often do something quite contrary to what he was supposed to have done. Coming through a real emergency or an imagined peril, he will color the details in the habit of all pilots, hunters, deep-sea divers and fishermen, and therefore will contribute to the temporary unbalancing of any newcomer.

The crew of the Mitchell heard many wild stories as they proceeded northward. They heard, for instance, that at low Arctic temperatures an exposed hand would freeze in ten seconds. They heard that without "proper winterization" they would crack up in some wilderness and that it might take months to find the wreckage.

At the time of the Gavin survey, airfield and building construction along the route was fouled up. He was unable to discover evidence of any program for its development.

However, every base had at least the following:

1. One or more usable landing strips in varying stages of completion.
2. A total Air Corps complement of thirty or more officers and enlisted men.
3. Substantial quantities of aviation gasoline and oil.
4. More Air Corps supplies than could be used or protected from the weather by existing personnel.

At no base on the entire route was there a commanding officer who knew definitely by what time his base would be ready, what function it was to perform upon completion, and whether it was to serve the Air Transport Command or the Eleventh Air Force.

Planes were found stranded throughout the length of the route. Early in March 1943 it was found that two derelict single-engine fighters had been at Whitehorse for eight months. No effort had been made to repair them. A twin-engine fighter had been parked on a ramp since 30 October, having been left by the pilot because of some small mechanical difficulty. A Skytrain, needed for transport along the route, had been grounded at Whitehorse for several weeks because the pilot and crew were sick. No relief crew had been provided.

Some of the situations were ludicrous. At Fort Nelson a plane was grounded in November for an engine change. After two months the engine was changed and, with the plane in a nose shelter, the propeller was installed. Then the propeller had to be removed in order to get the plane out of the nose shelter. The trained propeller man had left Fort Nelson, and no one else knew how to replace the propeller. In April the airplane was still waiting for someone to put back the propeller.

Northwest Airlines pilots were able to fly Skytrains for the Air Transport Command in Alaska solely because they depended on route bases for gasoline and oil only. Maintenance was provided in their own shops at Great Falls, Edmonton, and, when necessary, Minneapolis.

Although supplies were shipped, confusion started with an involved system of code names. Sometimes code names were changed, and some Army Transport Service officers actually did not know what code names were then in effect for their bases.

The tactical requirements of the Eleventh Air Force, which was in combat with the Japanese, had to take precedence over requirements of non-tactical bases, so that some of the equipment and supplies shipped on Air Transport Command projects were diverted to the combat units.

Probably less than half of the supplies and equipment authorized ever arrived. On the other hand, there were at every base more supplies of certain kinds than could be used. Because of the lack of buildings, much of what was not immediately used was left in the open. Air Corps supplies that were desperately needed elsewhere were often piled on the ground and covered with snow.

At Fairbanks the pool of supplies was not in buildings and segregated in bins, but strung out along a river bank in haphazard piles. Some supplies were covered with protective tarpaulins; all were buried in deep snow. Captain G. R. Jordan, making a supply inspection, tried to uncover some of the supplies. He probed the snow and looked into some of the unlabeled boxes. He exhumed generators, complete mobile depot units, complete instrument shops in boxes; he unwrapped countless spare tires and saw thousands of boxes of aircraft parts. Wherever he dug he uncovered another surprise. He saw nearly a hundred boxed Pratt & Whitney and other type motors covered with snow. All the supplies had been transported at great cost and consisted of innumerable scarce items. For hours Jordan roamed around pile after pile, many of which had no covering whatever. He found a complete mimeograph machine for which his companion said he had been trying to get an order through for months. He did not recognize the identifying symbols of many of the unopened boxes, but they looked like containers of Air Corps spare parts, tools, dies, belly-tanks, tires, and wheel assemblies.

Jordan learned that lend-lease aircraft for the Soviet were being delivered at Fairbanks usually lacking such removable items as flashlights, screw drivers, first-aid kits, and emergency equipment. The day before his arrival the first plane without a shortage had arrived; everyone seemed to consider this a remarkable event. At the same time Aircobras were arriving with expensive camera apparatus, and Mitchells were equipped with tow-target equipment for delivery to the Russians. The Russians reported that they had no use for tow-target gear. Colonel Kiselof, the Russian Commandant at Fairbanks, said: "We shoot at real targets." There was a continuing shortage of such vital items as spare tires, tubes, and equipment to repair radio sets.

At all bases the large supply of aviation gasoline had been scattered over a wide area for protection against possible fires and air raids. This haphazard dispersal frequently had been done by dumping the drums off trucks like so much firewood, with damage to the drums and difficulty in taking an inventory of gasoline. Lieutenant Dulevitz, Commanding Officer at Northway, discovered 50,000 gallons of aviation gasoline which had not been reported previously.

Frequently Air Corps equipment for the repair and maintenance of airplanes arrived at bases ahead of supplies for subsistence of the men and materials for construction.

At Galena in February 1943 *all* water for the camp had to be hauled one and one-half miles from the Yukon River in 32-gallon containers. There was no provision for bathing and laundry facilities. The underground water wells had been completed by the first of the preceding September and most of the piping was in place, but the pumps had not arrived. Galena yelled for pumps, but Fairbanks said that priority for flying in the pumps would be held off until January. In the meantime, Air Corps supplies not needed by the men at Galena poured in. It was obvious that one couldn't pioneer in the Arctic by the remote control of bureaucrats. Seven damaged Havocs at Nome needed some metal stocks. A requisition was sent to Headquarters, Eleventh Air Force, at Anchorage. After several weeks it was indorsed back with the requests to reduce the quantities "down to what is really needed." The Commanding Officer at Nome indorsed the requistion back to Eleventh Air Force, saying that there were no metals available at Nome and that what had been ordered was urgently required. Days later the requisition was again returned to Nome, noting that the supplies were not the responsibility of the Eleventh Air Force. The Air Transport Command Headquarters at Ladd Field was the proper source.

This problem of command was exasperating. At Galena the layout of buildings, operational areas, repair shops, etc. was not under the control of the Air Corps even though the Air Corps was charged with the operation of the Air Base. Control was held by Major Bowen, commanding officer at the local Alaskan Defense Command camp of engineers and infantry. Permission for even the location of a single hut alongside the runway apron had to come from paper-shuffling engineers at Anchorage. The Air Transport Command had to do the housekeeping at bases from Edmonton through Nome but had no authority to do it.

There were other command problems at bases scattered over the vast reaches of the air route, with almost every headquarters assuming responsibilities it did not have, and neglecting others that it was not aware it had been assigned. General Dale V. Gaffney, commanding general of the Alaskan Wing, eventually unsnarled the labyrinthine command and got it running correctly.

Morale of our Air Force men in the area was not improved by the realization that their living conditions were considerably below the standards of Canadian Department of Transport and Civil Aeronautics people living in the same places. Because of the freezing temperatures water was hard to obtain. Pipes were usually frozen where there were pipes, and baths were an impossible luxury during the winter. Drinking water and washing water generally were placed in GI cans alongside each other and always in a spot where there was warmth. Frequently this was in a lavatory and, if not there, in a kitchen.

When weather conditions were bad and planes were grounded, there were as many as thirty to forty pilots crowded in the one small barracks room available for transients. Sanitary conditions in many places were deplorable. At Fort Nelson, for instance, the drinking water was kept in the latrine in a large milk can alongside the GI can of water for washing purposes. All activity seemed to center around the stove in the latrine—shaving, washing socks, and usual toilet activities all occurred within six feet of the drinking water. Dirty hands dipped into the drinking water receptacle with paper cups, canteens, or the family glass. Epidemics of respiratory diseases were the result.

The Air Force did make efforts to look after its own men. There was no comparison, for instance, between the manner in which the Air Corps and the Quartermaster Corps handled the problem of providing winter clothing. The Air Corps seemed to have met the problem reasonably well, everything considered, although the first Commanding Officer of the Alaskan Wing, Colonel Tom L. Mosley, on one occasion had to fly to Minneapolis from Edmonton to bring back 850 pairs of felt boots.

On the other hand, the job done by the Army Quartermaster Corps was so inadequate that it placed a severe strain on the winter clothing supplies which the Air Corps had available. Lieutenant Bostick, commanding officer of a camp of forty-seven half-frozen engineers near Tanacross came into the supply office at Ladd Field and announced a sit-down strike until the Air Corps supplied him with forty-seven pairs of Arctic field boots. He stated that he recognized that the Air Corps had no responsibility for supplying Engineer Corps troops, but complained that his requests for proper footwear had not been filled by the Quartermaster Corps and that the temperature had been down to sixty-six degrees below zero for a couple of days at Tanacross. As his men were equipped with only field shoes and rubber overshoes or shoe-packs, frozen feet were common. Lieutenant Bostick sat down in the supply office to take off his shoes to display a pair of frostbitten feet. His men got their boots.

The heating of the temporary buildings, such as Quonset and Yakutat huts and Stout houses, produced a maximum of discomfort and fire hazard with a minimum of heat. Inadequate insulation and lack of circulation made these buildings too cold on the floor and too hot six feet above it. One precise soldier in a hut in Nome recorded temperatures of 85° to 90° Fahrenheit at 7½ feet and 40° on the drafty floor. One officers' hut in Galena registered a blistering 105° at 7½ feet and a frigid 42° on the floor; later in this hut it was 85° F. at 7½ feet and there was a coating of ice on the floor.

The quantity of firewood consumed at most of the bases was enormous, and this firewood had to be cut and hauled in midwinter by men improperly equipped for the job. At all of the bases, with the exception of Nome (where there was no wood at all), there was an abundance of spruce, but live timber could not be cut and used successfully as firewood.

By the following winter, the pyramidal tents had disappeared; the men were now living in comfortable wooden barracks. The pumps had finally arrived and running water was installed. The chilly nose hangars went out of use as new hangars neared completion. Supplies flowed in steadily and with the daily appearance of fresh food prepared by trained cooks, meals improved. With these improvements, the delivery of planes to the Russians grew from a small trickle to a steadily mounting stream.

CHAPTER XIX

Alsib

T HE COLD WAR and Soviet hostility have made many of us forget that for nearly four years the Reds were our allies. Few people ever knew that throughout the war we entertained a sizable Soviet military colony in North America, extending from Nome, Alaska, to Great Falls, Montana.

Censorship blacked out news about Operation Alsib—the wartime delivery of 7,000 Kingcobras, Havocs, and Mitchells from U. S. factories to Red airmen on our own soil. Allied unity and the desire for quick victory brought the Russians to our continent, established them in several key spots, and set up regular communications for them with Moscow. Alsib was so named because Alaska and Siberia were the principal way points. We turned our warplanes over to Russian pilots at Ladd Field in Fairbanks, who ferried the planes across the Bering Strait to Siberia and finally on to Russia's fighting front.

Hundreds of Soviet men and a few women lived side by side with Americans in Nome, Galena, Fairbanks, and as far south as Edmonton and Great Falls. Russian and American soldiers and officers ate in the same mess halls, shared their quarters, enjoyed the same games and movies, and perched on the same soda-fountain stools.

Alsib was a new and puzzling international problem with thousands of ramifications, such as the language barriers. There were conflicts of temperament, attitude, and outlook. The Russians, mostly veterans of the battlefields, had little patience with U. S. Army routine and "channels." Recklessly, one Red pilot brought in a Skytrain against all landing instructions, endangering the crew of another plane. The tower bawled him out in English and Russian, and an American officer ran down to tell him off.

"You've done everything wrong!" the American yelled.

The Russian viewed him calmly. "Me," he said, "fifteen Germans. You?"

A few early arrivals had chips on their shoulders. One of the first medium bombers arriving at Nome with a Russian at the controls buzzed the control tower. The Americans promptly clamped down on the pilot, delivered strong lectures to all others, and there was little further trouble. A few Soviet enlisted men tried to dominate the GI mechanics. But if the Russians were handled with the same toughness, everything worked smoothly.

The biggest barrier was mutual suspicion. The Red Army enlisted men were forbidden to fraternize, and we frowned unofficially on ordinary friendly advances toward the Russians. The Americans never were told what to do and say in the presence of a Russian. A large number of GI's wanted to know why America was giving planes to the Soviet, and they weren't sure the planes might not be turned against us. We should have instructed the men on the line from the very first day, but Alsib was in full operation for a year before anyone made that move. The orientation program was finally put into use to dispel rumors and misconceptions. General Dale V. Gaffney, who was Commander of the Alaskan Wing in 1943, laid down the law firmly. "Everything," he told the Americans in Alaska, "is secondary to the Russian movement."

Preconceived ideas hurt too. Our GI's remembered that not long ago the Soviets had been Hitler's pals, and they were critical of everything from the Russians' ancestry to their cleanliness.

So the Army in Alaska prepared unhappily for an onslaught of Red hordes when the AAF's ferrying division proposed that the Alaskan-Siberian route be substituted for the hazards of shipping crated planes through the U-boat wolf packs of the North Atlantic. To speed up these Lend-Lease planes for the embattled Russians, Alsib was conceived 26 June 1942 in an ATC order. By mid-August the advance guard of Russians arrived in Alaska. The first light bombers and single-engine fighters reached the exchange point at Ladd Field early in September, and a couple of weeks later the Russian crews appeared on Lacey Street in Fairbanks in their high leather boots with their full brown tunics hanging over blue breeches.

The newcomers seemed to have a single interest: to get a lot of planes moving as quickly as possible to Russia's battle fronts. Most of the fliers had been at the front themselves, and they realized the need for reinforcements.

At first, Americans felt that Russian demands on the condition of aircraft were excessive. Their search for faults, it seemed, put everyone to a lot of unjustifiable trouble. One little officer was called "Lieutenant Gremlin" by our mechanics. When they were sure a ship was in tiptop order, Gremlin still could point out flaws. The Russian standards were high. Our men often forgot that the Russians needed aircraft badly, that the planes must be in shape to go directly into combat, and that apparently there were few, if any, trained technicians at Siberian bases to correct faults that might appear during the long journey to the fighting fronts.

Americans felt and showed considerable animosity toward Russians at various stations, particularly in the early days. Sometimes this was understandable. The single permanent hangar at Ladd Field, for instance, belonged to Cold Weather Testing Detachment, an AAF unit trying to answer basic problems of cold-weather flying. When Alsib swung into action, CWT found out about cold weather the hard way; they were shoved outside to make room for Lend-Lease aircraft. Later the Russians constructed their own hanger on the far side of the field. Barracks equipment, of which CWT had too little, was transferred to the Soviet invaders.

The Russians could bring their wives and children to Alaska, but Americans could not. It wasn't easy for some of our men to work wholeheartedly with the visitors. Nevertheless, only one authenticated case of sabotage was uncovered at Nome, deliberate flooding of a Quonset hut which damaged battery carts and heaters and delayed movement of planes.

Meanwhile, the Russians continued to be completely realistic. While planes were en route to Fairbanks, AAF men often raided them for spare parts. Russian inspectors refused to accept delivery of these planes without every last item in place. They insisted on what was promised on paper.

These difficult allies had no use for ordinary courtesies and tact. Many American officers, fresh from Officer Candidate School, allowed themselves a certain amount of imagination and latitude in their relationships. The Russians, fresh from grim battle, just stuck to brutal facts.

Complicating all other difficulties was language. Most Russians picked up proper grammar and American slang with equal ease and used them interchangeably. "Vot's cook-king?" was one of their favorites, and they resurrected the ancient pleasantry, "I lof my vife, but oh you keed." Early in the game they learned the wolf whistle and if admonished, they were bewildered: "It is a compliment, no?"

The Russians' slang was generally coherent and orthodox. They said "okay" and "okie dokie" quite properly. On the other hand, one wit would lean from his cockpit after his plane revved up satisfactorily, grin broadly, and recite: "Okie dokie Pepsi-Cola, Piggily Wiggily Seven Up."

Teaching the Russians to fly our planes was the next problem. Proficient pilots with many combat hours, the Soviet airmen nevertheless knew only planes of Russian make. Now, learning to fly new types, they caught on rapidly. The first group needed just five days after a transition school was hastily organized by Major Fred J. Kane, Captain Thomas Harrell, and Lieutenant N. S. de Tolly. A White Russian, de Tolly spoke the Russian language fluently.

The training was conducted at Ladd Field and at Big Delta, Alaska. Ladd Field, of course, was the relay point where American pilots turned the planes over to Russia. The Red fliers then hopped across Alaska to Nome, jumping-off place for the flight to Siberia. On 29 September 1942, after the five-day transitional training, Lieutenant Colonel Nodosekin of the Red Air Force led the first flight of twelve light bombers out of Ladd Field, and headed toward the shores of the Bering Strait. They stopped at Nome for refueling and then disappeared into the westward mists. On 9 October Nodosekin's group was followed by Captain Finegenow with a flight of single-engine pursuits. These were the first of hundreds of flights in Operation Alsib.

The discussion of involved aeronautical problems was another language barrier. The solution was provided by the men of the Interpreters and Interrogators Detachment. All could speak, write, and read Russian. They were the link between the Red Army and the Americans. GI interpreters always were on hand, not only in the hangar, control towers, weather and communications offices, but they translated for the Russians in the movies, the hospital, or the barracks. Many were Russian-born, and even natives of the same towns as the Red Army fliers. All of Russian extraction, they not only understood the language but, more important, the Russian mentality and viewpoint.

The transition-training instructors explained procedures to interpreters who pointed, for example, to the instrument recording manifold take-off, and then the Russian pilot would memorize it.

If power were reduced at a certain point, the interpreters indicated that on the proper instrument. Instructions typed in Russian were pasted next to the English versions.

Calibrations were confusing. The Russians were accustomed to the metric system, but the red and green lines indicating safe operational limits were helpful. The Soviet fliers learned readily. As soon as they became familiar with our planes, which didn't take long, we marked only the new gadgets, changes, and warnings. Only a few weeks after the start, the transition school passed from the picture and Russian fliers checked out their own officers.

One of our instructors, in checking out a fighter pilot, was startled by his pupil's aptness. "He climbed into the cockpit, a girl interpreter got on one wing and I on the other. The pilot looked around at the instrument panel, grinned, and asked, 'How do you start it?' I told the girl, and she translated. He said, 'Da,' and then asked for the maximum pressure and RPM for the take-off. I answered that through the interpreter. Then he asked about how to keep the oil and coolant pressures up, and finally he wanted to know how to operate the radio. That's all the information he needed. The next thing I knew he was flying, and doing a good job of it too."

The Russians attitude toward field-control towers, particularly at Ladd Field where traffic was quite heavy at times, was highly unorthodox. They didn't know the procedure and made no effort to learn it. Our translators didn't know the routine either, so we trained tower operators in a new language. The Russians required instruction in two-way radio and telephone, since their communication had been largely based on code. At that time they used no voice radio whatever in their own planes. After realizing voice radio's tremendous value, they were enthusiastic about our use of radio ranges and tried to get them for installation in Siberia. At first the Russians scorned traffic control. Even though they snarled up let-downs in blinding snowstorms and avoided mid-air collisions by inches, they remained unconvinced. They believed in the old-fashioned system of getting on and off the ground as best they could. Despite their complete disregard for traffic patterns and a habit of flying at unconventional levels, they caused not a single disaster. Later, as flights and hazards increased, the Russians reluctantly came to accept our control methods.

The first pilot checked out by Lieutenant de Tolly did a slow roll barely off the ground with his wheels scarcely up. When he landed, the outraged de Tolly asked if he was trying to kill himself. The Russian replied: "What's the matter with you—afraid to die?"

By our standards, the Soviet pilots were crude in their handling of aircraft. They jerked planes off the ground, stunted at dangerously low levels, forced engines to the limit. Once a Russian pilot gave a fighter throttle such a vigorous blast in warming up for a take-off that the alarmed American mechanic shouted to the interpreter: "Tell him the engine won't last long with all that throttle." After the usual translative exchange the interpreter reported: "He says he may not last long either."

Another Russian revved up his Skymaster engines until they seemed about to jump from their mountings. Questioned, he explained that the engines should develop fifty-two inches of power and, though he'd run it and run it at full throttle, he couldn't squeeze out more than forty-six inches. Angrily, his instructor, Fred Kane, exclaimed: "We'd shoot one of our men if he mistreated an engine like that." The Russian, taking the remark as literally as all the Russians usually did, expressed the startled opinion that we were excessively severe with our men.

Many pilots in the first Russian mission insisted that their Russian planes were much better than ours. Their opinion of our Tomahawk never went very high, but their rating of American aircraft improved with their increasing familiarity until almost all of their pilots and ground staff agreed ours were good.

Because the Russians believed firmly in the value of firepower, they favored the Aircobra (supplanted later by the Kingcobra) and the Havoc because, aside from speed and maneuverability, these labyrinths of electrical and hydraulic mechanism were equipped with cannon. Members of the mission pointed out, unofficially, that their own Stormovik light bomber was more heavily armored underneath and so better suited to low-altitude work in front-line sectors because it was less vulnerable to ground fire.

Some of the younger Russian officers seemed determined to be unimpressed by anything American. They refused to admit that we had any superior material skills or mechanical progress, and they spent a great deal of time praising their own achievements.

Americans in Alaska soon admired the Russians' strength and physical prowess. All were regular Red Army men and obviously the product of a rigorous physical-training regimen. Captain Goubin, not a particularly massive man, ordered a can of beer in the Ladd Field BOQ, emptied it into a glass, then squeezed and completely collapsed the can in one hand. That looked so simple that an American tried it. He squeezed and squeezed, but nothing happened. In short order, all the Americans gathered around the bar were squeezing, too, unsuccessfully.

Meanwhile, quite likely, the Russians were drinking the Americans' beer, which they liked, though they usually preferred their own vodka or brandy, which they drank straight and "bottoms up." After draining their glasses in a gulp, a habit to which they attributed their phenomenal capacity, they would scoff at the Americans: "Russian—man! American—man or baby?"

Their parties always were the gayest and noisiest, with much drinking, singing, dancing, and laughter. There was no evidence to support the general idea that they are a gloomy people.

They were inveterate movie fans and liked American pictures, particularly animated cartoons and horse operas. Wherever a group of Russians was in a theater, a buzz competed with the dialogue as interpreters kept up their running account. Translating the gags of Joe E. Brown wasn't easy when everyone else was roaring with laughter. A picture called *Bataan,* starring Robert Taylor, greatly impressed the Russians. Fired by the story, they cheered repeatedly, but couldn't understand why the Americans lost the battle since the Japs had been slaughtered wholesale. Once a false rumor circulated that members of the Soviet mission were forbidden to see American movies. It turned out that no Russians were seen at the theater late in the evening because they invariably hurried to the first show.

One evening Lieutenant Colonel Shtriskov was asked about the array of decorations he wore. The Order of the Red Star, he explained, was for shooting down seventeen planes at Rostov; another award was for his participation in Stalingrad's defense, and so on. The Soviet flier was interested in the American's decorations too. "Tell me," he asked, pointing to the Asiatic-Pacific Theater ribbon, "what is this ribbon for?" The American captain blushed slightly. "Thirty days' service in Alaska," he acknowledged.

Was the Russian mission hand-picked to create a favorable impression? Americans who associated with them believe the original pilots may have been selected carefully. Later arrivals, however, probably were chosen only because of ability to do their jobs efficiently.

None of the Russians would discuss politics. They adhered strictly to Soviet policy and their viewpoint was the group's, not the individual's. They were equally circumspect in discussing military matters, and well trained in security and discipline. When General James A. O'Connor, Commandant of the Alaska Highway, asked Colonel Kiselev when he thought the war might be over, the colonel replied politely, "General, you are much senior to me. Therefore your own views must be much more accurate than mine."

We got along best when we could give them a "yes" answer. A "no" always provoked a violent reaction. The Russians showed no hesitancy in going out of channels to get what they wanted. For the first three or four months they doubted our sincerity. Spirited disagreements arose over honest differences on procedures in preparing and delivering aircraft. Friction could be erased when plane deliveries were on schedule. Delays in deliveries caused most of the squabbling.

Because the Russian ferry pilots had to be brought back to Fairbanks from the Siberian side, a transport routine was established almost at the start. Soon this service was expanded to provide a cargo service for high-priority freight. As time went on, the operation increased until it was a very important part of the Alsib activity. Cargoes westward included ammunition, spare parts, engines, and critical material of all descriptions.

The Soviet government was always suspicious of any American interest in ferrying across Siberian wastes and forests, about stations along the route, and how they operated. Only infrequently did Americans win permission to travel the route. Ambassador Davies, Wendell Willkie, and Henry Wallace were among the exceptions. Colonel Alva Harvey, who headed a mission that was to fly its own aircraft from Washington all the way to Moscow in August 1942, got only to Nome. From there he and one or two other members of his party were passengers in Russian planes.

Not long afterward, a mission headed by Major General Follett Bradley, after working with the Soviets in Moscow, headed back over the Alsib route. Their plane was forced down at Yakutsk. Major Kane, operations officer at Ladd Field, took off with ample supplies of emergency clothing and rations. Assigned to his crew were Russians as navigator and radio operator. The commanding officer of the Russian detachment at Fairbanks was helpful; everything seemed in order, particularly since the Russian embassy at Washington radioed permission for the flight. Kane thought that all diplomatic arrangements were set. But where Alaska ends and Russia begins, Major Kane ran into an impassable barrier. The Russian Commanding Officer at Nome was not satisfied with word from Washington; he insisted on Moscow's official approval. He steadfastly refused to yield, and after several days of waiting General Bradley was able to fly on to Nome without American aid. The general had seen only one Havoc between Moscow and

Nome. Somewhere along the route were many Havocs and Tomahawks.

We could only guess at what troubles the Russians were having with the planes that disappeared across the Bering Strait. We only surmised that they touched Vel Kal, Markovo, Seymohan, Yakutsk, and finally Okekminsk on the Trans-Siberian Railroad. Rumor said losses were high. At times consideration was given to adandoning ferrying over the Alsib Route, but the Russians seemed to be satisfied. They have never told just how many Lend-Lease planes eventually reached the battle fronts. It seems unlikely that we will ever know.

Inspection of planes which returned to Nome and Ladd Field from the Siberian side seemed to indicate from their mechanical trouble that repair and maintenance facilities across the Strait were limited. Most Americans thought that at least one reason for the impassable barrier the Russians set up on our travels to the Siberian side was their reluctance to reveal the limitations of their stations.

Nobody can say how important the Alsib route was to the Russian war effort. A few figures, however, will show the amount of help we sent. About 7,000 aircraft flew from American factories to the shores of the Bering Sea. In one critical year alone, 1944, about 3,000 were ferried, delivered, and accepted. During that same year only 19 Lend-Lease planes that left Great Falls failed to reach the transfer station at Fairbanks. Alsib continued to the war's end. Then the Russians moved out of North America.

PART III

Lifelines Across the Polar Sea

CHAPTER XX

The DEW Line, BMEWS, and Thule

GENERAL H. H. ARNOLD, who built the Air Force to its wartime
capacity to whip the Germans and the Japanese wherever
it met them, said about the northland: "If there is a third world
war, its strategic center will be the North Pole."

His colleague of many years, General Carl A. Spaatz, wrote that
every industrialized country is within reach of our strategic air
force through the Arctic skies. "America is similarly exposed," he
warned. "We are, in fact, wide open at the top."

General Curtis LeMay summed up the Air Force thinking about
the north country: "Our frontier now lies across the Arctic wastes
of the Polar regions."

One result of the warnings given by our air experts during the
years since the close of World War II has been an awakening of
public and governmental understanding of the nature of the menace
from the north. The Air Force was able to go to work to throw
up the barriers across the polar skies, and to advance rapidly its
own plans for quick retaliation should the massive attack ever
come. During the past few years there have been numbers of

191

Arctic military operations with these intriguing code names: Operation Frigid; Operation Muskox; Operation North Pole; Operation Frostbite; Task Force Williwaw; Task Force Frost; Task Force Blue Jay; Project Snowman; Project Mint Julep. I've been told that it's becoming difficult to find suitable synonyms for Arctic activities; the name is important because a well-chosen label is bound to generate enthusiasm, as Madison Avenue well knows.

The Arctic regions have been thrust into the center of the state of the new world strategy on both sides in the cold war. This change in the strategic shape of the globe has been forced by long-range weapons and far-reaching aircraft. Science has hammered down the Arctic's isolation.

The northland activity with which the people of the United States are most familiar is certainly the DEW Line, originally known as Project 572. Its name comes from its function; it is an invisible electronic wall of radar that is designed to provide "distant early warning" of an attack against this continent across the roof of the world. It is the most elaborate and ingenious alarm system ever devised; it has more than sixty manned stations, and it stretches north of the United States-Canadian border at roughly 70° N. Latitude for about 3,000 miles, from Alaska to the barren land of Baffin Island. It has been extended recently across the Greenland Icecap and into the waterlogged Aleutians. It cost the American taxpayer about $1,000,000,000.

The DEW Line across Canada grew from the insecurity created by the cold war. This link of prefabricated, air-conditioned, electronic stations in the continent's defense against surprise air attack was first proposed by the celebrated Lincoln Summer Study of 1952—an informal caucus of top United States' scientists. They concluded that an Arctic radar system was practicable and would provide from four to six hours' warning of the approach of hostile aircraft. The network would fill in the Arctic gap on the transpolar air approaches from Siberia to the North American continent.

The DEW Line was designed to supplement two other lines.

One is the "Pine Tree" system which links the Canadian and United States Air Defense Commands in a basic radar-warning and control system that stretches across the continent, roughly along the United States-Canadian border. The other is the mid-Canada radar line which crosses Canada about the 55th parallel and supplements the Pine Tree radar system. This vast warning system was extended by radar picket ships of the Navy and radar picket planes of the U. S. Air Force and Navy which range widely over the northern approaches to Alaska, Canada, and Greenland.

Military experts are divided on the worth of the DEW Line. Some argue that the DEW Line and its supplements do not constitute an impenetrable defense. These critics question the DEW Line's value against supersonic bombers, and claim that it is entirely worthless against intercontinental ballistic missiles. Soviet rockets, fired from launching pads in Siberia, can arch high and undetected over the Arctic en route to Canadian and American targets. This danger is well understood. In less than two years a billion dollar investment will result in the completion of large, complex, automated, missile-detection installations, called Ballistic Missile Early Warning System, that will alert us to a missile attack. The first of these, the BMEWS base at Thule, Greenland, was fully operational in the early autumn of 1960.

BMEWS scans the skies over the polar regions to provide early detection of ballistic missiles launched from Siberia, and to provide a reasonable prediction as to time and point of impact. The complete system includes not only the completed installations at Thule, Greenland, and at Clear, Alaska, seventy miles southwest of Fairbanks, but will have a third, at Fylingdales in the Yorkshire moors of England, scheduled for completion in 1963. The installations scanning the northern skies will provide at least fifteen minutes and, at best, a half-hour warning of any missile attack on the American continent.

The BMEWS setup operates automatically in transmitting data to an evaluation facility at our defense headquarters in

Colorado Springs, Colorado. Its heart is an air-conditioned combination transmitter-receiver unit which sends many times each second at a power level greater than that of one hundred large radio stations.

The Thule BMEWS is equipped with four of the world's largest radars. More than twenty-one miles of wave guide are needed to direct the radio-frequency energy transmitted to the high-speed scanning switch and antenna feed horns, which bounce the energy off four reflector antennae, each larger than a football field. With 1,500 tons of steel used in each reflector, they are built to withstand a 6-inch coating of ice in winds of 185 miles per hour. All of this is connected with a labyrinthian tunnel structure with miles of passageways on what is known simply as "J" site overlooking iceberg-strewn Wolstenholme Fjord.

Approximately twenty-seven million pounds of equipment went into the construction of BMEWS, much of it carried by air. The computers in their entirety, the detection radar take-off equipment, and the vast majority of all sensitive electronic equipment was airlifted in by Military Air Transport Service (MATS).

In occasional emergency situations MATS was called upon to carry to BMEWS heavy cargo not ordinarily associated with airlift operations. Some 375 tons of antenna steel which had been shipped in by sea failed to meet engineering specifications and had to be returned to the manufacturers for reprocessing, then returned to Thule by air. The defects were discovered after North Star Bay had been frozen over with ice, and the construction program would have been delayed until the following shipping season if airplane transportation had not been available. In 1959 alone MATS carried 5,500 tons of BMEWS cargo and 4,360 passengers.

The power supply for BMEWS in Thule is provided by a 5,032 ton freighter, a YFP-10 power ship, moored in North Star Bay. The vessel was first conceived and developed by the United States Navy as a stand-by device to provide power to Navy installations or as an emergency power source in the event of a major catastrophe in some coastal city. The ship is anchored in its own private dock where it floats in water that special equipment keeps free of ice; only a few feet away the bay ice is five feet thick.

The BMEWS installation represents only a beginning of a missile-defense system, most of which will also be based in the far north. Some scientists predict that missile-tracking systems, using a battery of satellites, will make BMEWS obsolete within the next half decade or so. Other research is already under way, connecting BMEWS with an electronic lethal device which would make the present equipment as obsolete as the Model T Ford.

We have also been building airfields located well above the Arctic Circle as further deterrents to Soviet aggression. The largest of these is probably the one at Thule, Greenland, where there was once the world's most northerly settlement of 130 polar Eskimos who recently were moved to a new settlement, Kanak, about sixty miles north of Thule on Red Cliff Peninsula.

The Eskimos said the noise and smell from planes and ships frightened away the walruses, seals, polar bears, and birds that they needed to live. The scale of the construction project was beyond their comprehension. Before 1891 the Eskimos in Thule had little contact with white men. In that year Admiral Robert E. Peary began his series of attempts to reach the North Pole. During the following eighteen years he wintered among the Eskimos several times. He taught them the use of modern firearms and, in turn, learned to eat their food, to live in their sod and stone houses, and to travel with dog teams. When he left them for the last time in 1909 after reaching the Pole, the Eskimos had rifles but no means of getting ammunition.

To meet their requirements the renowned Danish-Greenlander explorer, Knud Rasmussen, and the great bearded Danish explorer, Peter Freuchen, who had continued his explorations even after losing a leg through amputation, established a trading station in Thule in 1910. The Danish government took over the station after Rasmussen's death in 1932. Guns have replaced harpoons, cloth has replaced furs, feather beds are substituted for skins, and kerosene stoves supplant the blubber lamp.

The Eskimos still cling to many of the old ways of living. In the few months that the sea is ice free each year, they hunt seals, walrus, and narwhal from their fragile kayaks. During the rest of the year they travel for weeks or months with dog sleds, hunting bears and musk ox, and setting store traps for foxes. In the winter their food is meat and blubber from sea animals and in the summer it is supplemented by sea birds and fish.

The Eskimo earns money by selling fox and seal furs, bearskins, walrus, seal and whale blubber, and narwhal and walrus tusks to the government. In the shops he buys twine for nets, wood for boats, iron and steel for sledges, cartridges, kerosene, sugar, coffee, tea, and tobacco. Debt and idleness often replace initiative and independence; the Danish administration cannot reverse the effects of civilization.

When construction of the base began, some Danes feared it would mean the complete ruin of the native by making him entirely dependent upon the Americans. Consequently, the area surrounding the base was declared "off limits" to the airmen, a Danish liaison officer was installed at the air base, and contact with the Eskimos was forbidden. After two years it became apparent that the game was being driven away and the move to Kanak was made. Now the Eskimos have no problems concerning housing and heating as these are provided by the U. S. Air Force. Colonel Bernt Balchen and representatives of the Army District Engineers and contractors arrived at the site in February of 1951 for an initial survey. They found the Danish government's small trading post, a weather-reporting station, and a short, unpaved landing strip which, under the supervision of Balchen, had been bulldozed out of frozen soil in 1946.

Later that spring a convoy of 120 transport ships, led by the U. S. icebreaker *Adak,* cut through the heavy pack ice of Melville Bay and North Star Bay to Thule. The operation had the code name "Operation Blue Jay," and, although thousands participated in the project, the exact site was a well-kept military secret, not disclosed officially until the fall of 1952.

Thule Air Base is justly described as an engineering job comparable to the digging of the Panama Canal. The essentials of the base were completed in two years. Miles upon miles of broad concrete runways and parking aprons had been laid, and scores of buildings had been erected. The men endured the usual Arctic handicaps of poor weather, monotony, and darkness during the long winter.

During the summer the average temperature at Thule is thirty-four degrees above zero and in the winter the temperature averages about five degrees below zero. The lowest recorded temperature at Thule is forty-two degrees below zero, which is not unusual for some of our northern states. During the winter months the humidity is extremely low and there is little snowfall. Protracted periods of the low temperatures, however, make it necessary to restrict winter work to a minimum. The strong foehn winds, so characteristic of the margin of the icecap, are always a serious threat and slow down out-of-door operations. There is some accumulation of snow in the winter, but most of this is caused by the wind blowing it from the surface of the icecap. The area is sprinkled with shelters where anyone caught by a sudden blizzard can seek refuge.

Despite the relatively low temperatures and the long, dark winter period, which is generally thought to have a depressing effect upon men, the health of those on military assignment and of the civilian workers, mostly Danes in our employ, remained excellent and their morale good.

Today Thule is a self-sufficient community. Row after row of various types of buildings and workshops include steam-heated barracks with innerspring mattresses, a chapel, a complete laundry and dry cleaning plant, libraries, a fifty-bed hospital, an eight-lane bowling alley, and a gymnasium with equipment and instructors for such sports as basketball, fencing, tennis, judo, gymnastics, and weight lifting. The buildings house a hobby shop, a theater, Airmen NCO, Officers', and Service Clubs, glee club, a modern base exchange with barber shop, gift-wrapping window, special-order department, watch-repair shop, American Express and lay-away facilities, and a well-stocked commissary. Prices charged are attractive, but persons returning from Thule to the United States are subject to customs regulations.

Everything to make the base comfortable is found in Thule, including a long-line telephone circuit for personal calls to the United States. No incoming calls are received in Thule except in cases of emergency. Toll rates for out-going calls are computed from Quebec City in Canada. Private automobiles are not permitted at Thule, but this rule is not resented. There is no place to go.

Recreation on the base is kept at a lively pace, but off-base trips are severely limited by lack of transportation, rugged terrain, and the danger of sudden storms. The perils of traveling by inexperienced servicemen in Greenland were unhappily shown last summer when four men were killed and nine others injured on a sight-seeing trip to Russell Glacier near Söndre Strömfjord. A huge chunk of the glacier's face tumbled and crashed into the Watson River that flows from its base, while the sight-seers were taking pictures about 500 feet away. I was particularly upset by this accident, because I had observed the imminence of the ice avalanche in 1954 when I was studying the face of the glacier.

Fishing in the lakes near the base at Thule is encouraged, but hunting is forbidden because all available game is preserved for the Eskimos, even though they have been removed from the vicinity. Visiting native villages or hunting and fishing camps continues to be strictly forbidden.

Thule has many other trappings of a large American town. There are streets with their names on street signs, traffic signals, traffic policemen during the rush hours, and the world's third highest structure, a 1200-foot antenna tower piercing the low Arctic sky. Thule's radio station, which began broadcasting on 24 March 1952, is the voice of information, education, and entertainment. Its ratings are far higher than those of *Moscow Molly*, the Russians' answer to the *Voice of America*. The Armed Forces' television station, KOLD-TV, at Thule has been telecasting approximately sixty-two hours a week since 19 May 1955. State-side programming includes popular network shows. The telecast day ends with the Feature Film Theater.

The base newspaper, *Thule Times*, boasts that it is the "northernmost newspaper in the world." The 8-page multilithed paper, published weekly by its four-man staff, has won numerous Air Force journalistic awards. Its contents are of local interest principally, with a weekly inspirational column by the Commander, and includes interpretations of military directives, changes in promotion and rotation policies, and similar topics.

The base has a greenhouse with approximately one hundred plants, including an orange tree, cucumbers, tomatoes, and lettuce. Milk consumers at Thule know that their favorite beverage comes from a machine called a "mechanical cow," but few have ever seen its operation. During the course of a month the machine recombines 100,000 quarts of fat, powdered milk, vitamins, salt, and water.

Visitors to Thule see as many massive, rumbling waste and water trucks as they see aircraft overhead. Water and sewage lines are hard to maintain because of freezing temperatures, but satisfactory substitutes have been devised. Water is obtained for the base from Crescent Lake, located some five miles away. It is pumped from the lake into a modern treatment plant and fed by gravity through a heated 8-inch water main to specially constructed trucks which carry it to tanks at the base. Waste is trucked from buildings to sewage disposal plants.

The Thule project needed all the great physical, economic, industrial, and intellectual resources of the United States. Indeed,

Thule Air Base was organized and carried out with a determination and speed unusual in peacetime. Most valuable was the experience gained in establishing our wartime bases—Söndre Strömfjord, Narsarssuak, and Optimist farther south in Greenland.

Permafrost, the permanently frozen ground of Arctic and Antarctic land masses, is said by scientists to cover about one-fourth of the earth's total land surface. It proved the biggest headache to the architects and engineers who designed and built our big base at Thule, and it constantly hampers efficient maintenance of air strips as well as hangars and other permanent buildings.

Even in mid-summer the ground in parts of Alaska, depending upon the latitude and the vegetation, is frozen solidly from a foot or two below the surface to depths as great as 1,000 feet. In Greenland, scientists drilled 2,000 feet below the ground level and did not get beyond permafrost.

Army and highway engineers have for many years studied the characteristics of permafrost; residents of northern states in this country are well aware of the cost of road repairs that appear on their tax bills as their local highway departments ceaselessly fight the buckling of macadam and concrete because of winter's deep frosts.

During World War II permafrost was an unpredictable force in the Arctic. It buckled airfield runways and contorted well-constructed hangars almost beyond repair. Hangars would be mud-jacked several times, but the floors would still sink below the sides. Whenever anything built on permafrost contains enough heat to thaw part of the deep frost, irregular settling results. The weight or strength of a building or a runway is puny when pitted against permafrost, which can exert a stress of fourteen tons per square inch. Engineers have found only two solutions: one is to build where no chance exists for permafrost thawing, such as on solid rock or on gravel bars beside rivers; the other, more feasible for large-scale construction, is to build on permafrost and to insulate against thawing.

Buildings at Thule were set on timbers which elevated them several feet above ground. To prevent them from being carried away during high foehn winds off the icecap, reinforced construction was essential. Each building was heavily weighted with concrete blocks. Large buildings which had to be on the surface of the ground, such as hangars and heating plants, were constructed with ventilating chambers to permit cold air to circulate beneath the floor, thereby preventing melting of the permanently frozen soil.

Experience in the Berlin airlift of 1948 was of inestimable value in shipping supplies by air to Thule. Techniques of loading and unloading aircraft were utilized to effect quick turnabouts so that, during good flying weather, planes were not delayed on the ground.

The Thule Air Base, in the latitude of Spitzbergen, is only 931 statute miles from the North Pole and north of the magnetic pole. It is farther north than any point in Alaska. By air it is slightly closer to New York City than to Moscow, but also closer to our Pacific Northwest than to Washington. It provides the United States with a vital supply and staging point for the necessary weather stations scattered throughout the Arctic, and a base for long range, all-weather fighters which could surely blunt an enemy surprise attack. An attack by planes coming from the Soviet Arctic now could be picked up by radar networks spread over the Arctic and jet interceptors from Thule could take off almost instantly. Bombers based at Thule could be launched immediately on retaliatory missions.

Thule is now the staging point for a vast research project of the United States Army: the study of using the icecap as a refuge from nuclear bombs. Tunnels and ice chambers can be quarried from the icecap at moderate cost. Excavations large enough to hold our bombers have been dug out of the ice. Caverns beneath the surface of the icecap would be ideal for the storage of unlimited quantities of food, ammunition, supplies, and in an emergency could also be used for the housing of military personnel.

An atomic-powered city, Camp Century, has been built inside the icecap. Camp Century was dug with coal-mining machinery and has sixteen streets, railways, hot and cold running water, flush toilets, dormitories, cafeteria, gymnasium, workshops, a post exchange, a chapel, a hospital, and one hundred human inhabitants. Camp Century is free of dust, traffic noises, and changing weather. Building temperatures are set at 60°, and the temperature in the streets is kept at 20°. The power source is a portable nuclear reactor, capable of producing 1,500 kilowatts and built at a cost of $6,300,000. It has sufficient fuel, about one-tenth of a ton of enriched uranium, to provide light and heat for 24 months. Since it is estimated that 800 gallons of nuclear fuel will provide the heat and power derived from 850,000 gallons of Diesel fuel, it is obviously economic, despite the cost of enriched uranium, to use atomic energy on the icecap where the transporting of conventional fuel is prohibitively expensive.

Thule Air Base has been called a "pearl of great price," but it is one of our most important permanent defenses. It is no fly-by-night one-time station to be abandoned as our aerial strategy changes, for even in a peaceful world Thule will serve as a vital center for intercontinental air travel.

CHAPTER XXI

To Keep Them Flying

CONSTRUCTION OF THE Thule base provided more great experience in Arctic flying for Air Force pilots and for the crews of commercial aircraft. During the first year of construction, airlines under contract to the Air Force carried 19,000 passengers and tremendous loads of cargo from Westover Field in Massachusetts to Thule, all without a single casualty. There were a few forced landings and some damaged aircraft that were able to make it to an air base.

Navigation troubles, rather than weather, used to be the chief limitation on Arctic flying. Ordinary compasses on early aircraft had little value in high latitudes. Among the corrections made by science was a new method of navigation called the "grid." In these days, however, when vast scientific advances are everyday news and the launching of satellites may be bumped off the front pages by other news breaks, there are startling prospects ahead for navigators.

The new satellites that are being launched by the armed forces in increasing numbers can spin around the earth almost indefinitely, sending back information that will soon make commonplace an all-weather and precise navigational system for ships and planes, and eventually space ships. The navigational satellite, Transit II-A, had an accuracy when launched of well within one-quarter mile, far better than any instruments now being used can obtain by traditional methods.

It is true that air navigation in the polar regions will always have problems not found on other world airways. There aren't very many conspicuous landmarks for a navigator to pick up from the air, and those that do stand out can be quickly blotted from sight by driving snow, the peculiar vagaries of Arctic sunlight and darkness, or even the deadening monotony of most of the barren landscapes. The navigator must also stay alert to the extreme convergency of the meridians in the high latitudes. He finds that ice floe and sky are often uniform in color. He experiences the perilous white-outs, and his radio acts up because of ionospheric disturbances. The great distances between ground stations also makes him work constantly at his instruments.

Some of the wartime techniques of Arctic aerial navigation were passed on to the Scandinavians by U. S. Air Force personnel, and one of the results was a great step forward for commercial aviation. In 1952, Scandinavian Airlines System took delivery of its first Douglas 6-B four-engine aircraft at the factory in Santa Monica, California. Rather than use the conventional Atlantic route to get the plane home, SAS decided to take the short cut. The plane flew by way of Edmonton, Alberta, and Greenland to Copenhagen. The trip took less than twenty-four hours. The new Northwest Passage of the twentieth century was opened.

The pilot of that first SAS plane was a Dane named Povl Jensen. This was not his first experience in the north. Eighteen years earlier he had visited Greenland when Pan American Airways had employed him to survey a northern route connecting the United States and Europe.

Immediately after Scandinavian Air Lines System's historic

flight, SAS negotiated with the American government for a permit to make regular flights via Greenland and Canada to California. The route was officially opened on 15 November 1954. Colonel Balchen, who continued to be the inspiration behind so much of our Arctic activities, was a passenger on the preliminary experimental flight from California to Copenhagen in 1952, and in November 1954 he was at Los Angeles waiting to receive the first scheduled plane to fly from Denmark to California. In less than a year, the Great Circle Arctic Air Route was established as a commercial success. The schedule was extended to three flights a week, and in November 1955 a tourist class was introduced. Söndre Strömfjord was selected as an intermediate base, and there Scandinavian Air Lines System built a modest hotel for overnight guests which, with increasing traffic, had to be expanded.

Transpolar air service between Scandinavia and western America is proving of great importance. This has been recognized by two of our carriers, Trans World Airlines and Pan American, both of which fly a route from the West Coast of the United States via former Air Force Base "Crystal 2" in Frobisher Bay and over the Greenland Icecap to Europe. They do not use Söndre Strömfjord. The Danish government also actively promotes local air activity in Greenland, as does the Canadian government in its own Arctic and our government in Alaska.

Danish transport flights are made for the Greenland Department from Copenhagen to the air fields at Narsarssuak and at Söndre Strömfjord. The Danes have constructed a landing strip at Mestersvig in the lead-mining district on the east coast. Helicopters have operated for the mining company from this base since 1955 and they are being employed elsewhere in Greenland in geodetic surveys.

The first scheduled Europe-to-Japan airliner of Scandinavian Airlines, bypassing the bases of northern Greenland and crossing near the geographic north pole to Alaska and then on to the Orient, landed in Tokyo on 26 February 1957, fifteen minutes ahead of schedule. A sister plane which took off from Tokyo over the same route was delayed by head winds and landed in Copenhagen an hour and a half behind schedule. The two big aircraft missed a carefully planned rendezvous over the North Pole by only a few minutes.

Today the Arctic is a superhighway for commercial flights between Europe and the Orient. Six airlines—KLM Royal Dutch Airlines, Trans World, Pan American, Scandinavian, Air France, and Canadian Pacific Airlines—now use the Great Circle Route across or near the Pole for long distance intercontinental flights. The new route shortens the journey from Copenhagen or Amsterdam to Tokyo for propeller-driven aircraft by twenty-four hours compared with the former route via the Near East, Pakistan, India, Siam, and Hong Kong to Tokyo.

The polar route between northern Europe and the far Pacific cuts fifteen hours from another conventional route, the one across the Atlantic and America. This great advantage in time cannot be ignored, for in twenty-six hours after taking off from Oslo one can be almost halfway around the world in Tokyo, with stops made in Alaska and, if necessary, in the Aleutians. The distance is about 7,500 miles. From London to Tokyo via Rome, Cairo, Calcutta, and Hong Kong the time is more than 40 hours, including stops. The saving in time for jet aircraft, which fly at greater speeds, is correspondingly less.

Not so obvious and well known as the time factor are the safety advantages of favorable weather and smooth operation on the polar route. Precipitation in the Arctic and sub-Arctic is heaviest in summer, but surprisingly light for year-round average. Fifteen inches of precipitation, corresponding to semi-arid parts of our Midwest, is common to the northern area. Sections away from the coast have very little moisture from December to March.

Arctic zone temperatures vary much less than those of many areas of interior land masses in the temperate zones. Water acts as a stabilizing medium with its ability to retain heat. The natural tendency for temperature to decrease with an increase in latitude is offset in the Arctic by the sea around the Pole. (This is in sharp contrast to the Antarctic, which is a continent of ice-covered mountains.) Water acts as a radiator in the winter, preventing temperatures from falling extremely low, and as a refrigerator in the summer, keeping temperatures from getting very high. Therefore great extremes of temperature are found only in areas combining high latitudes, low elevations, and a considerable distance from the sea. The coldest spot in the northern hemisphere is around Oimekon in Siberia, inland about 200 miles south of the Arctic Circle. Temperatures there drop to 90° below. The coldest temperature recorded in Alaska and Canada is 79° below at Fort Good Hope, 20 miles south of the Arctic Circle and about 280 miles south of the coast.

To have high summer temperatures, a land mass must be away from the moderating influence of the water. The extreme heat record for Alaska, 100° in the shade, was observed just north of the Arctic Circle, at Fort Yukon near the center of Alaska. Fairbanks, 100 miles south of Fort Yukon, has recorded 99°. Days with 90° temperatures are not uncommon, and wheat grows regularly north of the Arctic Circle in lowland areas far from the cooling sea.

Counterbalancing the cooling effect of the sea in summer is the warming effect in midwinter. This comparative warmth comes both from the two currents—the Japanese and the Gulf—and from the radiation of some heat from the Arctic waters, even through a film of ice. It is unlikely that the temperature could fall much below −60° to −70° at the North Pole. The lowest temperature ever recorded on the Beaufort Sea coast of Alaska was 57° below zero. This is uncomfortably cold, of course, but 250 miles south of the ocean in the mainland of Canada it goes 30° lower than on the shore; in Siberia 600 miles south of the Arctic Ocean it also drops 30° lower than on the coast.

There are violent local gales in areas of the Arctic, but, in the main, the northern sea is one of the most placid areas in the world. Near land, and in areas where plateaus descend to the sea level as on the coastal area of Greenland, there are strong gales, and along the north coast of Canada and Alaska there are fierce autumn and early winter gales.

A midwinter sun that hangs over the horizon in sub-Arctic latitudes will not dissipate fog or low cloud. In some places, during periods of calm, layers of this mist start at 100 or 200 feet and remain throughout the day. Generally such mist is quite thin. The orientation of crystals makes horizontal visibility poor, while vertical visibility is good. Pilots have had the weird experience of seeing a landing strip clearly from overhead but being unable to make a landing.

The spring and summer periods are neither as long nor as warm as we are accustomed to in southern latitudes, but they do have much more light than ours. Men on the DEW Line can read without artificial light at midnight from mid-June to mid-July. The number of hours of sunlight does much to make up for the shorter frost-free period.

Pilots prefer the Great Circle Route over the far north because low temperatures and dry atmosphere are deterrents to engine and airplane icing. Turbulence is rare, and flying weather is consistently stable throughout the year. The safety record of the Air Force has been excellent. Commercial operations over the northern route have been free of casualties and even damage to aircraft. Fixed schedules have been adhered to closely. Although the Arctic routes cross thinly populated areas, there are many emergency fields adjacent to DEW Line installations, Hudson Bay Company posts, Royal Canadian Mounted Police posts, and weather stations that now dot the Arctic wastes, and no plane is ever more than two hours' flying time from a landing strip.

Even with the advances made in Arctic flying, costs remain high. All maintenance materials, supplies, and gasoline must be sent by ship to northern bases during the limited summer season and by air, at heavier costs, during the remainder of the year. There is need for continuing studies of weather, navigation, mapping, and magnetic surveys, as well as selection and care of personnel, including problems of their morale and adaptation to an inhospitable environment.

The Arctic weather forecaster's life remains an unhappy one. Land fragments of the Arctic produce oddities in clouds, fogs, and winds which play havoc with weather forecasting. In some areas of Greenland a serene calm can change in ten minutes to a raging blizzard with a velocity of more than 100 miles an hour, carrying with it brittle snow blowing off the icecap as well as sand and gravel from the snow-free marginal area. The Air Force for more than a decade has realized the need for more detailed information about weather in the Arctic. It has multiplied its weather-reporting stations in Greenland, the Canadian Arctic, Alaska, and stations on the polar ice. Regular weather flights are made from Fairbanks, Alaska, to the Pole and back. All meteorological information, of course, is provided to the commercial airlines flying through these regions.

Space technology holds some of the answers to forecasting. Some were solved with the launching on 1 April 1960 of Tiros I, the meteorological satellite. After 78 days of useful life as a weather eye, the satellite's twin TV cameras, riding 400 miles up, had transmitted 22,952 pictures of cloud formations. The two cameras took pictures of that part of the globe between 50° north latitude and 50° south latitude. More than 60 per cent of the pictures were good enough for meteorological research. They revealed the presence of jet streams, regions of moist and dry air, thunderstorms, storm fronts, and cloud fronts associated with tornadoes. Experimental weather use is being made of the data gathered from Tiros I.

Tiros II, launched on 23 November 1960 from Cape Canaveral, extended the cloud-cover experiment begun with Tiros I. It used two television cameras and carried several infrared radiation sensors to map solar and infrared radiation in various spectral bands. The Tiros satellites pushed far forward a U. S. program to have satellites provide world-wide meteorological information. There are other American projects in the satellite field which promise to revolutionize the entire navigational and weather field. Tiros IV weather satellite was placed in orbit on 8 February 1962.

The U. S. Weather Bureau, for example, is planning to launch a network of weather satellites called "Nimbus" which will circle on polar orbits. There is good reason to believe that someday they will be used as weather-control stations.

There is great need for accurate topographic maps of the Arctic. Until World War II, mapping of the entire polar region was in a primitive stage, and some areas still lack completely reliable maps. Navigators during the war found large blank spaces on their maps marked "unexplored." Well established landmarks were charted out of position, and closely grouped islands were shown as large land masses.

The Danish government has done much to correct this situation in Greenland, as have the Canadian and the U. S. governments in other northern areas. Modern air photographic methods have helped. The process is slow because there is still no substitute for field work. The helicopter has demonstrated its value in field work, as have the daring bush pilots who fly surveyors to out-of-the-way places.

Vast areas of the north country have been surveyed by a combination of aerial photography and conventional ground survey. This technique is called *Shoran,* an abbreviation for "Short Range Aid to Navigation." *Shoran* utilizes radar combined with triangulation to establish one fixed point after another, all geared to a previously determined starting point. Temporary radar stations on the ground are used in addition to established map locations. Field engineers translate electronic readings to linear measurements and thus obtain accurate distances.

Sketchy topographic maps are being rapidly improved, but some coast lines are still only approximately outlined and detailed inland features are too often incomplete. The most recent world aeronautical chart of the Smith Sound area of Canada-Greenland has on it such notations as: "Position and shapes of glacial lakes are approximate," and "numerous peaks and ridges partially snow covered." Elevations are followed by the indication that they are plus or minus, with a parenthetical word, "unreported," or "unsurveyed." This is the aeronautical chart for the air base at Thule. Unless a navigator has an unrestricted view and is familiar with the country, he will have trouble in fixing his position visually.

The mosquito is the scourge of ground surveyors in the otherwise pleasant Arctic summer. Anyone who has spent part of June, July, or August on the spongelike tundra knows that mosquitoes are the foe of anything living. They are always on the lookout for a meal of warm blood during the long bright days. They swarm about their victims, man or beast, attacking exposed skin or places where the hair is thinnest. They alight in countless thousands until a hand slaps them, a strong wind blows them off, or a chill rain disposes of them.

Magnetic surveys have been extended. The isomagnetic charts available for navigation during World War II were inferior. Teams of scientists have since been sent to various areas in the Arctic. They found that there is a magnetic pole and two minor poles and that the whole magnetic field of the poles is elliptical in shape. Yet the Smith Sound aeronautical chart published in 1957 has the notation, "lines of equal magnetic variation for 1955. Annual rate of change varies from 60′ decrease to 20′ decrease from the W to SE portion of the chart." An additional note is heavily printed: "Magnetic Note: Because of weak directive force and magnetic storms, the compass becomes increasingly unreliable approaching the magnetic pole from a distance of approximately 1000 miles."

The present position of the North Magnetic Pole appears to be north of Prince of Wales Island. The Magnetic Pole is currently drifting about four miles a year slightly east of north. The movement, however, varies from time to time in magnitude and direction. In 1831, according to Ross, the Pole was near Cape Adelaide on the west coast of Boothia Peninsula, and in 1904, according to Amundsen, about forty miles northeast of Ross's position. Since 1904 the average motion has been approximately north-northwest.

The position of the peripatetic North Magnetic Pole has been calculated for each year since 1946 from observations made at Dominion Observatory magnetic stations on the Arctic islands and the mainland surrounding the polar area, supplemented since 1948 by continuous records of the changes in magnitudes and direction of the earth's magnetic field at Resolute Bay and Baker Lake, and from magnetic surveys that have been made in Greenland for several decades.

The RB-47, the Boeing medium reconnaisance bomber that flashed into world headlines when it was shot down by Soviet fighters on 11 July 1960 over international waters, was mapping magnetic fields in the Barents Sea area in a survey intended to provide information for more accurate maps.

The Air Force is always troubled in Arctic operations in improving the comfort and morale of its men. Organization and equipment designed for temperate climates do not work.

Accurate and useful data on personnel performance in sub-zero weather has been gathered in recent years both in the Arctic and in Antarctica. Studies of physical and psychological reaction to cold are giving answers to such questions as: At what temperature is it safe to work actively? How long is it safe to work at particular temperatures? What are the signs of overexertion at low temperatures? If heated hangars are not available for aircraft maintenance, how long should certain operations such as changing a motor require?

It is one thing to work on a plane outdoors at Thule, quite another at Bolling Field, Washington. Such a simple operation as applying safety wire correctly becomes a choice between frozen fingers and the clumsiness of pliers held in a bulky glove.

The operation and maintenance of aircraft and other equipment in cold weather has been studied successfully ever since the establishment in 1939 of a Cold Weather Test Detachment at Ladd Field in Fairbanks. Four officers and fifty-one enlisted men were thought hopelessly mad. They hoped, with the temperature at fifty degrees below zero, that it would get colder. They burrowed and slept in snowbanks. They flew north of the Arctic Circle, testing electric underwear and shoes made of felt. If it was not cold enough at Ladd Field, they went where it was colder. Their wild antics permitted American aircraft to fly and fight in temperatures as low as ever recorded.

Their basic discoveries, which seem elementary now, were that engine oil was hardened by the extreme cold, gasoline would not ignite, rubber became brittle and shattered, landing-gear packings froze and cracked, delicately adjusted instruments and bombsights jammed. They tested photographic equipment, oil-tank immersion heaters, fire pots, heat guns, ration kits, emergency equipment kits and electrically heated clothing.

Twenty-six members of the Cold Weather Test Detachment gave their lives to save countless flyers in the stratosphere above Japan and Germany, across Arctic wastes, and above the Himalayan Hump. There were others who lost fingers and hands torn off by ground heaters; suffered frostbitten ears, faces, and toes; were burned and injured in crashes. They made flying safe in the coldest weather. Cold Weather Test learned that 90 per cent of the trouble could be corrected. The 10 per cent still needs attention and research.

There have been unprecedented Arctic research activities in areas other than those relating directly to problems of flying, such as the *Snow Man* and *Mint Julep* projects in Greenland. At Ladd Air

Force Base the areo-medical laboratory has included these areas in its work:

Report of studies on acclimatization—winter 1948–49.
Field test of Canadian snowmobile.
Relationships between low morale and personality structures.
Gloves as a factor in reduced dexterity.
Electroencephalographic study of men transferred from the sub-tropic to the sub-Arctic.
Personality alterations during reduced caloric intake under survival conditions in the sub-Arctic.
Field test of the bag casualty evacuation (experimental).
Arctic winter ration trials 1950.
The effect of prolonged Arctic light on night visual acuity.
A rapid oxygen analyzer.
Vitamin content of Arctic plants and their significance in human nutrition.
Survey of edible plants in Alaska.
Winter fire fighting in the Arctic—a study of clothing requirements.
Critical factor underlying the decision to extend or not extend the Alaskan duty tour.
Adaptive changes during exposure to cold.
Effects of weather factors on maintenance crews—Arctic area.
Heat loss from the respiratory tract in cold.
Nervous control of shivering.
Human acclimatization to cold.
Selection of men best qualified for sub-Arctic and Arctic duty.

The Arctic is not a region of nameless terrors where miracles are needed to survive. The man who tackles the north country for the first time must remember that winter cold can kill; that a single fire in camp can mean disaster; that Eskimos have been lost in blizzards within a snowball's throw of warmth and shelter.

Exploring parties, however, have crisscrossed Arctic lands and seas for hundreds of years, and long before the establishment of military air routes during World War II bush pilots and small commercial airlines successfully served a number of isolated Arctic communities.

Civilization is moving closer to the top of the world, but tourist traffic by air will not boom for remote regions. The few attempts that have been made to attract tourists to Greenland have ended in failure. Much of the Arctic probably never will be popular among tourists who are seeking excitement, but rewards exist for flying over the northern route. The flight within the Arctic Circle gives every traveler a thrill.

The settings of the air fields at Söndre Strömfjord, Narsarssuak and Thule are beautiful. Söndre Strömfjord and Narsarssuak are at the head of long fjords which empty into Davis Strait; each airfield is only a few miles from the great icecap which dominates all the scenery. In summer the approach to Söndre Strömfjord by air from the icecap to the east or the fjord to the west is breathtaking. Narsarssuak can be approached only up the fjord from the west. In winter, of course, the areas are dark, but winter is the season of the brilliant northern lights. Winter temperatures do not encourage outdoor activity. The air base at Thule, much farther north, is restricted to military operation. If it ever is open for commercial use, it will rival Söndre Strömfjord and Narsarssuak.

This is an air age, and long-range aircraft have changed our world. Places that are farthest apart by ordinary geography are much closer by air over the Pole. We can no longer overlook blank spaces on our maps. All military targets in the populated part of the globe over 35° are reachable. As Bernt Balchen has said, "the Arctic is no longer a cold spot, but the hot spot on this planet."

CHAPTER XXII

Ptarmigan

THE AIR FORCE has been studying the weather at the roof of the world since 1947. Four-engine planes have been flying to the North Pole since then in a schedule that has become so standardized and routine that it resembles a scheduled regular flight between New York and Los Angeles. These flights are called "Ptarmigan" missions after the feather-footed grouse found throughout the Arctic.

The first experimental weather flight to the frozen top of the globe was made on 21 July 1946 from Ladd Field. Only a dozen or so flights had been made by the following spring, when a Weather Reconnaissance Squadron was assigned to regular flights. Some critics viewed the project as foolhardy. It was a first long step toward providing the weather data needed for forecasting, and it was the first effort to harness Arctic forces.

The weather flights now serve several purposes. They provide accurate weather data collected from the polar basin where there are no ground stations except those maintained periodically on ice floes or ice islands; they provide periodic radar vigilance over

216

the Arctic Ocean; they carry out other assigned research projects such as the collection of air for detection of nuclear fallout and carbon-dioxide content of the atmosphere, the measurement of variations in compass readings, and observations of other phenomena.

The course of the flight covers 2,744 nautical miles, crossing the meandering Yukon River, spanning the rugged mountain ranges of northern Alaska, the flat tundra beyond, to the barren expanse of snow, ice, and occasional patches of open leads of salt water of the Arctic Ocean.

On 6 April 1960, exactly fifty-one years after Admiral Peary planted the American flag at the North Pole, I was a passenger on Ptarmigan's 3,015th mission flown with a standard nine-man crew in a WB-50. The pilot was Lieutenant Colonel Lawrence T. Keohane, a pleasant Air Force veteran and commander of Ladd's Detachment No. 1 of the 55th Weather Squadron. Captain Bobby Curtis was copilot.

Our airmen on the North Pole patrol are among the most skilled flyers in the world. They have learned all the tricks of Arctic weather and have keen extra senses for white-outs and raging blizzards. They know how to interpret drifting snow and the direction of open leads far below them. They fly in weather that would ground planes in more hospitable climates.

On the day before the flight we were briefed in Hangar 3—a building constructed by the Russians to house lend-lease aircraft during World War II. Seated next to me during the briefing, an airman with scores of polar missions to his credit listened as carefully as I did. The forecast was for heavy overcast as far as the coast line and fair weather with low-hanging, broken cloud cover over the Arctic basin. . . . We would be carrying 8,600 gallons of gasoline. . . . If communication failed we would turn back at position 5, which is 80° N., 600 miles from the Pole. . . . In case of a crash landing chances of survival and rescue are better if you stay with the plane. . . . If you parachute, try to join up with others instead of scattering separately. . . . Flight to 80° N. would mean full credit toward flying points. . . . Elmendorf in Anchorage would be the alternate field if Ladd should be closed by weather.

Then came the instructions: everyone will report to the hangar by six-thirty. . . . Everyone must have parachute and survival equipment. . . . Men will be in crash position for take-off. . . . Soviet territory will not be violated. . . . Outward flight will be at 700 millibars pressure and the return at 500 millibars. . . . Radar operators will change position at point farthest north. . . . Bail out only under extreme emergency and only on instructions from pilot.

All members of the crew had gone through an Arctic survival indoctrination program. They had been told that parachute descent through overcast or during heavy weather is extremely hazardous; that the parachutist's chance of survival in the Arctic, particularly in the polar sea, is slight. Survival records compiled by the Arctic, Desert and Tropic Information Center that I commanded during the war, do not make pleasant reading. Our staggering record of losses shows that men were frequently dragged to death, or were thrown fatally to the ground or ice, or were drowned when they landed in open water. The crews who remained with the distressed aircraft had definite advantages.

At six the following morning all men who were going on the Ptarmigan flight struggled into more than twenty pounds of protective flying clothing and foot gear. It was a major achievement. The garments, starting with long woolen underwear, then wool shirt and trousers, gabardine flying coverall, were topped off with a set of quilted, fleece-lined trousers and parka. Feet were kept warm in felt boots with three pairs of woolen socks and three sets of inner soles.

The plane's instruments were given a final check, last minute weather reports were received and studied, and the ground crew made a final inspection of the flying weather laboratory. A minor oil leak was discovered and quickly repaired. Each man, with parachute harness strapped over his cumbersome clothing, stood at attention for last minute instruction alongside his parachute and personal survival equipment—an extra change of woolen underwear, felt boots with inner soles, and a spare parka.

The plane had to be towed from the hangar, fully loaded and manned, to cool off in the morning air before take-off, so that ice would not form on the warm skin of the plane. Fire engines stood by. A crewman went over a check list of other emergency survival equipment. This additional equipment weighed two tons and would keep the crew alive for at least a month in the event of a crash landing. It included two walkie-talkie radios, first-aid kits, extra clothing, skis, snowshoes, rafts, sewing kits, two rifles, knives, fishing poles, sunglasses, a portable pantry—complete with dishes and plastic spoons—sleeping bags, flashlights, vitamin pills, and extra dehydrated food. On summer flights, I was told, the emergency equipment also included insect repellent and sun-protection ointment, for an airman downed in the interior of Alaska could experience temperature readings of 100° and encounter clouds of mosquitoes.

The box lunch provided for the flight contained fruit juice, choice of fried chicken or tenderloin steak (heated in the plane's portable kitchen), sandwiches, hot coffee, and a dessert.

Shortly before 8:30 o'clock, with another mission plane warmed up as a standby if a last minute substitution were necessary, we climbed aboard. There is no provision for passengers on the WB-50, but I was invited to make myself comfortable on the floor in the radio cabin, cushioned with the outer clothing we had shed upon entering the plane. The plane's officers, however, offered me the copilot's seat throughout most of the trip.

If everything went according to plan, we would be back at Ladd Field in twelve hours, the average time for these flights. If we needed it, the flying range of the WB-50 was adequate to keep us air-borne for twenty hours. Our gasoline allowed a margin for landing at the alternate field—Anchorage—if a set down at Ladd or nearby Eielson was impossible. (We consumed 7,500 gallons of gasoline on the entire journey.)

We were air-borne at 8:50 A.M. and, as we sped northward over frozen tundra and snow-covered foothills, we climbed quickly to 12,000 feet, passed the Brooks Range of mountains, and then let down to 10,300 feet as we approached Wainwright, the departure point over the Arctic Ocean from the coast of Alaska.

En route to Wainwright all instruments were given a final check, calibrated, and made ready for use, and the weather observer, seated in the Plexiglas nose of the plane, made additional preparations to take periodic samples of air for study by scientists at the Scripps Oceanographic Laboratory at La Jolla, California.*

Every Ptarmigan crewman has important duties. There is no opportunity for relaxation. The first of the carefully spaced weather observations and air samples was taken as the plane arrived over Wainwright. From that moment on the weather observers were busy. They had to make observations at fourteen specified points on temperature, atmospheric pressure, cloud type, amount, height, and direction of movement, relative humidity, wind direction, and velocity. A device called a dropsonde, which is dropped from the airplane by parachute, gathered data from all levels between the plane and the surface of the frozen Arctic Ocean far below. An instrument attached to the parachute sends back radio messages that are decoded aboard the plane. The dropsonde usually smashes when it hits the ice.

Each hour the information was radioed to the air-to-ground station at Eielson Air Force Base, twenty-five miles from Ladd Field. From Eielson the data are transmitted either to Ladd or

* One of the glaciology and polar cap findings of the International Geophysical Year is that the change in rate of melting ice in the North Polar regions is greater in recent years than that encountered in the South Pole regions. An hypothesis advanced by Scripps oceanographers at La Jolla and a group of specialists at the University of California relate this phenomenon *on* the quantity of carbon dioxide in the atmosphere of the two hemispheres. (The air samplings being taken on our flight were for examination of carbon dioxide content.)

McClellan AFB, where they are checked, evaluated, and dispatched by radio teletype or land-line teletype for use by weather stations throughout the world. Within hours, forecasters everywhere have weather information gathered on the Ptarmigan flights.

The course of each of the 3,015 flights has usually been the same, and new reports from fixed places are compared to earlier observations. Weather data are gathered not only at the same geographical location but at a uniform altitude. After leaving the coast on the way north, the plane maintained an elevation of 10,300 feet. On the return flight to Ladd it cruised at 18,000 feet.

We had unlimited visibility over the Arctic basin, but even in the clear air we could see nothing but an endless expanse of ice punctuated by an occasional salt-water lead of deep blue water. Near the coast line the leads were numerous, but they thinned out so that at 80° north only a few were in sight. None was observed as we reached the vicinity of the Pole, although they are not uncommon at that latitude. The surface of the ice appeared rough and serrated, and the bright sun cast sharp shadows from the hummocks and pressure ridges.

The winter Arctic basin, seen from the air as a vast, dull and rumpled carpet, is crisscrossed with long, jagged pressure ridges. In the summer the hummocks and pressure ridges become a chaotic jumble surrounded by pools of water and slush. The whole ice pack from 18,000 feet looks like a dry river bed with rivulets running haphazardly through it.

The polar sea is not a solid mass of ice even in winter. Actually it is an animate shell of ice, about ten feet thick, floating over a body of salt water that in places reaches depths of more than two miles. The "pack ice" moves in a slow, clockwise eddy, with smaller eddies here and there on the margin. Not even in February or March, the most frigid months, are there extensive unbroken stretches of ice. Because this mass of ice is in constant motion, carried by wind and currents, there are always leads and lanes of water. Explorers seldom travel over the ice surface more than twenty or thirty miles before coming to an opening which may be anything from a few inches to a few miles in width. Peary, on his expeditions toward the Pole, found open leads to be his greatest obstacle. The crack may be open water or it may have a covering of ice that varies from a thin film to several feet in depth, depending on the recency of the opening.

Some open water is caused by the grinding of floe on floe, one breaking up on another to form a pressure ridge. Leads that open in winter are quickly cemented by the cold-producing areas of level ice that explorers find favorable to sled travel and that aviators use for landings and take-offs.

The permanent ice which occupies most of the polar basin is not uniform around the Pole. The Gulf Stream still has enough warmth in it after passing between Iceland and Norway to prevent ice from forming there; and this effect pushes the pack ice toward the Alaskan side of the Arctic basin. The center of the ice-covered area is about 400 miles to the Alaska and western Siberia side of the North Pole.

In winter the ice of the Arctic Ocean comes flush up against most of the northern coasts—Greenland, Canada, Alaska, Siberia. But drifting salt-water ice is never seen along the Norwegian coast because the pack is always kept back by the comparatively warm water. Coastwise mail steamers in Iceland seldom have difficulty with pack ice as they circle the island at all seasons of the year.

The movement of the pack ice is constant. Although the ice is only seven to ten feet in thickness in an ordinary winter, the grinding and heaping movement may cause thicknesses of 100 feet as one floe crashes into another. The angular blocks and piles of ice are called pressure ridges.

Floes that have been built up by pressure ridges are comparatively stable, although in constant sluggish motion. One can live on them through the winter. But it rains at the North Pole, as well as at every other point in the Arctic Ocean, and this rain with midsummer sun thaws the ice and snow, toning down and rounding the blocks of ice. Within four years all appearance of the block structure has been lost, and the ice looks like a rolling prairie with hummocks about fifteen or twenty feet high.

A forced landing on the frozen surface of the Arctic Ocean need not be fatal. Because of the excellent visibility during our entire journey, Colonel Keohane and Captain Curtis kept a sharp lookout for possible emergency landing zones where a WB-50 might be brought down with a minimum of damage. Large salt-water leads that have been frozen are best for smooth landings, but there is no way of telling from the air whether the ice is thick enough to take the impact of a heavy plane. Pilots minimize the danger of plunging through the ice, preferring to take that chance to the risk of landing among heaved ridges. Once a downed plane has been located, rescue is quite feasible. Ski-equipped planes, helicopters, and glider snatch have proved successful.

Our two navigators checked the grid heading and position constantly, using celestial navigation procedures. Since navigational aids are practically non-existent over most of the route followed by the weather-reconnaissance planes, navigators have to be good. Aircraft instruments are not absolutely dependable. As likely as not, the magnetic compass in the north will spin dizzily, and even the radio compass and gyro compass may act up. A navigator unable to make a celestial observation may find himself flying in circles.

Our plane was completely dependent on electronics. Without instruments the crew would have been virtually helpless in stormy weather. Even in good weather over the Arctic basin the navigator has no conspicuous visual features as check points.

The navigator depends in the summer on fixes on the sun and in winter on fixes on the moon and stars. The twilight moods during the fall and spring equinox have posed one of the more annoying navigation problems. During these periods the Arctic sun falls so slightly below the horizon that it leaves a colorful glow in which the moon and stars cannot be seen. The navigator is stumped, and the pilot has difficulty in judging elevation and distance. The technique of locating invisible stars and the Pfund sky compass have helped navigators. The Pfund device determines the spot on the horizon directly above the hidden sun. Improved radar and other electronic instruments also are used, but standing instructions on all Ptarmigan flights are to turn back at 80° N. if radio contact has been cut off because of polar magnetic storms or for any other reason. Beyond that point the turn around would be made immediately upon radio failure.

Although the flight on which I was a passenger was as uneventful as the other 3,014, each take-off constitutes a challenge. Trouble need not arise from mechanical deficiencies, but may be the result of ignorance, carelessness, bad judgment, or lack of training. Selecting the wrong course when the turn around is made at the Pole may take the plane to the Canadian Arctic Archipelago, Siberia, Lapland, or Spitzbergen. On one such occasion a plane (not on weather patrol) became lost in a twilight haze when farthest north and, hindered by loathsome weather, chose a wrong south and landed at Thule—luckily, without misfortune. None has yet headed for Siberia.

Our return from the Pole was in clear weather, but the unexpected, predicted during briefing session, did happen. The meteorologist failed to take his last observation over the radar station on Barter Island, and we had to return, thus delaying our scheduled time of arrival at Ladd by thirty minutes. By now it was completely dark, but south of the Brooks Range we could see here and there at great distances the blinking lights of a trapper's hut. Far on the horizon the lights from Eielson Air Force Base, Ladd Field, and Fairbanks brightened the sky.

CHAPTER XXIII

The Assault on the Arctic Ocean

THE MONOTONY of our Ptarmigan flight was relieved by constant radar and visual searching for "ice islands." These formations, descriptions of which appear in early polar literature, have probably broken off an ice shelf which fringes the north coast of Ellesmere Island and which shows characteristics very similar to ice islands. It is not clear whether the shelf is of glacial origin, a relic from the time when ice covered much more of north Ellesmere Island than it does today, or whether it has grown *in situ* mainly from the freezing sea water. Recent investigations by glaciologists suggest that both processes may be responsible.

Many centuries old, the ice islands have a yellowish hue caused by glacial dust. The surface ice has revealed large and small boulders and gravel accumulation, as well as plant stems, blossoms, twigs, roots, leaves, mollusk shells, a 400-year old sponge that through the years had worked its way up to the surface, bones of a fish at least a foot long, and a complete set of caribou antlers. This evidence gives weight to the theory that the ice islands were formed on land.

Higher elevations on the ice islands in the form of ridges vary from twenty to twenty-five feet above sea level. In the middle of the islands the gullies between the ridges are shallow, but near the border they are more pronounced, some being as much as fifteen feet deep.

The first sighting of an ice island, more than 200 square miles in area and much thicker than the surrounding pack ice, was made on 14 August 1946 by the crew of an Air Force Photo Reconnaissance plane flying over the Beaufort Sea, less than 300 miles north of Point Barrow. Since its radarscope return was similar to that of land, it was at first believed to be land, and this gave rise to the name "ice island." It was named T-1 (T for Target), and was tracked visually and by radar for more than three years, during which time it wandered a distance of 1,400 miles at an average rate of approximately 1.2 miles per day.

Ptarmigan crews in 1950 were instructed to try to locate other ice islands along the route to and from the Pole. A second ice island, T-2, about 300 square miles in area, was detected on a clear day in July of 1950 by an alert crewman who recognized it because of its color, homogeneous appearance, and strikingly unique surface features. Eight days later, a radar search resulted in the discovery of T-3, the smallest of the ice islands discovered and plotted, and one that became prominent in our polar research effort. Large numbers of extremely small, tabular ice islands, not much larger than good-sized icebergs, have also been observed.

The discovery of the three ice islands was a military secret until November 1950. Their existence was revealed at the Alaskan Science Conference in Washington, D. C., by Colonel Joseph E. Fletcher, commander of the 375th Air Reconnaissance Squadron, Ladd Field (the forerunner of the 55th Weather Reconnaissance Squadron) when he read a paper on the subject which he had prepared in collaboration with Major L. S. Koenig.

Air strategists hoped to use the islands as floating landing fields. The idea of ice airfields wasn't new. When submarine warfare was at its height during the war, Prime Minister Winston Churchill suggested floating airfields of ice, using them for anti-submarine activity by aircraft. Others suggested using manufactured ice for an airfield in East Greenland on the ferry route to Europe, and even as bases for air operations against Nazi Germany.

With the beginning of the cold war three possibilities for the development of airfields on ice were explored: ice islands, ice floes, and manufacture of reinforced ice. During World War II an ice compound, Pykret, made of wood pulp and water, was tested and found capable of withstanding attacks by bombers and torpedoes launched by submarines. Pykret has now been found unsuitable and an alloy of ice and Fiberglas is presently being tested as a more satisfactory substitute. The Fiberglas alloy is found to be ten times stronger than pure ice. While aircraft require natural ice thickness of at least four feet, experiments have demonstrated that an alloy six inches thick is sufficient to support a moderately large airplane.

Ice islands are superior to ice floes as floating laboratories. They provide opportunity for neglected research in geology, meteorology, and oceanography in the polar sea.

Early Arctic explorers had not been particularly concerned with scientific investigation of the polar basin; the first motive had been to find the Northwest Passage. The magnet later was the North Pole. The desire to reach the Pole was a competitive race among nations, with little scientific motivation.

The first proposal for a north polar voyage was made in 1527 to King Henry VIII when Robert Thorne, an English merchant, suggested a northern route to Cathay and India. During the early voyages in search of this northern route, John Davis in 1586 sailed through the strait which bears his name as far as latitude 72° 12′ N. Between 1594 and 1597 William Barents made three voyages to the north, during which he discovered Spitzbergen, and reached 79° 49′ N. Henry Hudson circumnavigated Spitzbergen in 1607 and sailed to 80° 23′ N. This remained the farthest north voyage until 1773 when Captain Phipps, commanding a Royal Navy expedition in which Horatio Nelson was serving as a midshipman, penetrated twenty-five miles farther north in the same region.

In 1827 Parry attempted to reach the North Pole by hauling sledges over the ice rather than sailing through it. His party set out from Spitzbergen, but the ice drifted south almost as fast as they traveled north and on 26 July they had to turn back south at 82° 45′, only 435 miles short of the Pole. The British Arctic Expedition of 1875–1876, commanded by Sir George Nares, wintered in North Ellesmere Island. A sledge party under Lieutenant Albert Markham managed to reach 83° 20′ N., 400 miles from the Pole, when an outbreak of scurvy prevented further progress. His achievement was beaten by four miles by Lieutenant Lockwood in 1882, the first time an American held the farthest north record.

In 1893 Nansen attempted to reach the North Pole by freezing his specially constructed vessel, the *Fram,* into the impenetrable polar pack and drifting with it. The drift did not follow the course he expected, and two years later, when it became clear the ship would not pass near the Pole, he and Johansen left the ship and traveled over the ice to the most northerly point to have been reached by man, 224 miles short of the Pole.

In 1901 Lieutenant Cagni of the Italian Navy led a group, with two supporting parties from the Duke of Abruzzi's expedition, over the ice from Franz Josef Land, and on 24 April the jubilant Italians hoisted their flag at a spot exceeding Nansen's farthest north by about twenty miles. One of the supporting parties never returned, and no one ever learned what happened to the group.

On 21 April 1906, Peary, traveling north from Ellesmere Island, beat Cagni's record by reaching a new high latitude of 87° 6′ N. In 1909 Peary again set out by sledge from Cape Columbia with a number of supporting teams and on 6 April with Matthew Henson, a Negro, and four Eskimos, reached the Pole after many years of effort.

Some scientific knowledge was compiled by the early explorers. Greeley's studies laid the foundations of Arctic meteorology, which was not fully appreciated until World War II. Nansen's remarkable studies of polar drift were applicable to our establishment of research stations on the floe ice of the polar sea.

After Peary's success, North Pole activity waned. Amundsen planted the Norwegian flag at the South Pole on 14 December 1911. Although Byrd and Bennett were the first to fly over the North Pole on 9 May 1926, followed two days later by a flight by Amundsen and Ellsworth in a dirigible, it was more than a decade later before an aircraft made a planned landing on the ice pack near the Pole. This, however, was not the first successful landing on the ice pack.

George Hubert Wilkins and Carl Ben Eielson flew northwest on 29 March 1927 from Point Barrow, Alaska, for a distance of approximately 500 miles. Engine trouble developed and for repairs they were forced to make the first landing with ski-equipped plane on the ice pack. Wilkins took soundings and found the greatest Arctic Ocean depth recorded up to that time—more than 15,000 feet. After fixing the engine they were air-borne for only ten minutes when a second landing had to be made. Once again in the air, they were buffeted by a sudden storm. Fighting strong headwinds, their fuel supply was exhausted and a third forced landing without accident was made about 100 miles from Point Barrow. The ice floe drifted them eastward. When Wilkins calculated their position to be eighty miles from the nearest land, they abandoned the plane and walked to the Alaskan shore at Beechey Point, building snow houses for shelter on the way, and struggling on hands and knees over upended ice blocks covered with soft snow. It took almost two weeks to reach the coast.

A decade later, on 21 May 1937, the Papanin North Pole drift expedition, sponsored by the Soviet Northern Sea Route Administration, disembarked at the Pole from an orange-colored, four-engine aircraft to establish the first of many scientific stations on the drifting ice.

The Papanin expedition, now called North Pole 1 by the Russians, was serviced by large, ski-equipped transport planes belonging to the Northern Sea Route Administration. They were based on Rudolph Island in the Fridtjof Nansen archipelago, the major base for all Soviet Polar Basin research. It is 450 miles from the North Pole and is the nearest Siberian point to Greenland and Canada.

The elaborately equipped scientific station on the floating ice pack provided the Russians with comprehensive year-round data on the central polar basin. The four men comprising the expedition drifted for 274 days on a zigzag course, traveling 1,200 miles south before the ice floe that had been home for the expedition broke up off the east coast of Greenland. There the scientists were rescued by two Soviet ice breakers.

Four years later, in 1941, another Russian aircraft made three landings on the ice north of east Siberia in the vicinity of 80° N., a region called the "Pole of Relative Inaccessibility," a concept introduced by Stefansson. This unrelieved area of ice floes has no permanent geographical significance, but until World War II it was considered that part of the Arctic Ocean about which least was known. It was not accessible by surface transportation. A number of hasty scientific observations were made during the short time the aircraft spent at each of the three landing areas. These flights and planned landings initiated a new phase in the exploration of the Arctic Ocean. They demonstrated again that aerial landings of men on the drifting polar ice for scientific observation or military purposes are possible.

The early success of the Soviets in the Arctic can be attributed to several decades of planning and exhaustive study on Arctic problems. These studies began shortly after World War I. By the time the first flights had been made to the Pole they had developed ski-equipped, four-engine aircraft, had devised by aerial observation a technique for determining the weight-bearing capacity of sea ice, and had tested a variety of automatic scientific recording instruments.

The Soviet studies of the central Arctic had to stop during the war, but were renewed on a much more imposing scale in 1948. During the three succeeding years, polar aerial expeditions landed groups of scientists at eighty-seven locations on the Arctic Ocean to conduct short-term observations in oceanography, meteorology, terrestrial magnetism, and gravimetry. These comprised an impressive study of the central Arctic basin and resulted in some important geographical discoveries, including an undersea volcano and detection and survey of the underwater Lomonosov Ridge—named for the Russian scientist, poet, and grammarian of the eighteenth century. This great, submerged geological feature extends from Siberia toward Canada and Greenland and divides the ocean into two great rotating current systems that have a pronounced effect on drift ice. In its length, height, and rugged outline, the Lomonosov Ridge matches in grandeur the world's great mountain ranges. Soviet geologists studied the composition of the ocean floor while other scientists probed the ocean depth and measured the extent and limits of distribution of the layer of Atlantic water that had infiltrated the Arctic Ocean. Meteorologists brought back valuable data on the structure and movement of the polar atmosphere.

These postwar observations in the polar basin, however, were made during limited periods of time. They were carried out principally in the spring season, March through May, when weather and ice surface conditions were most suitable for aircraft operation. In order to gather more detailed and thorough information about the nature of the central Arctic during an extended period of the year, the Soviets in 1950 established a second drifting station like that of the Papanin Expedition of 1937 (North Pole 1). This new project resumed scientific investigations and provided regular weather data. An area north of Bering Strait was selected as the site for North Pole 2, because ice drift and currents had not been studied in that portion of the polar sea.

The scientific program projected was ambitious. The oceanographers proposed to conduct hydrobiological studies, make systematic collections of plankton, make basic hydrochemical analyses of water samples on the spot, and carry out long-range, continuous observation of currents. Other scientists were to investigate the thickness of sea ice, the relationship between air temperatures and ice thickness, compute the heat balance of the ice cover, determine the water content variations of the ice, observe gradients of wind, temperature, and humidity of the air immediately over the ice, influence of currents on the breakup of floes, and other matters. The results of these investigations were published in four volumes, three of which have been released. The fourth, on gravity measurements, is classified as a secret document by the Soviet government. Even during the International Geophysical Year the Soviets were reluctant to release information about gravity measurements because they have military implications. Local variations in gravity affect the paths of long-range missiles.

The first party of sixteen, led by M. M. Somov of the Arctic Institute, was landed on 1 April 1950 on the designated floe, about 300 miles northeast of Wrangel Island. The spot selected for the drifting station was a large stable floe about ten feet thick. The first meteorological report to the mainland was transmitted the next day by radio.

The pack ice surrounding the floe on which the camp was constructed stretched beyond the horizon—a great, boundless waste that was in constant motion, moving and churning, carried by the winds and currents. Fissures in the seemingly solid expanse would appear suddenly, threatening the camp. Precautions were taken to stay afloat should the station suddenly be immersed. Two rubber boats were kept ready. These boats were used for transportation during the summer when a wide lead opened between the camp and airfield.

Polar bears appeared at the drifting station eight times. Three were killed, the others were chased out of camp. A sentry was posted to prevent the surprise appearance of bears, and no one was permitted to go beyond the limits of the camp unarmed. The skin of any bear killed was to be awarded to the man who first spotted a bear, not to the one who killed it. The rule worked so well that not a single bear got into the camp undetected.

It is surprising that the Soviets, considering other measures they took to insure safety on the ice and their experience in the Arctic, neglected protection from fire. Apparently they thought that a fire in a tent is no particular threat except that the tent might be damaged or destroyed. They soon learned differently. A kerosene stove exploded and the tent housing the radio station burned in two or three minutes. The radio station was ruined. A makeshift creation, assembled by an ingenious technician from odds and ends of electronic equipment, was made to work. Fortunately, data on scientific observations being prepared for dispatch were saved. (A fire at the main Soviet station in Antarctica took the lives of eight men on 3 August 1960. The victims were six Russians, a Czech, and a German—all scientists.)

The snow at North Pole 2 began to melt about the middle of June, and this was followed by the melting of the ice which continued through July and the first half of August. During this period it was warm enough to work outdoors in shirt sleeves, but working conditions on the rotting, saturated ice floe were intolerable. Although the sun shone only on rare occasions, it was not particularly welcome since it accelerated the melting process. Great quantities of melt water accumulated on the floe, forming fresh-water ponds and puddles, many a foot or two deep, interspersed with occasional small areas of relatively dry ice. Movement about the camp became increasingly difficult. It was impossible to get rid of the insidious dampness that penetrated every corner of the living quarters.

The water created problems in addition to the physical discomfort it brought to the men. The mountings of the instruments loosened, the anchors for radio masts melted away, the airfield became a fresh-water lake, and twice during the summer period the work and living quarters had to be moved to elevated spots. The problem of melt water was solved partially during the early thaw period by boring holes through the puddles and draining the water out. Later, when the level of the fresh water on the floe was the same as the ocean, draining through bore holes was no longer effective.

During the summer months there were observations of plant and animal life other than bears, both in the water and on the ice. A large number of birds appeared in camp—snow buntings, gulls, and ducks. Several of an unidentified species of whale were seen, and seals often appeared in the open leads. Foxes, which usually prefer the mainland, were found following the plundering bears. Some were seen at North Pole 2 even in late autumn.

The party on the floe received a proposal from the Northern Sea Route Administration on 12 August to maintain the camp for an entire year. Everyone volunteered to remain. A landing strip was completed in late October, and on the twenty-fifth two planes made the first landings on ice in the central Arctic during the polar night. Kerosene torches improvised from tin cans lighted the runway and made the landing possible. About twenty tons of food, clothing, fuel, and additional housing were flown in.

Eleven men remained at the station for the entire winter period. It was a difficult time, much more so than the melt period during the summer months. The bitter cold and darkness were bad enough, but the unexpectedly quickened movement of ice during the winter months kept everyone apprehensive. There was thunderous crashing and crunching of hummocks, accompanied by strong, vibrating shocks which were felt in the camp. Their anxious position was endangered when the floe on which the drifting station rested was reduced to 120 x 210 feet in size. If the compression of ice continued, it was apparent the camp would be literally chopped and crushed to pieces. A more stable floe was discovered nearby on 17 February, and several days later all vital supplies and equipment were removed to it. But the new floe was also doomed, so that on 11 April 1951 the entire crew of North Pole 2 was flown to Wrangel Island and two days later departed for the mainland. They took with them the results of a year's research from one of the world's least known and most desolate areas.

Three years later, on 28 April 1954, at 75° 5′ N. and 184° 40′ E., a portion of the abandoned airfield of North Pole 2 was sighted from a reconnaissance plane. On 6 June a helicopter from the nearby recently established Station North Pole 4 landed a group of scientists on the floe—among them a scientist who had spent the year at North Pole 2. Several remarkable changes were noted. The tents, which were black when erected, were now almost white but in an excellent state of preservation. Most startling was their position. They stood like mushrooms on pillars of ice five feet high. The reindeer skins, used on the tent floors for protection from the cold in the winter, had insulated the ice from the warm air above during the summer so that the floe melted substantially everywhere except beneath the tents.

A study of the thickness of the floe revealed the uniformity of the thickness of the ice. It measured ten feet when the station was evacuated in April 1951; it was ten feet thick when measured in 1954. The floe had been growing on the underside as rapidly as it had been melting above.

North Pole 2 followed for 376 days a twisted path in the ice for more than 1,600 miles, but moved only 400 miles in a straight line.

The drifting stations had strategic significance. In 1954, therefore, the Soviet Union established additional stations. North Pole 3 and North Pole 4 were erected at 86° N. 176° W., and at 76°

N. 175° W. North Pole 5 was set up in 1955 at 82° N. 157° E., at which time North Pole 3 was abandoned. North Pole 6 was established in the spring of 1956 as a part of the Russian International Geophysical Year program, and North Pole 5 was abandoned that fall because it had drifted close to one of the Soviet controlled islands that already had a research station. North Pole 4 was evacuated in the spring of 1957 in the vicinity of northeast Greenland after having been in continuous operation for three years.

All of these stations were on pack ice with the exception of North Pole 6 which was on an ice island similar to T-3, twenty miles in circumference but only between thirty and forty feet thick. After the annual relief in the spring of 1959 the current carried North Pole 6 station, as expected, into the Greenland Sea. It was abandoned on 15 September 1959 at a position about 150 miles from the northeast tip of Greenland. During the three and a half years it was occupied, the station traveled approximately 5,800 miles as it moved on its tortuous path, and over 1,600 miles in a straight line.

The men on North Pole 7, who had experienced unusually low temperatures, were airlifted to the mainland in June 1959 after the floe had drifted to within 180 miles of Greenland. Since that time, Canadian flyers have observed the ice island well within Baffin Bay, off the coast of Labrador. While it is possible that the mass of thick ice negotiated the passage between Ellesmere Island and Greenland, it is far more likely that it was caught in the swifter currents that course the coast of Greenland, and moved around that island swiftly over the seasons to be borne by the northward-moving seas into Baffin Bay.

Meanwhile, North Pole 8, which had been established on sea ice in April 1959, some 500 miles northeast of Wrangel Island, drifted west-northwest. By November it was still 500 miles from Wrangel, but had drifted to a position due north of it. Summer melting on the floe was so extensive that aircraft landings were impossible until the freezing period began in September. North Pole 8 was located geographically near the spot that had been the starting point of North Pole 2 in 1950, but, strangely, it had followed a substantially different course to that of its predecessor which moved northward, then eastward and southward to form a circle in a clockwise drift.

An American aircraft landed on the ice pack in the spring of 1950. This first landing was by a ski-equipped Skymaster of the 10th Air Rescue Squadron under the leadership of Bernt Balchen, called back from retirement into active service when the Air Force expanded its operations in the north country. By the end of the year Balchen had developed a well-trained crew in polar navigation and operation, and they had made 150 successful landings and take-offs from the pack ice.

The first American camp on the ice was established in February 1951. Eight men were landed on a floe about 115 miles north of Barter Island in the Beaufort Sea. They erected their prefabricated huts, installed their scientific equipment, established radio contact with the mainland, and settled into a routine that lasted for only twenty-two days.

Early in the morning of 10 March, the wind picked up and soon it was blowing a violent gale; the whole camp vibrated as the wind screamed in the radio guidelines; the blowing snow, mixed with sea spray, reduced visibility to just a few feet. The pack snow began to move. There were sounds like the distant rumble of thunder. The formation of pressure ridges could be heard all around as the ice roiled into turmoil. Squalls blotted out ice and sky. The camp site sustained a succession of violent shocks as the floe broke up and a broad crack opened 100 feet from the camp. The men moved from the camp to a safer spot from which they watched in the hazy light as their huts were demolished. They radioed for help. The party was picked off the floe at noon by a plane that made a dangerous landing on the only frozen lead left on the floe. Three days later a plane flying over the area reported that all trace of the camp had disappeared.

Enthusiasm for drifting stations in the polar basin now vanished. The tentative scheme to establish a series of them was abandoned. The Russians, whose camps had also disintegrated under them, were proceeding with the installation of additional ice-floe stations. They were outstripping us rapidly in scientific and military knowledge of the Arctic basin.

CHAPTER XXIV

Ice Islands and Ice Floes

COLONEL JOSEPH FLETCHER, the Air Force officer who discovered the ice islands, wouldn't be dissuaded from further attempts at scientific stations. He discovered in 1951 that T-3, the smallest of the islands that had been located during the Ptarmigan flights, was slowly approaching the North Pole and was scheduled to reach it the following spring.

T-1 and T-2 had been temporarily lost, so T-3, because its position close to the Pole made it favorable for research purposes, was the best prospect for a permanent floating scientific station. Colonel Fletcher saw the Arctic Ocean as one vast floating landing field during most of the year, but he said that a floating island would be a fine platform for a scientific expedition. Suitable runways could be prepared easily so that supplies could be flown in during most of the year. He also said that submarines could be used for delivering supplies, since open water had been observed on one side or the other side of the ice island as it drifted in the pack ice.

Colonel Fletcher found an enthusiastic supporter in Major General William Old, Commander, Alaskan Air Command. The first landing was made on T-3 in a ski-equipped Skytrain on 19 March 1952. At the time the ice island was 103 miles south of the North Pole. The expedition was called "Project Icicle," and the landing party included Major General Old; Colonel Fletcher; Captain Mike Brinegar, assisting Colonel Fletcher; Captain Lou Erhart, the pilot; and a civilian scientist, Dr. Kaare Rodahl, who has described the venture in his excellent book, *North*. Navigation for the flight, which began in Thule, Greenland, was provided by three accompanying Skymasters.

The party found that T-3 measured approximately five miles in width and nine miles in length. The surface of the island on its outer edge varied from five to ten feet above the pack ice. Colonel Fletcher, Captain Brinegar, and Dr. Rodahl remained for thirteen days to study the possibilities of setting up a permanent camp. Their report brought additional men, supplies, and equipment for a year-round scientific station. The island was designated "Fletcher's Island" and since has been popularly known by that name, as well as "T-3" and more recently as Station "B" or "Bravo."

The scientific program included meteorology, glaciology, oceanography, and geophysics. These studies were continued for more than two years by rotating groups of Air Force personnel and scientists. They stopped because T-3 had drifted close to the weather station "Alert" on the northern tip of Ellesmere Island. The camp was temporarily evacuated, but a small party of scientists again occupied it from April to September 1955.

Following this period, scientific investigations by the United States in the Arctic Ocean came to a virtual standstill. Then on 15 June 1956 the National Academy of Sciences requested logistic support for Arctic research on ice islands as part of the network of stations being organized for the world-wide effort known as the International Geophysical Year. The forerunners of the International Geophysical Year—the first International Polar Year of 1882–83 had fourteen meteorological stations in operation, twelve in the Arctic and two in the Antarctic, and added much to our knowledge of meteorology; the second International Polar Year of 1932–33, with ninety-four stations manned in the Arctic, made further great advances in meteorology and initiated additional studies of the ionosphere, but meteorology was again emphasized because of the progress and potential of polar aviation. For the first time reliable information was provided about polar weather.

The International Geophysical Year involved sixty-six nations and carried out a wide range of research in many sciences. The United States Air Force established and supported two IGY ice stations. The project was called "Ice Skate." T-3 or Fletcher's Island was one station, and the second, in the absence of another suitable ice island, was constructed on an ice floe and called "Alpha." In the meantime the Soviet also planned to man two drifting stations during the IGY.

Finding a suitable floe for Alpha was difficult. In March reconnaissance flights resulted in the tentative selection of general areas for the station. Major Richard E. Freeman, who had been designated commander of the installation, Father Tom Cunningham, a weather-beaten Jesuit missionary to the Eskimos of Point Barrow, who from thirty years of first-hand studies knew the pack ice intimately, and Fritz Awe, another special adviser to the Air Force for Arctic operations, made a landing on a tentative site 600 miles north of Point Barrow, the northernmost spot in the United States. In the unsuccessful 1951 attempt to establish a station on an ice floe there was some criticism because of its closeness to the coast line. This time the station would be well within the pack. Even so, everyone realized that a station established on an ice floe, following the Soviet pattern, would not have as long life as one on an ice island.

The ice floe was two miles wide by two and a half miles long. A safe landing was made as the aircraft used less than a thousand feet of the uneven ice. The temperatures were so low the engines of the plane were left running while the party scouted the floe. In the short time they were on the floe they drilled holes to determine the thickness of the ice; they were pleased to find it to be fifteen feet in spots, thicker than the average. Three men were left behind to carry out further studies on the suitability of the floe for research purposes. In less than two weeks after the first landing, the tentative site was accepted as the location for establishing a permanent installation and two Skytrains landed with construction equipment. On 19 April two huge, four-engine Cargomasters air dropped heavy equipment, including a 16,000-pound caterpillar and an Arctic weasel, a tractor-like vehicle that had a comfortable heated cabin and two-way radio equipment. On 27 May the first Cargomasters were able to land on the runway, dynamited and bulldozed into shape over the hummocky sea ice. Airlifting cargoes in support of Alpha continued as an uneventful operation about a month, and by June the research program was under way.

The summer months and the following year passed easily. The station complement, consisting on the average of from six to nine scientists and ten to fifteen Air Force supporting men, was relieved periodically. Everyone adjusted to the monotony of isolated camp life. Scientific studies ranged from probes of the depths of the sea to observing the aurora borealis, which draped the polar night with its bright colors. The camp was always aware of weather, either summertime slush and numbing water that seemed to cover the entire icescape, or winter blizzards that beat their way across the frosted sea. The everlasting roar of the ice floes ripping each other apart was joined by man-made echoing explosions as the scientists sought to find the floor of the ocean.

Occasionally a bear shook up the camp. Two Eskimo huskies were flown in to serve as watchdogs, and men were instructed not to leave camp unless they were armed with rifles. The polar bears were no surprise. They have been reported at sea as much as fifty miles away from land or from the nearest floe. They can swim almost as fast as the average man can run, and they float so high in the water that it is easy for them to rest while voyaging.

The bear lives mainly on the sea and catches his food there, practically all of which is seal. This white giant with an elongated neck, sometimes weighing 1,600 pounds, migrates south with the ice pack in the winter and follows it northward in the spring.

Generally an inoffensive and even an amusing animal, the hungry polar bear is a dangerous animal, a great traveler, a powerful predator with the agility of a cat. In Northwestern Greenland in 1955 a polar bear that had climbed the Greenland icecap was killed 200 miles from the coast where its food source was located. In June 1959 a polar bear attacked six unarmed Frenchmen, members of the International Glaciological Expedition while they were preparing a camp 6,600 feet above sea level on the Greenland icecap, almost 200 miles inland from Scoresby Sound on the east coast. All escaped. A female sled dog fought a bloody battle with a polar bear to save the life of the commander of one of the ice-floe stations in the Beaufort Sea, several hundred miles from the nearest land.

The seal is the only other large mammal which is found all over the northern sea at all times of the year. The walrus is unable to make a hole in the ice for feeding as the seal does, so never ventures far into the ice. There is evidence that whales, especially Beluga or white whales, cross the Arctic Ocean in midsummer. In the sea the small animals eat the plants and the large animals eat the small animals. The seal, for example, eats the shrimp and now and then a fish; and the polar bear eats the seal. The walrus, a friendly animal allied to the seal, has deadly tusks which extend as much as two feet, but lives almost entirely on small animals, mainly clams. An exception to the general rule is that most of the whales live mainly on tiny animals and plants.

The Soviet exploratory campaign and our most recent efforts during the International Geophysical Year have uncovered much information on resources of the northern sea. It was generally believed that the Arctic Ocean teems with life, but it has been found to be one of the most barren of the world's oceans. The

IGY studies involved measurements of the amount of photosynthesis taking place in the Arctic Ocean and of chlorophyll and nutrients in the water. The poverty of the Arctic Ocean in nitrate and phosphate nutrients makes its productivity level one of the lowest in the world.

Everyone on Alpha dreaded the coming of February; they had been told that the floe would be most dangerous then, but nothing happened. The tension which developed during the dark winter months vanished when the sun returned in March. By the end of April the men on the floe were experiencing twenty-four hours of daylight, and basking in the warm sun whenever it penetrated the fog and clouds. April, however, brought increased ice pressure and movement in the form of an ice ridge. There was fear of the camp breaking apart, but after reviewing the situation the Alaskan Air Command decided to continue the operation on a day-by-day basis. A nearby floe was earmarked as a substitute location for the station in case of emergency.

Although visitors by air could not reach the floe during the melting period, the group was surprised to have guests from underwater. In 1958 the USS *Skate,* a nuclear-powered submarine, was sent north to navigate beneath ice floes or possibly to locate openings in the ice cover—long cracks called "leads," lakelike areas that had been labeled *polynya,* a word borrowed from the Russians.

The *Skate* surfaced on 14 August in a polynya fifty yards from the main camp. At the time there were twenty-nine men stationed at Alpha. The crew of the *Skate* were the first visitors for months. All air traffic had been called off because the runway was immersed in melt water. The visit was cut short by the movement of the pack ice that threatened to close the polynya before the sub could submerge. The *Skate* exchanged ten gallons of ice cream for polar-bear steaks, took on mail, and departed.

The months passed quickly in hard work. In October the sun

again sank below the horizon. The increased movement of the pack ice hinted of trouble. Fresh leads yawned and new fractures appeared daily, one cutting directly across the runway. A late October storm reduced the size of the floe by about 30 per cent from the original area which had measured several square miles. On November 6 a furious storm, whirling wildly with snow, hit and raged through the night. Its fury broke the station in two. The runway was separated from the main camp area of 21 buildings by one and a half miles of open water, and was so broken up that no stretch of it was more than 2,000 feet in length.

Even though the men had thought they were ready for any crisis, they now were frightened and sent out an emergency radio alarm. They told the Air Force that they were marooned on a piece of ice 1,000 feet square, and that what remained of the island was continuing to break apart. An air cover was quickly organized. Two transport planes and a weather reconnaissance craft from Thule were assigned to fly over the floe constantly until a rescue plane could snatch the party and remove it to safety. The air-cover and rescue plane flew out into the long night and the thick weather. The perverse Arctic weather momentarily abated. Flare pots along the abbreviated landing strip on the ice were used to augment the moonlight. The twin-engine transport slid in for a ski landing. The men and valuable records were hustled aboard and the plane with the assistance of jet boosters took off again.

At the time of its evacuation on 7 November 1958, drifting station Alpha was 300 miles from the North Pole, 960 miles northeast of Point Barrow, and 600 miles northwest of Thule. The party was rescued just in time. The ice floe was disintegrating so rapidly that another day might have been fatal.

The breakup of drifting station Alpha did much to augment the IGY research being conducted on T-3 and to extend investigations begun on Alpha. The next step was drifting station "Charlie," originally labeled "Alpha 2." This was a joint Air Force-Navy responsibility, with the Air Force responsible for supply. During

March 1959, Navy patrol bombers and Air Force Weather Reconnaissance planes conducted an extensive search for suitable ice-pack fields. On 10 April two Navy planes from the Navy's Arctic Research Center at Point Barrow landed on a site 225 miles north of Point Barrow. Air Force Captain James Smith, former commander of Alpha, and Max Brewer, Navy Arctic expert, were flown in a Cessna to the ice pack and landed on a small, recently frozen lead. The floe was surveyed and found acceptable, so on 15 April a Skytrain, piloted by Air Force Captain James H. Graham, landed on the frozen lead with a construction party of fifteen. Within hours Cargomasters began dropping equipment and supplies. Favorable weather prevailed for two weeks, and in this period the supplies dropped included housing, weasels, tool kits, food, and clothing. Ninety per cent of the material dropped, an unusually high figure, was recovered; in contrast, one drop at the Soviet North Pole 2 lost everything.

Station Charlie's floe measured approximately five by seven miles and floated in a mosaic of a thousand other floes. In late May an area about one mile wide broke away from the southeast and west sides. This was the only notable loss from the floe during the spring and summer period, although areas of a hundred feet or so sheared away or ridged occasionally.

During the warm months of 1959 melting was severe. Early in August ice-temperature profiles were taken and revealed that the ocean water was colder than the ice at any level except where ice and water were in contact. The ice cracked, opening a number of natural drain holes that emptied great quantities of melt water into the ocean. Melt water also formed small lakes reaching depths of more than three feet. Sometimes the bottoms of the ponds became so weakened that they broke loose and bobbed to the surface like corks. The edges of the ponds were undercut as much as ten to twelve feet, creating a hazard in the operation of heavy equipment. The runway, which was on ice originally six feet three inches thick, melted until toward the later part of the summer it measured only four feet ten inches. Except for trash disposal, all vehicle operations outside the immediate camp area had to be stopped in mid-July.

Weather conditions varied from raging blizzards to placid days with sunny skies until late October; then temperatures dropped as low as 30° below zero. The highest temperature, 39°, was recorded at the beginning of August. Monthly averages were above 30° during June, July, and the first half of August. Very little freezing occurred until the first of September. Fog and low ceilings prevailed throughout the period, and rain on several occasions made life on the floe even more miserable. Sometimes rain and temperature combined to melt the ice so rapidly that the men felt their lives might be in danger. On the other hand, nine inches of snow fell during one three-day period in July. It melted almost as quickly as it fell, and the run-off added to the size of the pools on the ice. They were now taking on the appearance of small lakes.

Official weather records for 140 days—from the fourteenth of May through the thirtieth of September—revealed only 6 per cent clear days, 20 per cent partly cloudy, and 74 per cent completely overcast. Visibility of less than one-half mile was recorded approximately two-fifths of the time, so that even if the runway had been available for aircraft landings the weather would have prevented them. The winds blew ceaselessly and often maintained velocities above twenty-five miles per hour.

The runway surface deteriorated rapidly in June. Snow melted and ran off into puddles, and no new snow fell. The ice runway was now almost unserviceable, and only emergency flights were permitted. The water level of the ponds was the same as the sea level, so it was not possible to drain them. There were no large capacity pumps available. An attempt to freeze the pond water by chipping and shaving ice into it didn't work. When a Caterpillar tractor broke through the edge of one pond, operation of heavy equipment was halted in the immediate vicinity of ponds and near the edges of the floe. Despite all precautions two other major items of equipment, a Caterpillar and a weasel, were lost through the ice. Fortunately, no operator suffered more than a minor scratch or wet feet and, in one case, a good ducking. In the heart of the Arctic everyone longed for freezing weather.

The runway was closed on 16 June, having by then taken thirty-one landings by four-engine aircraft and eighteen by twin-engine planes. The field was not open for operation again until 109 days later, 3 October, when a four-engine plane arrived at the station. During the time intervening, two and a half months, the station personnel was dependent upon air drops for mail, supplies, and equipment.

Meanwhile, the floe drifted out of range for twin-engine cargo planes. The path the floe followed was a meandering one, but it migrated in a general northwesterly direction. The distance traveled in a straight line was 450 nautical miles; the actual distance traveled, however, was easily three to four times the direct distance. A total of twenty-eight men, twelve military and sixteen civilians, manned the ice floe station over the summer period. Nineteen were quartered in Jamesway huts, four in helicop huts, two each in the oceanographic and sound laboratories, and one in the weather-bureau office.

During the construction period, while the runway was being leveled and all housing accommodations were being constructed, the schedule called for everybody to work fourteen hours a day. On 1 July this was reduced to eight hours a day, seven days a week, as the work load slackened. Twice during the melting season all structures had to be removed from ice pedestals that had grown to elevations of one and a half to two feet, because the buildings had insulated the ice beneath them from the sun.

Communications with the mainland and overhead aircraft were always maintained. In addition to their normal duties, communications' personnel provided a daily newspaper and phone "patch" through a "ham" in Peru, Indiana. The paper was brought out by the "Nowhere Publishing Company," and telephone service was provided by the "Arctic Basin Tel & Tel.—Northernmost Modern Dial Telephone System in the World." A telephone directory was published monthly, though no new listings occurred between 1 July and 1 October when the runway on the floe was closed to air traffic. The paper carried some serious pieces written by the commanding officer as well as many tongue-in-cheek columns. The classified section included advertising of such sprightly items as "Hydro-holes dug. Reasonable rates. Specializing in submarine geology and biology." Another promoted "Gast and Perry, winch operators. Arctic Ocean bottom samples by appointment. Haircuts our sideline specialty."

Even though by 1959 the Air Force had considerable polar experience and the problems of living in isolation were well known, for some reason extensive screening, testing, or training of the men assigned for duty at Station Charlie was ignored. Selections were made from a casual review of personnel records, and no attempt was made to determine if any men would be unsuitable for life on an ice floe. Selectees, some of whom were bad choices, were taken to Elmendorf Air Base at Anchorage, given routine physicals, and then told to report to the Project Officer.

Much of the equipment for the ice floe never went through Elmendorf where the airmen were supposed to be trained in its use. A man might see a new instrument for the first time when it reached the ice floe.

Five civilians landed with the first party. These included two carpenters, an electrician, and two Eskimo equipment operators, one of whom had participated in construction of Station Alpha and was well acquainted with building problems on an ice floe.

Morale was at its highest at the beginning when the work was so demanding that it called for extra effort. There was a noticeable decline, however, when life at the camp reached a routine, even though there was plenty of work. A few personality clashes did occur. Status, either military or civilian, did not appear to be a particularly important factor, even though the civilian pay was far higher. The civilians were on a controlled schedule and knew when they would be relieved, but those on Air Force assignment were always more or less uncertain about when they would be able to leave the floe.

Isolated unpleasant incidents ran all the way from minor complaints regarding personal hygiene and pipe smoking of bunkmates to the serious matter of a recommendation by the contractor's representative that a contract for further services at the station not be renewed. He argued that the Air Force had not kept its promises about some comforts to which he thought he was entitled. Most of these were isolated incidents. Delayed shipments, items damaged during air drop, lack of fresh food, tobacco, movies, and mail were major vexations. To avoid irritations, no heavy, noisy equipment was operated during normal sleeping hours, and activity that would interfere with delicate instruments used in research was eliminated.

Although Station Charlie was planned as a modest research installation and the military complement was usually a fixed one, no definite figures were ever firmly established governing civilians who were to be on the floe as construction workers, scientists, or visitors. Too often the first information received on the ice floe of visitors en route to the station was notification of their arrival at Ladd Field where they would await further transportation. The huts, the only oases of comfort on the floe, were frequently crowded.

The problem was further complicated by the irregular arrival and departure of construction workers. A carpenter, an electrician and an Arctic advisor, specialists in their fields, departed before their assignments were completed on the last aircraft to leave before the runway was closed in June for the summer months. On the other hand, two members of the IGY scientific team, although advised they might be marooned for months, decided to take their chances on relief and continued their studies. As it turned out, they were not able to leave until October.

The selection of qualified airmen for the ice floe did not improve with the passing of time, and there were some bad choices at the station. Some of them believed that by accepting assignment to Charlie they were escaping from the world. Rotation of military personnel began with the first aircraft landing of the fall season. Five airmen arrived on the first plane, but three were found unsuitable for duty on Station Charlie and had to be returned to the mainland. One, a heavy equipment operator, had had no experience with Diesel or construction equipment; another heavy equipment man became ill with a stomach ulcer after three days on the ice floe and was not available for duty after that; the third, a supply man with a history of frostbite, was virtually one-handed so far as outside work was concerned, and it was immediately apparent that for him exposure to low temperatures was out of the question.

The summer and fall months turned into a sunless and cold winter. The weather was abominable and flying conditions were risky. Mindful of the problems involved in evacuating Station Alpha on a day's notice, plans were made for an emergency departure from Charlie. Floe ice is unstable, and a vicious storm can quickly break up a floe. Withdrawal plans took into account not only the evacuation of men but also the salvage of equipment and instruments. Everything would be removed to Point Barrow, now at a distance of approximately 400 miles.

Late in December the camp radioed that the floe had begun to erode at an alarming rate and general conditions were described as "unstable." The runway scraped out by bulldozers during the summer was reduced from 5,000 to 3,700 feet but was still long enough for twin-engine cargo planes. The floe had been slowly reduced to approximately two by four miles in area. Then, without any more warning, the breakup came. The ice floe heaved and bucked and suddenly sheared to about one-fourth its size. The station's situation now became desperate. On 7 January 1960 the removal plan went into effect. It was expected that the withdrawal would be orderly and could be accomplished in five to seven days.

The Air Force acted instantly when it received the message that requested immediate relief. Other agencies took the radio call differently. The air waves were filled with alarming messages. Newsmen evidently said the first thing that came to their minds. The Voice of America, as reported from Tangiers, said that the floe was capsizing. A broadcast received by the men at the station told them that seventeen of them had drowned. The men managed to quell the rumor through "ham" operators in the United States and Canada. The main problem for them all was to get off the station as quickly as they could.

The sixteen scientists were supposed to leave with their data and equipment as rapidly as possible. The thirteen Air Force men were to be the last to leave so they could pack and load equipment on cargo planes. On the first day, four of the scientists were taken to Point Barrow. On 9 January four airmen who were transport experts were flown to Station Charlie to pack expensive equipment.

The buffeting of the sea now was reducing the size of the floe alarmingly. There was only a brief daily period of twilight, and all work was hampered by the darkness. Then a 3,500-foot section of the floe was separated from the main portion by a lead sixty feet in width, bringing the edge of the floe to within three quarters of a mile of the base camp. The floe continued to shift and break. The big split had reduced the runway by a half mile in length. On the following day, the tenth, another 200 feet of the already dangerously short runway broke off, leaving about 3,500 feet of useful length. Ice deterioration and pressure-ridge action continued, reducing the island to about one-fifth its original size. Routine withdrawal was now out of the question. The evacuation operation had to be accelerated.

On 13 January, when sixteen persons still remained on the floe, Brigadier General Gordon H. Austin, Commander 11th Air Division, and Captain James F. Smith, Project Officer for Charlie and the other installation, T-3, flew to Charlie for a personal inspection. They were accompanied by a Navy officer who was to supervise removal of specialized equipment. On arrival General Austin and Captain Smith saw the immediate danger and issued new orders to hurry the evacuation. By the time the General's party had taken off, new cracks appeared within 500 feet of the base camp. Five more men were removed on the thirteenth. Two days later ice station Charlie became just another broken chunk of ice lost in the blackness of the Arctic Ocean when an Air Force plane carrying the last of the men lifted its wheels from the cracked runway.

The final act performed aboard the crumbling floe was the lowering of the Stars and Stripes. The men who remained to the end stood at attention in the sub-zero weather to salute the wind-tattered flag. Then they removed the flag and carried it with them to Ladd Field where it was presented to General Austin.

The Air Force had successfully completed the second aerial evacuation from an ice floe in less than fifteen months. This time, however, in addition to airmen and officers, the rescue planes had carried away almost 120 tons of scientific and supporting equipment valued at a fifth of a million dollars. Although the ice island was rapidly disintegrating, Air Force planes and men landed and took off regularly to carry out removal operations planned long in advance, based on experience gained when ice station Alpha broke up. The only equipment left on the island for nature to bury in the shifting ice pack were expendable Jamesway huts used for work areas, the mess hall, and the flare pots and runway lights needed for the last take-off in the darkness of the Arctic day.

On 15 January 1960 some of the Jamesway huts and the barren flagpole were all that could be seen from a plane of the remains of station Charlie, still flirting with huge ice ramparts. The floe had practically disappeared.

CHAPTER XXV

Bravo

ON 8 APRIL 1960 I took off for Bravo, the new elaborate station on T-3, from Ladd Air Force Base in an Avitruc twin-engine cargo plane. As we flew over northern Alaska at 10,000 feet the pack ice and frozen, snow-covered tundra below congealed into an unbroken crust, glistening white in the clear sun. It was impossible to pick out the ice-encrusted coast line. Although outside temperatures were well below zero, the inside of the cavernous plane was kept at near room temperature. Six enlisted men and five civilian construction specialists, all flying in for a tour of duty on the ice island, perspired freely in heavy layers of Arctic clothing topped with a cumbersome parachute.

The weather was clear, and, with the radio beacon working to perfection, the flight lasted only three and a half hours. Glistening in the bright morning sun, Bravo's slightly yellowish hue and one elevated edge made it stand out conspicuously from the surrounding ice pack. Although not split with fissures and leads of open water as were the surrounding ice floes, the island viewed from above had a recognizable drainage system which gives it the

254

appearance of a huge, irregular washboard. But to rely solely on visual methods to locate Bravo, a floating ice cube far out in the endless mass of pack ice covering the Arctic Ocean, would have been useless. The best navigator requires the aid of electronic devices. Even in good weather it is a tough job to locate an ice field, land passengers and cargo on its frozen surface, then take off and fly back to the mainland.

Between the time of take-off from Ladd and arrival at Bravo the weather can change all the way from clear, unlimited visibility to blizzards and perilous white-outs. There were times when a plane flying on instruments would circle the neighborhood of Bravo for an hour or so without seeing clear sky or ice surface and, sweating out a dwindling gas supply, would have to return to the mainland without having landed on the island. The homer beacon, an electronic necessity for locating Bravo, is of no help to the pilot who has no depth perception in a white-out.

Fortunately, the weather was fine on our flight and the landing was as smooth as going into Idlewild. When the cargo doors opened, a blast of minus 29° air swished upward. The mercury dropped 90° in a matter of seconds, and it was an effort to breathe. The high wind ripped at my face and bare hands as I stepped out on the ice to take pictures of the hurried unloading operation. In minutes my movie and still cameras began to perform sluggishly and my perspiration-matted hair instantly turned into icicles. The unloading operation was so well organized that in less than an hour the plane had discharged its cargo, including the most welcome shipment of all, a large sack of mail, had then taken on cartons of clothing being sent to Ladd for laundering, and had flown off in a swirl of snowflakes for Fairbanks, with a refueling stop at Point Barrow.

There were thirteen scientists and fifteen GI's who lived on Bravo. The six enlisted men on the flight relieved six who were being rotated to a post in a warm climate. The customary duty on Bravo was three to six months, and was never extended beyond six months. During this period the airmen were separated from the outside world and its diversions except for radio programs, occasional private radio-telephone conversations with home through a "ham" operator, and mail brought in fairly regularly by plane or by drop when landing conditions were unsuitable.

The men on Bravo knew they were the shock troops in a battle for understanding and control of one of the world's most lonely yet critical areas, an area which some believe could be the center of any future war. As front-line soldiers in the battle of the Arctic Ocean, they looked to their first skirmishes not with men but with the elements. They were briefed to expect winds with gale velocities, blizzards that prevent all outdoor activity, and white-outs thicker than pea soup. They were reassured by the knowledge that the mercury in the thermometer would not drop as low as it does at the other end of the world and on the Greenland Icecap. Indeed, a young man from northern Minnesota discovered that winter on the polar sea is not much colder than back home. The lowest recorded temperature on Bravo during the entire period of its occupancy as an IGY station was minus 65°, lower than that experienced on the thinner ice floes near the Pole. The wind velocity during most storms ranged between thirty and sixty miles per hour, whereas winds of greater force were not nearly as commonplace as they are at Air Force installations in Greenland and in Antarctica.

Men on the ice island were isolated in a physical world as unreal as the moon and which, after a few months, began to seem almost as alien. This was the loneliest and most forbidding of all our military outposts. For mile on mile the icy barren offered no relief. There was no tree, no shrub, no greenery of any kind, and no animal life except an occasional fox, polar bear, sea bird, or seal on the pack ice surrounding the island. In summer the sun rarely showed itself through the murky overcast, and in winter it stayed below the unrelieved horizon. When the summer sun did shine, the island had a ghostly attractiveness—glistening white, pinnacled, and hummocky, like a lunar landscape covered with snow. But the visions of beauty were only occasional and fleeting. More often than not, snow and sleet driven almost horizontally blotted out the hummocks, the runway, and the huts, and in the distance the moving pack sounded like the roar of surf. Day and night the wind played mournfully among the wires supporting the radio mast and huts. Sometimes it howled and sometimes it moaned, but it sounded incessantly over the dreary shingles of this fantastic world.

The only place for the men to go to get away from the boredom of the camp was the edge of the ice island, there to look out over the shifting pack ice piled high in blue-white ridges and hummocks, sometimes reaching upwards to seventy feet. When torn by the wind, the pack split—shrieking, groaning, and grinding, and building still more lofty ridges.

Bravo consisted of a number of prefabricated huts, each about as large as three small rooms placed end to end. In a typical one there were six bunks with mattresses, warm woolen blankets, and clean sheets. Each man had his private cubicle with a shelf for small personal objects and hanging room for his clothing. The paneled walls were decorated with marked calendars and pin-up girls. At one end of the hut was a tiny lounge with a day bed, a couple of comfortable armchairs, a writing desk, and a study lamp. The oddest sight on Bravo was to see each hut perched, sometimes precariously, on a column of clear blue ice six feet high. To reach the hut rough steps were hewn into the ice and a rope hand rail put up for support and guidance. In the summer the huts served as insulation for the ice beneath them and, as melting occurred around them, the huts were left stuck in the air like mushrooms. Periodically they had to be moved to flat areas where the process of melting was repeated.

There were no needlessly contrived duties on Bravo. With all hands busy, morale was no problem. From interviews with men on the ice and others who had spent time on Bravo, I learned that all had adjusted well to their strange surroundings; they seldom quarreled, and, although there were the differences of opinion found in any human society, none was brushed with even a trace of bitterness. The same attitude of co-operation that had distinguished the lonely life on Alpha and Charlie was found on Bravo. It was sincere; consideration of each member of the island's population for the daily problems and anxieties of his associates left no room for clash of personalities.

The IGY group on Bravo had learned from the mistakes made during the earlier occupancy of the island when it was known as T-3 or Fletcher's Island. During the first nine months, when T-3 was still in an experimental stage, there were distressing personality clashes between the commander, an Air Force Major who had had Arctic experience and from his record seemed well qualified for the post, and the rest of the men. The Major's background of polar work, however, was no guarantee that he possessed the qualities of leadership, and he became a serious encumbrance to the success of the scientific program. His administration of the work on the island resulted in a series of directives, many of which were contradictory, all of which were confusing, and most of which were not worthy of execution. Some of the airmen were so perplexed by his behavior that they ominously questioned his mental stability. One of the more mature scientists on the ice island contemplated sending out a report of the Major's conduct with a recommendation that he be removed. A competent psychologist who was sent to the island to study the situation concluded that the officer was not actually mentally ill but a pronounced eccentric.

The observer found the Major entirely lacking in personal daintiness, untidy, wearing tattered, grease-stained clothing, and even boasting that he had not had a change of garments in months. While not in any sense an alcoholic, he fermented liquor from fruit. Repeatedly he lost his temper, particularly at meal times, when he chastised the enlisted men and scientists for not carrying out chores which apparently he had never assigned. The Major would let no one forget that he was an Arctic explorer and, there- fore, by some twisted reasoning was justified in insisting that everyone on the island "rough it." By this he meant, among other things, sleeping in unheated quarters. The Major permitted policing of T-3 to be neglected; buildings became filthy, and haphazard disposal of garbage and excreta constituted a danger to health. Filth set the tone of the station, and the stench was pervasive and steady. He complained that the group on the ice was becoming soft because it was supplied with too many comforts. A frosty social climate was the result. In short, even though on paper he looked good, the commander had been an unfortunate choice for a position of leadership.

The airmen on Bravo were carefully selected volunteers. Their technical proficiency was superior, and they passed rigid physical examinations. Anyone with a history of marital or dis- ciplinary problems, with neurotic tendencies, or any kind of troubled past, was eliminated. Even the health of a man's im- mediate family was taken into account. Finally, each man had had at least five years of creditable military service, but former Arctic experience was considered to be of secondary importance.

Bravo at that time was a kidney-shaped, 42-square mile mass of ice floating in an ocean of salt water, completely surrounded by frozen pack ice. It was about 170 feet thick. In the summer, as on Alpha and Charlie, fresh-water ponds developed in the low areas and rivers formed from which fresh water could be drawn for the camp. During one mild summer season the surface level dropped three feet by melting. In the winter the ponds, lakes, and rivers on the island froze over, but one pond was pierced daily for the water supply which was hauled back to camp in barrels on a sled.

The freshness of the water was no mystery. Bravo was of glacial ice, centuries old, and the frozen pond from which the water was drawn was only about twenty feet deep, no lower than the level of the surrounding sea ice, so it remained crystal clear glacial water, absolutely free from salt, as palatable as water drawn from an artesian well.

For the decade Bravo has been under surveillance it has journeyed along an irregular path, but generally southwestward. At the time of my brief visit the island was traveling through shoal water off northern Alaska, and there was some anxiety about when it would turn north again. Earlier it had seemed to be headed straight toward Siberia. In early April of 1960 there was only 170 feet of water between the bottom of Bravo and the continental shelf.

In its twisted travels Bravo also moved around and around slowly with the shifting wind and currents, so that from time to time one might enjoy a sunset and sunrise from the same window or watch rivers on the ice reverse direction as the island was tilted by the shifting winds. Incoming pilots were never sure when they left Ladd Field what the orientation of the runway on Bravo would be. As an interesting check point, they used the ice-covered shell of a Skymaster that arrived there some years ago and never managed to get off the island. It now sits on a fourteen-foot pedestal of ice that was shaded by the plane's body and did not melt.

In the camp were two cooks, both staff sergeants, who prepared delicious high-calorie meals, comparable to any found in quality restaurants. Bravo was no place to diet. The bountiful breakfast usually included cereal, fruit, bacon, fresh eggs, coffee, tea, and milk. Luncheon was comparable, and the hearty evening meal usually consisted of an appetizer, fresh vegetables, steak, salad, and dessert. Apart from emergency stocks cached a short distance from the main station as a fire precaution, the camp carried food for only thirty days as Bravo could always be supplied by air.

The principal attraction after the well-prepared food was the camp movie where recent films were shown. This was located in a special hut which had been turned into a movie house seating about a dozen men, each with an overstuffed armchair. The same picture was shown twice every night so that the men could choose the early or late show. This arrangement also made it possible to accommodate the busy scientists who kept unusual working hours determined by the demands of their instruments.

No effort was spared in looking after the comfort of the men. They had recreational facilities, guns for hunting, fishing gear, skis, snowshoes, and, for the less athletic, indoor activities including cards, Ping-pong and hi-fi music. Even so, regular receipt of mail was the major factor in high morale.

Most of the men did not feel that living on Bravo was nearly as bad as they had expected it to be, even though a low temperature of −65° F. was reached. Some felt the work was monotonous, routine, and perhaps unnecessary, and they regretted that there was little opportunity to improve their job performance. One of the most important contributions to the morale of the men on Bravo was the provision for unimpeachable medical care. They knew there were adequate medical supplies on hand and that radio contact was maintained regularly with other bases. A realistic and satisfactory medical evacuation program was planned, and knowledge of this was most satisfactory.

Fire hazards were given strict attention, but many valuable records and equipment were destroyed in the one fire they experienced on the island. The fire occurred about a mile from the main camp in a 6 x 8′ wood and canvas hut used as a laboratory. The blaze was spotted by one of the civilian scientists who noted a deep red glow in the Arctic night, but the hut had burned to the snow before the men reached it. Only a few feet of charred seismographic records were salvaged.

The research program was comprehensive, including studies to determine the nature of the earth's crust under the Arctic Ocean, evidences of changing climate, ocean currents, the sun's radiation, aurora borealis, gravity, and sea life.

One of the interesting studies on Bravo was being conducted by a marine biologist. The investigation was designed to treat the earth's oceans as gardens, using fertilizers to force the growth of plants for food for fish, thereby leading fish to predetermined spots to be caught. In the relatively barren Arctic Sea, such an experiment might show remarkable results.

The structure of the ice was examined for clues to past climates. To do this the scientists bored a hole fifty-two feet into the island. The core, four inches in diameter, that came out of the hole disclosed fifty-eight identifiable layers of dirt. The scientists who studied the boring found the top layer thicker than that underneath. If the smallest dirt layer was a single year's accumulation, they reasoned that from the evidence of the top layer, the present warming climate has lasted for a century.

We can now plot roughly the currents which move the ice pack and ice islands from a study of the paths over the polar sea covered by Storkerson, the Papanin North Pole Drift expedition, ice island drifting stations on ice floes, and by ships (occupied or abandoned) drifting along with the ice which beset them. There is a basic clockwise current around the Pole, with a number of secondary eddies on the outskirts of the main drift, most of them located off the Siberian coast. An ice floe at the North Pole, such as the one on which the Papanin expedition was landed by plane, would gradually drift to the North Atlantic. The North Pole is itself a way-station on the migration of ice, and not the center.

The ice floe which is fairly close to shore will start on a long, twisting, tortuous journey all around the Arctic Ocean before it finds itself over the North Atlantic. A piece of ice off Point Barrow, for instance, in successive years will be west of Wrangel Island, north of Siberia; farther west the next year, north of Franz Joseph Land; then, it drifts westward and southward, past Spitzbergen, into the gap between Norway and Greenland.

This route of the drift is supported by the experience of several iced-in ships of explorers, as well as the more recent drifting scientific stations. The *Karluk,* of the third Stefansson expedition, was caught in the ice about twenty-five miles north of Alaska and drifted westward until she was crushed, less than four months later, fifty miles northeast of Wrangel Island, near the northeastern tip of Siberia. De Long's *Jeannette* started to drift in 1897 near Wrangel Island, went in the same western direction along the coast, and was crushed a year and a half later north of the New Siberian Islands. Nansen's *Fram* was caught in the ice near these islands in 1893, and after almost three years of uncontrolled drifting, passed the top of Europe and came free of the ice near Spitzbergen.

But there are great eddies to complicate this drift. This is proved by the paths of three ships, the *Navareh,* the *Bavchimo,* and the *Maud,* which kept reappearing in the same regions in which they had been caught.

The majestic 14,235-mile tour of the Arctic Ocean which Bravo has been making since it broke off Ellesmere Island seems to have come to an ignominious close. On 25 May 1960 it was grounded on the shoals about eighty miles northwest of Point Barrow, Alaska, so close to extensive research facilities at Point Barrow that its value was seriously curtailed.

The summer of 1960 saw the break-off from Bravo of a section of the floe 3.5 miles in area, followed by a series of smaller fractures. On 16 July a favorable wind released the floe from captivity and started it on its leisurely travels, but in less than two weeks and twenty-seven miles of wandering, it was back to its originally grounded position. It was there in December 1960. Some were confident the station would again break loose, and the scientific program was continued although reduced and oriented toward a non-drifting station. . . . Bravo was abandoned late in 1961 but reoccupied by three men from the University of Alaska's Arctic Research Laboratory in February 1962 when it was discovered drifting 180 miles northwest of Point Barrow. Bravo's final destiny remains at the whim of winds, currents, and the tenacity with which it again some day may cling to the continental shelf.

Whatever the fate of Bravo, we need constant reminders that the Soviets have a definite edge over the United States in the investigation of the Arctic Ocean. This is apparent from the scope of publications that have been released. According to these, in the past few years the Russians, as part of a huge exploratory effort, have landed by air the staggering total of more than 700 research parties on widely scattered ice floes in the Arctic Ocean. These are in addition to the nine stations which have been manned for extended periods of time. The temporary camps have been utilized principally for measurement of ice thicknesses for possible use as landing strips.

This widespread and concentrated Soviet attack on the Arctic has virtually blanketed the barren area from the Siberian to the Canadian and Alaskan coasts. Some landings that were announced publicly were alarmingly close to the northern coast of Alaska, the Canadian archipelago, and Greenland. In 1955 the Soviet disclosed that one of their expeditions, while 1,075 miles from the nearest point of Siberia, was only 750 miles from Thule; another Soviet Arctic research party was working 775 miles from its mainland at a point 690 miles from Point Barrow, Alaska. Most of the landings were made with ski planes operating from more permanent stations either on the mainland or on ice floes.

On 16 June 1957 the Soviet proudly announced that two of their ski planes had landed at the North Pole. That was the first landing since 3 May 1952 when one of our ski-equipped Skymasters made a short flight of 135 miles from T-3 to the Pole, where the accompanying scientists stayed a few hours to measure the depth of the ocean. The Russian aircraft stayed at the Pole for six hours while an automatic weather reporting station, one of thirty they had installed in the Arctic Ocean, was set up.

The intensified effort to explore all areas of the Arctic continues. The Moscow radio reported in April 1960 that a team of scientists had relieved the staff of North Pole 8 and that yet another advance party of Soviet explorers had landed on a drifting floe at latitude 77° 23′ N. and 163° E. to establish North Pole 9. Moscow radio said on 2 April 1960 that researchers had to be taken off a floe not further identified. It was probably North Pole 9 which split in two one night, taking huts and stores away from the main camp. The broadcast said that earlier stores and equipment had had to be shifted eleven times as the floe kept shrinking.

The Soviets are making scheduled flights similar to our Ptarmigan missions over the Arctic Ocean and, according to one news source, a reconnaissance plane on a photographic mission has taken pictures of BMEWS in Thule.

Soviet attacks on the scientific problems of the Arctic have been well conceived, massive, realistic, and vigorously pursued. Military problems combined with geographic and strategic objectives certainly receive major attention during the course of these investigations. In planning and performance, study of the entire Arctic area has become a national undertaking. For years the Soviets have been acknowledged experts on Siberia. Now it is apparent that they are determined to become experts on the area embracing the Arctic Ocean.

No matter how often they say that their imposing polar investigations have only peaceful motives, we must not forget that the Soviet effort is comprehensive and vital, and that our effort in comparison has been meager and wavering. During the last decade, which has seen an impressive Soviet assault on the Arctic, we have landed approximately 100 research parties. Other than the abortive attempt to establish a station on an ice floe in 1951, there have been only three floating stations manned by the U. S. Air Force in the Arctic Ocean, whereas the Soviets are occupying at least their ninth, and the pressure for more Russian research in the Arctic continues. During an extended period in the summer of 1960, Soviet aircraft and our own have searched the polar sea for new sites for drifting stations.

Understanding of the polar sea is crucial to our own security; the barren waste separates North America from Siberia and provides an avenue of approach for Russian attack. The bombers and missiles of any future war would be propelled over the Arctic's desolation. The country with ice island or ice-floe missile bases would have an enormous advantage—an advantage the Russians would capitalize on for they have probably experimented with the launching of rockets in the North Pole area. Most of their 1961 nuclear tests were conducted in the Arctic regions. They have developed specialized equipment for polar work including ski planes; ours are not built as such but are converted wheel aircraft.

We have made great strides in our comprehension of the polar basin in the past few years, but we will fall farther behind unless our program is sharply expanded. Much more needs to be done. To catch up with the aggressive Soviets we need to push hard to establish further emergency strips on the ice pack, as well as rocket-launching sites, improved weather reporting, and general planning for war in the Arctic should it ever come.

Large sums of money are needed for enormous programs like those necessary in the Arctic, but when a doubting Thomas looks at a polar projection he observes only northern Alaska as the frontier of concern to us and fails to recognize that we have assumed *de facto* sovereignty over much of the remainder. The mass of the Arctic coast line belongs to Canada, and that country cannot possibly afford a major share of the cost of establishing a defense system covering the great Arctic expanse under her control, though she is doing a good job erecting and maintaining her own stations as well as joint operations with us.

Military uses apart, the scientific stations located in the Arctic Ocean serve many useful peacetime purposes. They are essential for the safe operation of commercial airlines over polar routes.

The dreams of the early explorers and air prophets have been largely realized; we Americans have finally discovered the Arctic.

The necessity of air fields, research and meteorological stations in the Arctic in global strategy as well as commercial flying has been convincingly demonstrated and should be universally evident. The one-time vulnerability of Greenland and Alaska has been weighed, and their positions as stepping stones over the Great Circle Route to Europe and Asia are clear. We are building military stations in the North based logically on the instrument of air power; we are utilizing wartime experience and postwar exploration and research to further commercial exploitation of the air. We can keep our northern frontier inviolable by remembering the past, by sustaining the means that will best insure the future.

For the Arctic Ocean, no matter whether it is crossed by air or under water, is a bridge between the two hemispheres which could serve as a pathway for peace instead of war. Our men on ice islands and ice floes have laid effective groundwork for safe air travel over the Pole. Our efforts to tame the ice-encrusted northern seas are successful, yet on our part the contest for control of polar routes is still in the preliminary stages. On its outcome may depend much of the future history of America, Europe, and Asia.

Selected Bibliography

The Army Air Forces in World War II, Plans and Early Operations, January 1939 to August 1942, W. F. Craven and J. L. Cote, editors. Chicago, University of Chicago Press, 1950, 788 pp.

Balchen, B., Ford, C., and LaFarge, O., *War Below Zero.* Boston, Houghton Mifflin Company, 1944, 127 pp.

Carlson, William S., "Movement of Some Greenland Glaciers." *Geological Society of America Bulletin,* Vol. L, Part I, No. 2 (1939), pp. 239-55.

———— *Greenland Lies North.* New York, The Macmillan Company, 1940, 304 pp.

———— "Aerology and Meteorology—Report of the Northern Division of the Fourth University of Michigan Greenland Expedition 1930-31." *University of Michigan, Scientific Series,* Vol. VI, Part II, chapter ii (1941), pp. 65-135.

———— and Brodsky, G. D., "No Mean Victory." Manuscript, Personnel Narratives Division, Office of Information Services, Hq. AAF (May 9, 1945), 590 pp. (typewritten).

"Comprehensive Report on Operations of Task Force 4998-A and the Ice Cap Detachment in Greenland 1942-44." AFCTR ADT Branch, Orlando, Florida (June 15, 1945) 182 pp. (typewritten).

Dempster, Cecilia I., "Report of a Survey of the Literature of the Greenland Ice Cap." Manuscript prepared under contract for Research Studies Institute, Maxwell Air Force Base, Alabama, by American Geographical Society, 143 pp. (typewritten).

Eilbert, L. R., Glaser R., and Hanes, Randall M., *Research on Problems of Isolation of Personnel for Duty at Isolated Stations.* Pittsburgh, American Institute for Research, 75 pp. (draft copy).

Geography of the Northlands, Dorothy Good and George H. T. Kimble, editors. New York, The American Geographical Society and John Wiley & Sons, Inc., 1955, 534 pp.

Greenland. Copenhagen, Royal Danish Ministry for Foreign Affairs, 169 pp.

"The Greenland Ice Plateau." *Air University Quarterly Review,* Maxwell Air Force Base, Alabama (spring, 1955), pp. 78-90.

"History of the Air Transport Command in Greenland," 177 pp. (typewritten).

Howard, R. A., *Down in the North*. Arctic, Desert and Tropic Information Center Research Studies Institute, Air University, Maxwell Air Force Base, Alabama (1953), 42 pp.

Joerg, W. L. G., *Brief History of Polar Exploration Since the Introduction of Flying*. New York, American Geographical Society, 1930, 95 pp.

Kayser, O., *The Inland Ice, Greenland,* Vol. I, chapter xxi. Copenhagen, Commission for Geological and Geographical Investigation in Greenland, 1928, pp. 357-422.

Kirwan, L. P., *A History of Polar Exploration*. New York, W. W. Norton & Co., Inc., 1960, 374 pp.

Mirsky, J., *To the Arctic*. New York, Alfred A. Knopf, Inc., 1948, 334 pp.

Project Mint Julep, Part I (Introduction, Narrative, and General Reports) and *Part II* (Special Scientific Reports). Arctic, Desert and Tropic Information Center Research Studies Institute, Air University, Maxwell Air Force Base, Alabama (1955), 82 pp. and 100 pp.

Rodahl, Kaare, *North, the Nature and Drama of the Polar World*. New York, Harper and Brothers, 1953, 237 pp.

Simpson, C. J. W., *North Ice, the British North Greenland Expedition*. London, Hodder and Stoughton, 1957, 384 pp.

Small, Frederick A., "The Inland Ice of Greenland." Submitted in partial fulfillment of the Degree of Bachelor of Arts at Goddard College, Vermont (1952), 98 pp. (typewritten).

Somov, M. M., "The Drift of the Scientific Research Station of 1950-51," trans. by Geophysics Research Directorate. Air Force Cambridge Research Center (1955), 27 pp. (typewritten).

Steffansson, V., *Greenland*. New York, Doubleday, Doran and Co., 1942, 338 pp.

Sullivan, Walter, *Assault on the Unknown*. New York, McGraw-Hill Book Co., Inc., 1961, 460 pp.

Summary Report, 14 April 1959 to 21 October 1959, Station Charlie, Project Ice Skate, APO 731, Seattle, Washington, 15 pp. (typewritten).

Williamson, G. W., *Changing Greenland*. London, Sidgwick and Jackson Limited, 1953, 280 pp.

Classified Materials Consulted

"Arctic Survival and Research Reports, North Atlantic Area," compiled by Oron P. South. Documentary Research Division, Air University, Maxwell Air Force Base, Alabama (July, 1949), 162 pp. Ms. restricted.

"U.S. Operations in the Northeast 1940-1950," prefaced by the Directorate, Historical and Reference Services. Headquarters, Northeast Air Command (January, 1953). Restricted.

DATE DUE   ECHEANCE

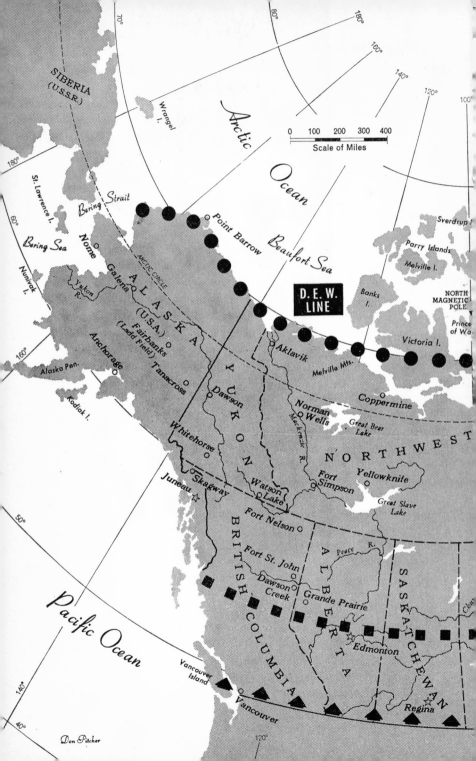